RENO, LAS VEGAS, AND THE STRIP

Wilbur S. Shepperson Series in Nevada History

RENO, LAS VEGAS, AND THE STRIP

A Tale of Three Cities

EUGENE P. MOEHRING

UNIVERSITY OF NEVADA PRESS / RENO & LAS VEGAS

Wilbur S. Shepperson Series in Nevada History
SERIES EDITOR: Michael S. Green

University of Nevada Press, Reno, Nevada 89557 USA
Copyright © 2014 by University of Nevada Press
All rights reserved
Manufactured in the United States of America
Design by Kathleen Szawiola

Library of Congress Cataloging-in-Publication Data
Moehring, Eugene P.
Reno, Las Vegas, and the Strip : a tale of three cities, 1945–2013 /
Eugene P. Moehring.
pages cm. — (Wilbur S. Shepperson series in Nevada history)
Includes bibliographical references and index.
ISBN 978-0-87417-955-2 (cloth : alk. paper) —
ISBN 978-0-87417-956-9 (e-book)
1. Reno (Nev.)—History--20th century. 2. Las Vegas (Nev.)—History—
20th century. 3. Las Vegas Region (Nev.)—History—20th century.
4. Reno (Nev.)—Economic conditions--20th cenury. 5. Las Vegas (Nev.)
—Economic conditions—20th century. I. Title.
F849.R4M64 2014
979.3'55033—dc23   2014012354

ISBN 978-1-64779-155-1 (paper)

The paper used in this book meets the requirements of American
National Standard for Information Sciences—Permanence of Paper
for Printed Library Materials, ANSI/NISO Z39.48-1992 (R2002).
Binding materials were selected for strength and durability.

This book has been reproduced as a digital reprint.

*For Fr. Wally Nowak, dedicated priest,
educator, and counselor of students at* UNLV

CONTENTS

	List of Illustrations	ix
	Preface	xi
	INTRODUCTION | Reno, Las Vegas, and the "Strip City"	1
One	RENO AREA | Gambling Gains Ascendancy, 1945–1970	8
Two	LAS VEGAS AREA | Laying the Foundation, 1945–1975	41
Three	RENO AREA | The Growth Wave Rises and Recedes, 1970–1990	69
Four	LAS VEGAS AREA | Recession Turns to Boom, 1975–2007	103
Five	RENO AREA | Transition and Depression, 1990–2014	139
Six	LAS VEGAS AREA | Depression and Some Recovery, 2007–2014	169
Seven	THE RENO AND LAS VEGAS AREAS | A Comparative View	207
	Notes	229
	Bibliography	251
	Index	259

ILLUSTRATIONS

PHOTOGRAPHS *(following page 138)*

Truckee River flooding in downtown Reno, 1950
Elegant Mapes Hotel, ca. 1965
Aerial view of downtown Reno, 2003
Aerial view of MGM Grand Hotel in Reno, ca. 1980
Aerial view of downtown Las Vegas, 1968
Aria hotel-casino, 2013
Wynn Las Vegas, 2013
The Palazzo, 2013
The Fontainebleau, 2013

MAPS

MAP 1.1. Historic Downtown Reno Casinos and Other Past and Present Points of Interest	10
MAP 1.2. Reno-Sparks Metropolitan Area	19
MAP 2.1. Downtown Las Vegas: Major Casinos and Other Points of Interest, ca. 2013	43
MAP 2.2. Las Vegas Strip	46
MAP 2.3. Las Vegas Metropolitan Area	49

TABLES

TABLE 1.1. Resident Minorities, Reno Area: Percentage of Population	40
TABLE 4.1. Latinos, Las Vegas Area: Percentage of MSA Population	124
TABLE 4.2. Resident Minorities, Las Vegas Area: Percentage of Population	125

PREFACE

MUCH HAS BEEN WRITTEN about the histories of Reno and Las Vegas, but rarely are the two cities examined together. This book will survey the development of both metropolitan areas from the postwar decades through the Great Recession up to 2014, although coverage of recent history (especially after 1970) will be more detailed. This coverage will include the debut of major resorts, key trends, public policies, voter actions, and contemporary opinions from a range of people, along with a variety of noteworthy events. Part of the book's purpose is to explain the separate trajectories each metropolitan area took in the latter decades of the twentieth century into the twenty-first. Reno slowly moved away from a full-scale commitment to gambling as its major industry, while the Las Vegas area more fully embraced gaming-related tourism in the years after 1980. These actions resulted in various consequences for the economies of both metro areas, as did the rise of Native American gaming and the advent of America's "Great Recession."

Reno and Las Vegas are not the book's only focus, however, because viewing historical events simply from the perspective of these two cities alone distorts the picture. Although Sparks, which began almost forty years later than its neighbor, certainly can claim John Ascuaga's Nugget and a few other places, Reno remains the central city in its metropolitan area. But Las Vegas, although it is the mother city for its metro area, functions today as just part of the story. While Henderson and North Las Vegas deserve attention, the Strip and its suburbs, in both physical size and population, really constitute the valley's largest "city" and should therefore be regarded as such. This role became increasingly important after 1985, when the Strip city's roaring economy vaulted Las Vegas up to the title of

America's fastest-growing metropolitan area. After 2007 the Strip city again played a key role when the national recession damaged the economies of both metro areas and forced leaders to put greater emphasis on economic diversification, university research, and the role of private-public partnerships. In the Las Vegas area the Strip helped promote metropolitan revival and insulate the place from the corrosive effects of Native American casinos and the growing popularity of Internet gaming.

Besides the analysis covering the numerous factors affecting the varying development trajectories of Reno and Las Vegas since World War II, then, this book's central thesis, in extended form, is that Reno and Las Vegas aggressively pursued a different development path than other cities in the United States by embracing vice and ceding much of their downtown blocks to casino gambling and twenty-four-hour bars. As in other municipalities, there were residential, business, and other pressures to confine the largest clubs and full-fledged gaming to a red-lined, restricted area downtown, which both cities did for many years. But south of the city of Las Vegas, in the 1940s and 1950s, entrepreneurs developed the Strip, which was not subject to these restrictions and had abundant acreage for the expansion of casino resorts.

Over the course of seven decades, the county commissioners and hotel owners who ran the Strip and the city that grew up around it developed the resort industry in new directions and to heights that their counterparts in Reno and Las Vegas never dreamed of. In so doing, they gradually sculpted a unique world venue for leisure and convention activities that drew, and continues to draw, tens of millions of visitors each year—a model for gaming that today influences Macau's Cotai Strip as well as the many other places where the pastime has been or may soon be legalized.

Finally, having been flexible enough to embrace a notorious resort economy based on gambling and other "vices" for many years, residents of the Reno and Las Vegas areas once again are looking to diversify their economies by embracing innovative and cutting-edge industries. These longtime maverick cities are today using the metropolitan base created by seven decades of gambling, liberal marriage and divorce, twenty-four-hour liquor sales, and adult forms of recreation to aggressively pursue alternative energy, data storage, robotics, and similar industries.

In terms of this book's structure, the first six chapters alternate between coverage of the Reno and then the Las Vegas metropolitan areas. I have included the Strip-city coverage in the Las Vegas–area chapters, rather than giving this area its own chapters, because many events and trends in southern Nevada affected the three cities and the Strip simultaneously and they (especially Las Vegas and the Strip) often had a symbiotic relationship.

Numerous people have advised me on these issues and assisted in the preparation of this book. Michael Green and Alicia Barber read an early version in its entirety and offered myriad helpful comments, which I have implemented. Former Nevada state archivist and historian Guy Rocha aided in the resolution of various issues related to state and metropolitan governance. I would also like to thank Betty Glass, Jessica Maddox, Kim Roberts, Glee Willis, and Jacqueline Sundstrand at the Mathewson-IGT Knowledge Center at the University of Nevada, Reno (UNR), who found a number of key documents for me in Special Collections. The same is true of their counterparts at the Lied Library of the University of Nevada, Las Vegas (UNLV), especially Peter Michel, Sue Kim Chung, Tom Sommer, Claytee White, Delores Brownlee, Joyce Moore, and Kelli Luchs. I also appreciate the assistance extended to me by Michael Maher, Eric Moody, Phillip Earl, Lee Mortensen, and Sheryln Hayes-Zorn at the Nevada Historical Society in Reno and by Dennis McBride, Crystal Van Dee, and, for many years, David Milman at the Nevada State Museum and Historical Society in Las Vegas. At the University of Nevada Press, Matt Becker, Joanne O'Hare, and Kathleen Szawiola were particularly helpful. As usual, my history colleagues at UNLV were very supportive, as was my wonderful wife, Christine.

RENO, LAS VEGAS, AND THE STRIP

INTRODUCTION

Reno, Las Vegas, and the "Strip City"

WHEN MOST PEOPLE THINK of Nevada and gambling, they think of Reno and Las Vegas.[1] Both the Truckee Meadows and the Las Vegas valley (*valley* is the popular term, but technically, it's a basin) served as oases for nineteenth-century travelers. Reno began as an overnight stop for Comstock-bound wagons; the railroad came later with the town's birth in 1868. Like most urban communities on the mining frontier, Reno was a wide-open place with its share of saloons, prostitutes, opium, and gambling clubs that only grew as railroad traffic increased in the twentieth century. But Reno also was an agricultural community surrounded by farms and ranches for its entire history. In the early twentieth century the city began forging its notorious reputation as a divorce mecca. By the time of Reno's incorporation as a city in 1903, most western states, including California, had adopted the one-year waiting period that was standard in the East. Nevada remained a holdout at six months. But Progressive state legislators briefly shamed it into virtue by banning most games of chance in 1909 and then changing the waiting period from six months to a year during the 1913 session. Liberal divorce, however, was too important to the town's coffers. So, after much prodding from Reno interests, the state legislature in 1915 restored the six-month waiting period, and the boom was on, heightened further by actress Mary Pickford's headline-grabbing divorce in 1920. In 1927 state lawmakers cut the waiting period to three months, and four years later, during the Great Depression, they reduced it again to six weeks—on the same day they legalized wide-open casino gambling.

The Depression, with its destructive effects upon Nevada's mining, farming, and ranching industries, led the state to embrace easy divorce, gambling, and tourism. Reno profited mightily from this in the 1930s and especially during the chaotic years of World War II, when quickie marriages and divorces were especially popular. Divorce, gambling, and auto tourism teamed with railroad-related industries, centered along its tracks and in its railroad repair-shop suburb of Sparks, to keep the Reno area prosperous through the war years and beyond. Led by Harolds Club and other prominent midcentury casinos in and around Virginia Street, postwar Reno grew steadily, albeit slowly, and remained the state's largest city until 1953, when Las Vegas finally passed it in population.

From its earliest days Las Vegas catered to travelers.[2] In the 1830s it served as a desert oasis for those plying the various trails linking Southern California with Arizona and Utah. After the Civil War a few ranch-farms sprang up in the valley to act as hostels and supply points for weary travelers crossing the remorseless Mojave. The town of Las Vegas (incorporated as a city in 1911) grew slowly and almost anonymously after its founding in 1905 and during its salad days as a transshipment point on Senator William Clark's railroad system connecting Los Angeles with the East via Salt Lake City. His Las Vegas & Tonopah Railroad, which began in 1907, allowed Clark to forward supplies to and mineral shipments from the booming mines around Tonopah and Goldfield. Las Vegas prospered through World War I into the early 1920s, when Clark finally sold his line to the Union Pacific. A union town, Las Vegas struggled with labor tensions during the national railroad strike of 1921, after which the Union Pacific moved its valuable repair shops to Caliente and replaced them with smelly stockyards. The real trouble began after local residents antagonized Union Pacific executives with militant unionism that included roughing up the company's scab workers in the yards—a move that brought in the state police and martial law for a time.[3]

In the 1930s the Boulder Dam project literally rescued Las Vegas from oblivion by creating more than five thousand jobs in the area and orienting it more toward serving tourists. Starting in 1931, they came by the thousands to see the latest man-made "wonder of the world" under construction. With gambling relegalized and Prohibition ended, locals and out-of-state businessmen opened clubs and gambling halls on Fremont Street, on the Los Angeles Highway—US 91 (today's Strip)—and on US 93 (the early Boulder Highway), which, after the dam's completion, delivered an increasing number of tourists from Arizona.

By World War II Fremont Street was ablaze in neon. It was the center of the city's gaming district, because, like Reno's Virginia Street, it was near the railroad station and served the heart of downtown upon which all nearby US highways converged. War also brought heavy defense spending and more business. The 1941 arrival of the US Army Air Corps' Flexible Gunnery School invigorated Thomas Williams's old 1917 community that later became the city of North Las Vegas, just as the Basic Magnesium Plant laid the seeds for the eventual city of Henderson. During the war thousands of weekend gamblers flocked to Las Vegas from the factory and base, as well as soldiers and sailors from military installations in Arizona and California. These customers, along with workers from defense plants in both states, patronized Fremont Street's growing casino district.[4]

Not all the action, however, was in the mother city. The small clubs and motor courts that sprang up along the highway approaches to Las Vegas also did a brisk business. The real breakthrough came in 1941, when California hotelier Thomas Hull opened his sprawling El Rancho Vegas casino resort[5] on fifty-seven acres of desert flats just south of the city line on San Francisco Street (today's Sahara Avenue). In the following year R. E. Griffith and his nephew William J. Moore joined Hull on US 91 with their Hotel Last Frontier, a mile south of the El Rancho. Four years later, thanks to the efforts of Hollywood publicist Billy Wilkerson and the legendary Bugsy Siegel, the Fabulous Flamingo opened even farther down the highway. Then in 1948 Marion Hicks and Cliff Jones unveiled their Thunderbird casino resort, just south of the El Rancho, across US 91.[6] It was not long before club owner Guy McAfee dubbed the new line of resorts the "Strip." McAfee, a former Los Angeles Police Department vice commander, named it for the Sunset Strip whose line of clubs (with their illegal bars and gaming tables) in the 1920s drew periodic federal raids. After Prohibition's repeal in 1933, the Sunset Strip's increasingly popular club scene featured such rising stars as Tony Bennett, Sammy Davis Jr., and others who would soon headline on the new Las Vegas Strip.[7]

Still, even for a few years after World War II Fremont Street continued to dominate the scene, with its access to both railroad and highway. But in the 1950s this changed, as more sprawling resorts began to fill the open desert abutting US 91. By 1958 the Desert Inn, Sahara, Sands, Riviera, Dunes, Hacienda, Tropicana, and Stardust had all opened. While the casino kings of downtown Reno and Las Vegas certainly transformed their city's streetscape with properties designed to appeal to American postwar consumers, the growing number of themed resorts on the Strip did everything in their power to embrace postwar mass-culture patterns. Gradually, they began to offer much more than downtown Reno or Las Vegas or the Sunset Strip or the fabled Agua Caliente hotel-gaming complex in 1920s Tijuana, which drew its share of famous and infamous Californians. With their landscaped grounds, spacious casinos, star-studded showrooms, shopping arcades, ethnic restaurants, ample parking, azure pools, and palm tree–lined sundecks, these casino resorts on the "Strip" soon became the preferred spot for Southern California motorists rather than the crowded blocks in and around Fremont Street in the central city.[8]

Low-rise apartment complexes, some stores, and a few subdivisions linked by two-lane roads began to appear behind the resorts, as the Strip spawned some of the first traces of development that would eventually ring the burgeoning job zone for miles around. In the 1940s and 1950s the once pristine, largely empty desert began its gradual transformation into something bigger—something that, by century's end, would become a true phenomenon: a national and even global destination for tourists, convention delegates, and millions of new residents. This was a new entity—a city in itself that would forever set the Reno and Las Vegas areas apart in their historical development.

The Strip served as the steadily expanding nucleus of an informal city that soon became larger than its mother city and much larger than neighboring Henderson and North Las Vegas (in fact, some of the bedroom suburbs for the Strip's resort and other workers extended into these cities). The Strip city, though never formally incorporated into a municipality, was controlled by Clark County commissioners. It developed near the center of the Las Vegas valley on former ranch lands and vacant desert between these three municipalities. For the most part it was the Strip city's spectacular development over the next seven decades that transformed the Las Vegas valley and beyond into a metropolitan area. By 1970 the Strip city claimed the lion's share of coverage from the county's growing fire and police departments. County public works focused on building enough roads, streets, sewers, curbs, gutters, and pavements to serve the growing number of homes, hotels, motels, restaurants, and other businesses and residences springing up in the Strip city. While the courts and federal, state, and local government offices remained largely downtown in Las Vegas, some county departments, the school district and other government agencies, the gas and power utilities, and a few major companies relocated to the Strip city, where they could be near the big resorts and most of the valley's residents.

As the Strip city's population soared in the years after 1960 and especially after 1980, the three surrounding municipalities also gained more residents. Some of this can be attributed to the natural birthrate and each city's promotional efforts, but a lot of this growth resulted from the growing number of jobs and businesses in and around the Strip. While officially cities in their own right, Las Vegas, North Las Vegas, and Henderson increasingly functioned as suburbs of the steadily expanding Strip city located in the heart of the emerging metropolitan area. The county seat of Las Vegas, a bedroom suburb of the Strip but also a casino center and government administrative center in its own right, sat to the Strip city's north and west.[9] The lower-income suburb of North Las Vegas (with affluent Aliante appearing after 2000 in the extreme northern end of its township) lay north and east of the Strip city. Henderson, the onetime factory town and now a largely middle- and upper-income city, served as a bedroom suburb south and east of the Strip city, while the old dam town of Boulder City was a more distant appendage in the extreme southeastern portion of the metropolitan area.

By the 1990s, as high-rise megaresorts replaced the Desert Inn, Sands, Dunes, and the other low-rise hotels catering to the midcentury car culture, the Strip, with its erupting volcanoes, Eiffel towers, and Egyptian pyramids became a postmodern icon all its own—quite simply, there was nothing else like it in the world. The surrounding city it inspired exploded far outward, becoming a candidate for what journalist and scholar Joel Garreau called an "edge city" in his 1991 book.[10] In that work, however, Garreau rejected the Strip and its county suburbs as an edge city, characterizing them instead as an "Edge City *paragon.*" He was right. Although it did meet some of *his* criteria, it did not fulfill the criteria for edge-city status set by many scholars in the field. For example, the Strip area's streets were *and* are not "hierarchical, consisting of winding parkways (often lacking sidewalks) that feed into arterial roads and freeway ramps." The Strip is "not exceptionally distant from other urban centers," such as the cities of Las Vegas and North Las Vegas. The Strip is no longer a place where "low elongated buildings predominate." Moreover, the Strip is not "a winding main axis from which secondary streets lead off . . . [to] various quarters, habitually known as villages," nor are the Strip and its surrounding lands located "in a campus-like environment full of lakes, woods, pedestrian paths and bike lanes."[11] So, because this urban area is not really an edge city in the strict sense of the term, I will refer to it instead as the Strip city—an agglomeration larger than many of Garreau's edge cities and in many ways more interesting.[12]

Like many American edge cities, southern Nevada's Strip city was presided over not by a mayor and city council but by county commissioners who were hardly household names—even to residents. Nevertheless, the commissioners' power was considerable. By the 1990s they reigned over many square miles of development generated by the casino resorts on Las Vegas Boulevard. The commissioners established policies and made decisions that enhanced the growth not only of the Strip, but also of the lands extending outward for miles in all directions. In the late 1950s, along with their counterparts in Las Vegas, the county commissioners erected the valley's first large convention center and kept enlarging it into the twenty-first century. This was a forward-thinking policy that attracted ever-larger meetings and kept all major conventions in the Strip city rather than in Las Vegas, which in the 1980s constructed a smaller convention center near downtown. Then in 1960, to ensure the Strip city's continued dominance, the commissioners built a modern jet facility, McCarran Airport, south of the Strip on the same road as the convention center.

In the 1980s into the 2000s, it was the Clark County commissioners, not the city of Las Vegas or some regional authority (as in the Reno area), who steadily enlarged McCarran into a sprawling international airport capable of handling more than a thousand flights per day. It was also the county commissioners who financed and built a fifty-three-mile beltway that circled most of the valley, connecting the cities of Las Vegas, North Las Vegas, and Henderson and the county's unincorporated townships with the Strip job zone and its myriad suburbs. The urban agglomeration of Henderson–Boulder City had been growing toward the Strip city since the 1960s and '70s; the same was true of the Las Vegas–North Las Vegas agglomeration. The beltway simply reinforced this conurbation process. It was the county commissioners and their staff of engineers and planners who built the Desert Inn Super Arterial in the 1990s and made hundreds of decisions affecting the installation of infrastructural systems and traffic arteries that served the resorts' needs while simultaneously opening new suburban frontiers to the east, west, and south in the years after 1970. County authorities also helped the Strip city snare five exits on the new Interstate 15 in the 1960s, compared to the city of Las Vegas's three. Additionally, county leaders in the 1980s and '90s led the campaign to establish an affordable valley-wide bus system for lower-income commuters, while also spearheading the effort to design an effective flood-control system that so far has protected the metropolitan area from devastating floods. Finally, it was the county commissioners who dug up Las Vegas Boulevard in the 1990s to provide the additional sewer capacity to accommodate the new MGM Grand and the Strip's other recent megaresorts, with their four to five thousand hotel rooms, their time-share towers, and the high-rise condominiums they supported.

In short, the Strip city was built by no mayor, no city machine, and no Robert Moses–like power broker. In the Las Vegas valley county commissioners played a major role, along with Nevada's congressional delegation, state and city officials, members of various regional government bodies, and business leaders, in sculpting much of the metropolitan area that today hosts nearly two million residents and an average of one hundred thousand visitors a day. In myriad ways the Strip and its city fueled the spectacular growth of the Las Vegas metropolitan area far beyond what its namesake city could ever have done. No such phenomenon occurred in Reno, because, as will be shown, conditions there were not conducive to Strip-city or edge-city formation.

Although Reno inspired the formation of a small metropolitan area of its own after 1970 with help from neighboring Sparks and Washoe County, this urban agglomeration never approached the size of its southern counterpart. Nevertheless, Reno's development was crucial for Las Vegas, because Reno, much like the pioneers celebrated in the famous mural fronting Harolds Club, "helped blaze the trail" for Las Vegas. Reno's successful courtship of gambling and tourism in earlier decades encouraged its southern rival to adopt the same maverick culture that powered "the Biggest Little City's" transformation from an obscure railroad entrepôt on the Sierra's eastern edge into an iconic destination that put Nevada on everyone's map.

In many ways Reno led the way, developing the successful tourist and gaming economy that Las Vegas later embraced. Over time, both towns inspired the early Strip, which eventually blossomed into an even larger city than Reno and Las Vegas combined.

Chapter One

RENO AREA

Gambling Gains Ascendancy, 1945–1970

RENO ENTERED THE POSTWAR ERA in a strange jumble of moods. World War II and the years immediately afterward cemented the city's place in history as America's divorce center. Even more than Las Vegas, midcentury Reno was the place where thousands of people still came to get divorced and married *quickly*. By 1952 the number of Reno marriages outnumbered divorces, a trend that would accelerate once other states slowly began to liberalize their divorce requirements. Gambling flourished also. During the war the presence of so many nearby military bases and defense plants, especially in California, made Reno a convenient weekend getaway to relieve the stress of wartime living. In the immediate postwar era the trend only intensified, as it did in Las Vegas, with Californians enjoying the postwar affluence that inflation, prosperity, and civilian life brought. Much like the smaller Las Vegas, Reno saw its tourism and gaming revenues increase into the 1950s. But, unlike Las Vegas, there were many citizens who, concerned about gaming's growing influence at city hall and their community's future direction, wondered aloud whether Reno should begin to diversify its economy, move away from its longtime maverick culture, and become more like other American cities.

In 1950, despite the presence of Stead Air Force Base and various small industries, Reno's main business was still tourism and, increasingly, casino gambling. This was its economic legacy, especially from the Great Depression and war years. During these years as well as earlier ones, unrestricted gaming had thrived along the railroad tracks by Commercial Row and Virginia Street and in Douglas Alley, just east of Virginia. At midcentury the largest casino in Reno and the world was Harolds Club, with Harrah's and the Golden Bank Club still distant runners-up. By the late 1940s Reno boasted a number of fine hotels, including the Mapes, the Riverside, and the Golden, along with the El Cortez and a few other places. Charlie Mapes's establishment was the best in town. When it opened in 1947, the twelve-story Mapes was the tallest building in Nevada and the first venue in Reno to feature big-name entertainment. Frank Sinatra, Liberace, Sammy Davis Jr., and a host of other celebrities all appeared in the Sky Room long before they performed at Harrah's, the Sahara, or the MGM Grand. But the Mapes had competitors in entertainment during the early 1950s, especially over at the El Cortez, where the Trocadero Room flourished for almost a decade. The Hotel El Cortez itself had opened in 1931 and offered gamblers roulette, craps, and slot machines and competed into the 1950s with the Mapes for casino play.[1]

In addition to these existing properties, many new gambling spots appeared in the 1950s, as gaming began to expand its presence downtown. William Harrah, for one, kept buying up old clubs and gradually spread his business into sections of Center and Virginia Streets. Other operators also gobbled up properties in an effort to serve Reno's ever-growing number of visitors. The demand for new casino space began to price real estate offices and similar businesses out of the area, once lot owners realized they could make more money leasing or selling their buildings to men like Harrah. As a result, in the 1950s the gaming industry oozed steadily southward down Virginia Street toward Second Street and downtown's retail and office district—something store owners and other business groups did not welcome.

Among the new gaming establishments was the Holiday Hotel-Casino, which opened in 1956 on Virginia Street across from the Riverside. Once Ernest Primm convinced a new, more pliable city council and Mayor Len Harris to extend the city's red-line zone to allow unrestricted gaming licenses on the west side of Virginia Street, he opened his Primadonna (later the Sahara's/Flamingo's Virginia Street entrance) in 1955. This encouraged a series of new clubs next door that included the Horseshoe (1956), the Silver Dollar (1959), and the Silver Spur (1968), which joined the Nugget (1947) to create a line of small casinos down to the railroad tracks across from Harolds Club. In 1950 Harolds Club (then the largest business in Reno), the Nevada Club, and Harrah's constituted the casino core of downtown. At the time the Colony (1946–84) and Palace Club (1888–1979) by the railroad station on North Center Street and the Waldorf Club (1920s–48) and Club

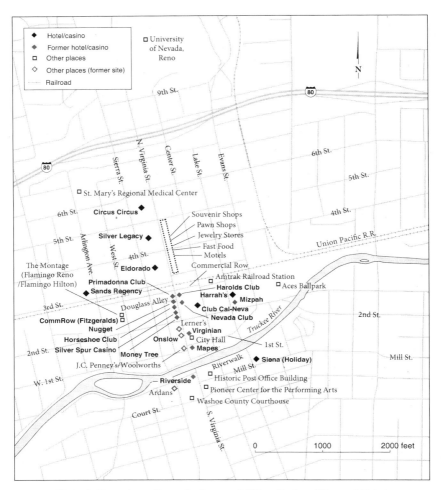

MAP 1.1. Historic Downtown Reno Casinos and Other Past and Present Points of Interest

Cal Neva (1948–), farther down Virginia Street just north of the Truckee River, offered gamblers worthy alternatives.[2]

Even more than Las Vegas, which was really a small place before World War II, postwar Reno profited from its longtime reputation as America's divorce mecca and from its maverick subculture that embraced vice, especially the green-felt world of wide-open gambling, booze, and prostitution. For years the city's reputation had profited from publicity generated by gossip columnists from New York and other large cities who covered Reno's divorce colony. This included the activities of the wives of prominent men spending the required six weeks there to qualify for a Nevada divorce. Reno also catered to gamblers, vacationers, and other visitors arriving by car and train. In addition, the town staged annual events to exploit Americans' nostalgia for the Old West, which drew even more visitors. In 1935, for instance, local rodeo enthusiasts formed the Reno Rodeo and Livestock Association to raise funds to build a rodeo facility that year for the Reno Rodeo (called the Reno Round-up after World War I), which became an annual event drawing thousands to the city. At about the same time Las Vegas promoters organized the Helldorado Rodeo to accomplish much the same thing. In Reno and Las Vegas, although western-themed casinos dominated early, nonwestern places, especially in the years after World War II, also appeared. In Reno, while some of the city's clubs and bars harked back to the Old West and Comstock days, places such as the Mapes and Harrah's, along with many others, did not.[3]

Aside from Las Vegas, no other American downtown looked like this, and many local residents were uncomfortable with it. As historian Alicia Barber has observed, "two Renos," one the western vice and gambling town and the other the staid small-town community, coexisted for decades. As she describes the scene, "Expanding clubs were interspersed among traditional businesses. . . . Locals uninvolved with the gambling or divorce industries continued to work and shop downtown, where jewelry and stationery stores, banks, and hardware stores shared space with the clubs, cafes, and restaurants patronized heavily by locals, as well as divorcees and other tourists." Published guides to Reno reassured visitors that although it was a city of pleasure, it was also a traditional community of stores, homes, and churches where they could feel comfortable. These two Renos lived side by side well into the second half of the twentieth century.[4]

In the 1950s, however, Reno tourism faced growing challenges from new vacation getaways gradually opening in the Caribbean, Hawaii, Florida, Southern California, and Las Vegas. Despite the increased competition, many Renoites preferred that their city be marketed more for its bucolic setting than as a divorce center. By the 1960s they largely got their wish. With many states liberalizing their divorce laws, this industry in Reno slowed markedly. Gambling soon became the city's main draw, partly thanks to Las Vegas's meteoric rise, which helped popularize Nevada.

Gradually, as Harold and Raymond I. "Pappy" Smith, Bill Harrah, and other operators expanded their business into larger casinos in the 1950s and '60s, more downtown stores and offices found themselves being pressured, as gambling and the hospitality industry began usurping more and more space in what was never a very large downtown area. The same was true in Las Vegas, where hotel-casinos, smaller gambling emporiums, souvenir stores, pawn shops, and other businesses catering to gambling and non-gambling visitors filled most of the lots on Fremont Street and its nearby thoroughfares from the railroad station down to and past the El Cortez in the two decades after World War II.[5]

Clearly, the postwar gambling boom was on. In the Reno area the widening of US 40 from California, the opening of a new airline terminal, the 1959 creation of the Washoe County Fair and Recreation Board (which became the Reno-Sparks Convention and Visitors Authority [RSCVA] in 1981) to build a convention center, and the chamber of commerce's hiring of Jud Allen as its aggressive new general manager in 1959 convinced growth advocates that their city was on the verge of spectacular expansion.[6]

But threats lurked everywhere. Las Vegas continued to make inroads into Reno's Pacific Northwest and Bay Area customer bases, and the growing popularity of skiing produced major winter getaways in Sun City, Aspen, Park City, and Mammoth that competed with Lake Tahoe. Even worse, after the 1960 Olympics, Reno experienced an economic slowdown. In 1962 the Riverside and the nearby Club Cal Neva, a downtown mainstay since 1948, temporarily closed, as gamblers increasingly headed to Las Vegas, where the Desert Inn, Dunes, Sands, Sahara, Stardust, and Tropicana delivered gaming, luxury, and big-name entertainment in larger and more glamorous venues than Reno.

In the early 1960s the city faced a tourism crisis that required Harrah's, Harolds Club, the Mapes, the Riverside, and a few other places to increase their contributions to the chamber of commerce to enhance its marketing efforts. But the hotel owners were slow to respond. According to chamber of commerce head Jud Allen, "With a short tourist season, a bad highway (rather than a modern interstate), little air service and the hotels and casinos having no tradition of working together, it seemed like there was no solution to reviving a stagnant economy" in 1959. At the same time, the chamber of commerce operated on a small budget. The largest contribution from any casino was Harolds Club at seven hundred dollars per year.

Not surprisingly, the chamber's deficit was thirteen thousand dollars. After much effort, Allen convinced executives first at Harolds Club and later at other casinos as well as nongaming businesses to give more, but it was a struggle. This was in stark contrast to Las Vegas, where hotels on the Strip and downtown worked together in the 1940s to support a variety of initiatives pushed by the chamber of commerce as well as the 1950s effort to build a convention center.

Reno's promotional effort was still meager even on the eve of the Winter Olympics. Into the late 1960s the city's casino-resort economy remained largely seasonal and not overly ambitious, marked by a relative lack of cooperation between the hotels. As Allen complained, leading casino owners such as Bill Harrah and Charlie Mapes rarely coordinated promotional efforts; in fact, they hardly met at all. Their shared interest in thwarting initiatives by the Culinary local and other unions was about the only issue that periodically brought them together.[7]

Except for Mapes, Reno's big casino executives were slow to build hotel rooms, if at all. The year 1960 marked the silver anniversary of Harolds Club, which had opened in the midst of the Depression in 1935, four years before Harrah opened his Tango Club in Douglas Alley. The Smiths never built a hotel, and Harrah took his time. Over the years he had greatly enlarged his casino and used its profits in 1955 to open a new casino and showroom at Stateline at the south shore of Lake Tahoe. But he did not build his twenty-four-story hotel tower at Harrah's Reno until 1969. Why? Because in the 1950s and early '60s, gambling still did not dominate Reno's economy the way it would later. Besides tourism and its still vibrant railroad economy, the city was also an important manufacturer of wood components such as doors, floors, window frames, and other home supplies for construction firms that profited from the postwar building boom blanketing the West.

As in Las Vegas, where the existing city sat near the center of a broad valley with plenty of undeveloped desert extending outward in all directions, promoters and political leaders in Reno-Sparks recognized that their valley was capable of sustaining much growth—if it came. There was much developable space as well as affordable housing. In 1956 the area counted 17,000 housing units. By 1960 the number had jumped to 20,300, thanks to the construction of new split-level and ranch-style homes in suburban subdivisions mostly near downtown. Water was also abundant. One state report released in 1960 indicated that the Reno-Sparks area had more than enough underground water to support development for the foreseeable future.[8]

Sparks also benefited from this growth and played a key role in helping to form the budding metropolitan area of 1960. But that had not always been the case. Laid out in 1903 on former ranch lands and swamps, Sparks was the railroad's new repair town just east of Reno. Despite its incorporation as a city just two years later, Sparks developed slowly. Over the years it functioned as an appendage to Reno and a small supply point for local farms until the rising popularity of Reno gambling and tourism after World War II roused Sparks from its doldrums. Just as suburban development resulting from the growth of Las Vegas and the Strip city linked them physically with Henderson-driven development by the late 1970s and early 1980s, Sparks and Reno also grew toward each other.[9]

The initial connection was a meager one, along the street railway line the two cities shared in the 1920s. But it was cars and the auto suburbs they spawned that really brought Reno and Sparks closer together. The main connecting road, US 40, created in 1926 from the old Victory Highway, promoted the initial conurbation process, which intensified in the postwar decades, as Reno became a popular gambling center and Sparks began to function as its eastern bedroom suburb. Interstate 80 reinforced this relationship in the 1970s by providing a high-speed commuter link between Sparks and the metro area's main job center in downtown Reno. In the 1950s the old railroad repair town also developed a small casino zone of its own for visitors and especially for residents who wanted to gamble closer to home. In 1955 Dick Graves opened the Nugget, which his general manager, John Ascuaga, purchased five years later. Ascuaga slowly expanded the gambling hall into a full-fledged casino resort. His Celebrity Showroom debuted in the 1960s, but the hotel section came much later, with the East Tower opening in 1984 and the thirty-story West Tower in 1996.[10]

The growth of Reno-area tourism, while welcomed, also brought more population, and more population meant more government spending on services and higher taxes. In time the gaming community's growing influence at city hall began to raise questions among residents about Reno's policy direction and the need for reform. Reno, like Las Vegas, reflected the rising dominance of progrowth, business-oriented administrations in postwar Sunbelt cities. In Phoenix, Dallas, and elsewhere, business groups increasingly took over city hall in the 1950s, sometimes to replace corrupt machines with more efficient administrations and sometimes to push ambitious growth agendas that included new airports, convention centers, expressways, and other projects to stimulate business downtown or in the suburbs. In Reno business reformers sought to wrest control away from mayors who struck them as too willing to please downtown gaming executives. A number of events helped guide the city's progress in the 1960s and '70s. The first was a reform of municipal government, which involved changing Reno's charter to eliminate what many voters considered the excessive power wielded by the mayor and city council. Following a series of expensive and controversial public works projects in the 1950s that included a new city hall and downtown street improvements, Reno's mayor Bud Baker (1959–63) and the city council slowly lost the public's confidence. In 1960 concerned residents formed a citizens committee led by former Washoe County school superintendent Earl Wooster, which pushed a new city charter to reform the municipal government.[11]

Las Vegas voters acted similarly, choosing dark-horse candidate Oran Gragson, a businessman and store owner, who ran on a platform touting honesty in government and reform. Gragson won the 1959 race, replacing former city engineer and two-time mayor C. D. Baker, who carried the reform banner just eight years earlier. The immensely popular Gragson was reelected three times, holding office until 1975. In Reno the reform process was similar, although several mayors served under the new charter.

Following its approval in 1961 by the state legislature and a year later by city voters, the Reno committee worked to recruit respected members of the community to run for office in 1963. All of these reform candidates shunned political contributions from the gaming community. Roy Bankofier, a laundry owner who ran for city council under this new regime, served as mayor in the late 1960s and early 1970s. This was when the leaders decided, among other things, to abolish the controversial red-line ordinance, which had confined unrestricted gaming licenses to a few streets downtown, a situation that seemed to favor influential gamers such as Harold and Pappy Smith, Ernest Primm, and Bill Harrah.[12]

In keeping with the spirit of reform, the new city charter strengthened the office of city manager by making that person more independent of the mayor and city council. Under the new charter the city council appointed Reno's mayor. The charter also created a seven-member city council. Though all city council races were now citywide, five councilmen still had to live in their ward, while the other two held at-large seats. This arrangement continued into the late 1970s, when growth advocate Bruno Menicucci served as mayor. After a city charter revision in the mid-1970s once again made the mayor's office elected, "managed growth" or "planned growth" advocate Barbara Bennett defeated Menicucci in 1979.[13]

Although the slow-growth movement did not become really popular until the late 1970s, even in the 1950s there was evidence that residents did not want to spend the money to make Reno a first-class destination. Take the issue of building a convention center. Early in President Eisenhower's administration Congress reformed the nation's tax laws to allow deductions for travel-related expenses to exhibit goods and for professional development at conventions and smaller meetings. Shortly afterward Reno officials began serious discussions about building a convention center, but twice local voters rejected bond issues for the facility. Although residents understood the importance of filling Reno's rooms with delegates during the week when hotels were empty, they did not want to help pay for a convention facility. Clearly, the advent of the passenger jet in 1957–58 and the opening of Las Vegas's convention center in 1959 helped inspire the proposed bond issues, as did the fact that Dallas and Seattle, as well as smaller cities, were spending the millions necessary to draw conventions to their towns. Reno leaders recognized that casino gambling would help their effort to attract conventioneers and acted to build a modern facility.[14]

The problem was how to pay for it. By the late 1950s Las Vegas and other cities saw the value of enacting a hotel/motel room tax as a way of circumventing the opposition of frugal voters. Reno and Sparks also opted for this approach. Once the 1955 state legislature allowed counties to create a fair and recreation board to construct convention facilities, Washoe County established a board with representatives from the two cities and county. Unlike Las Vegas and Clark County, however, several years elapsed before authorities moved forward with the project.[15]

The major problem was where to build the center. In 1959 Reno had little more than a convention director, and the city itself hosted only forty-six meetings that drew just over thirteen thousand conventioneers to its small meeting halls. But this was expected to change quickly once Fair and Recreation Board members moved forward with their project. In January 1960 the board selected a downtown site just north of Mill and east of Lake Streets as the convention center's location. All five members would have preferred cheaper land, but the acreage was near the city's casino core. This choice led one member of the board, Sparks city councilman Edward McGoldrick, to vote no, because he wanted the facility located somewhere in southeast Reno, where Sparks's hotels were more accessible to conventioneers. This had been the case in Las Vegas a few years earlier, when city and county commissioners agreed not to build the convention center downtown, where large tracts of space were relatively scarce, but rather east of the Strip, where land was cheap, available, and more accessible to guests at the major hotels.

Much to the board's surprise, the location it preferred near the river and close to Reno's big casinos generated much opposition from officials, the public, and the press, because the property was expensive and not large enough. A site north of the railroad tracks near today's National Bowling Stadium may well have been the best site for Reno's hotels, but it was not available because leaders were still locked in a protracted debate over the downtown route for Interstate 80. Critics then championed a number of alternatives, all of which drew opposition. Eventually, the probusiness *Reno Evening Gazette* struck a responsive chord with boosters and board members when it declared: "There never will be a convention hall here if every site is attacked on the grounds that a better one might be found later." Obviously, the editor reasoned, no matter what site was proposed, the cost would be high, because "blue chip real estate cannot be bought for a song." Indeed, if the cost of land was the main criteria, "then the only place to put the hall would be far out in the desert or down in the swamp."[16]

The selection process was complicated by bitter divisions marking the debate. Chamber of commerce general manager Jud Allen's recollection of the interests surrounding the site's selection illustrates the factionalism already forming in the community regarding the role tourism would play in future development. As Allen recalled, a committee of fifty representatives from around the metropolitan area studied sites and recommended the Southside School location (later the site of Reno's old city hall). But Harrah's and Harolds Club executives considered the place too far from the casino district and convinced the Fair and Recreation Board to reject it in favor of land around Wingfield Park, near the river. That area, however, was a notorious flood zone and had no space for parking, so the Washoe County Regional Planning Commission, created in 1947 to recommend planning measures for the two cities and nearby county areas, opposed it.[17]

This reopened the debate, which quickly degenerated into a free-for-all. Some Reno councilmen insisted on building the facility downtown, while some Washoe County representatives suggested that the suburbs would be even better, removing conventioneers far from the "gambling scene." There were also suggestions that putting the convention center on the edge of town might spawn another Strip—an idea that casino owners in the urban core hardly relished. But an "arena" in the southern suburbs would allow many upper- and middle-class Renoites to attend UNR basketball games (the Lawlor Events Center on the university campus did not open until 1983) and other local events, a convenience that would only encourage voter support for the inevitable bond issue.

After months of bickering, which even involved the state legislature and Governor Grant Sawyer, all sides agreed to bring in consultants from Stanford and abide by their decision. The consultants chose the Southside School location that the committee of fifty had picked. But the politics continued for more months. In the end the Fair and Recreation Board chose the South Virginia Street site, where the convention center is today, three miles from downtown. For many in the community this was ideal. But it did little to make Reno a popular convention destination. As Sands Hotel owner Pete Cladianos observed, "The convention center should be in a place where there's several thousand rooms nearby." But it wasn't. When it opened in 1965 the facility was in a location on the very edge of the city. At that time most of the built-up part of Reno ended at Plumb Lane, and there was no hotel in the vicinity. Cladianos recalled that whenever the chamber or the Fair and Recreation Board tried to recruit large meetings, "We [had] to tell them we're going to have to put [delegates] all over town. That means you've got to bus people out to the convention center and back." Cladianos, like many other downtown hotel owners, considered the convention center's site selection to be a fatal mistake and characterized it as an "absurd... political decision" made by board members who were not knowledgeable about the meeting industry.[18]

Some landowners on the city's periphery and in the county lands beyond hoped the facility might encourage formation of a strip of resorts, given the sudden need for hotel rooms nearby. But except for the Atlantis and Peppermill hotels, no strip of resorts has emerged out there in a half century. Not building Reno's main convention center near the casino core downtown or by the airport was a mistake that weakened the area's

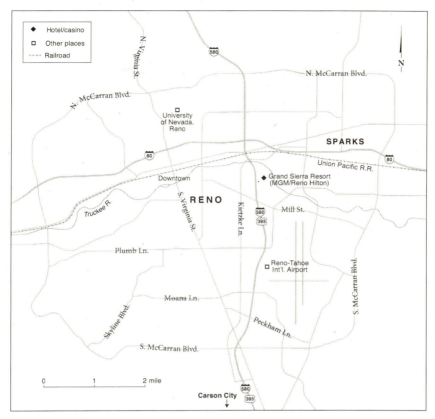

MAP 1.2. Reno-Sparks Metropolitan Area

ability to attract large meetings. The Centennial Coliseum certainly was big enough; in 1965 it was the sixth-largest convention facility in the West. In the mid-1950s when Clark County and the City of Las Vegas quickly agreed to the location for their new convention center, a vibrant Strip of resorts already existed south of the city line. But this was not the case in Reno, and the development of the Peppermill and Atlantis resorts took years to occur. The convention center's location in south Reno only diverted business from downtown to the suburbs and to other American cities, because meeting organizers generally preferred a downtown location that they could not get in Reno.

Once the site on South Virginia and Peckham Lane was formally adopted, Jud Allen concluded that "it was apparent that the existing hotels and motels [downtown] were going to be sacrificed in the gamble to attract a strip of resort hotels on Virginia Street near the facility"—a decision that hardly pleased him. So, in order to placate Harrah's and the other downtown hotels and clubs, there had to be a compromise to "split the master plan" and build what Allen called the "Pioneer Auditorium" in the core area, which "would allow smaller conventions to locate within walking distance of the three hotels." The only available site was that of the old Nevada State Office Building, which was built in 1926 as part of the Transcontinental Highway Exposition. The state had erected the building on a lot in Powning Park, Reno's first public park, across from the county courthouse. In 1966 the Washoe Fair and Recreation Board demolished the structure to make room for the new Pioneer Center for the Performing Arts. Allen recalled that the board, still under fire for putting the convention center way out on South Virginia Street, was "far more receptive to the compromise than it would have been before the transaction," and the architect was able to devise a plan for a fifteen-hundred-seat theater and auditorium.[19] The Pioneer Center opened in early 1968, but it was an abortive attempt at constructing a convention hall. Why? Because the theater-type building, with a main floor and balcony, lacked the flexibility to host different types of meetings. Downtown would have to wait until the Livestock Events Center and Reno Events Center opened years later. But the flawed 1960s effort to locate a convention center downtown at least gave the city a facility, which ultimately became a cultural center for the larger community.

The process of building the Centennial Coliseum (the name commemorated Nevada's centennial in 1964) also reflected, especially for Allen, the lack of citizen support for Reno's badly neglected convention industry. As he reported in his 1997 memoir, two bond issues to build a convention center had failed because of what he called "a widespread negative attitude toward local gamblers."[20] These events helped demonstrate the fact that Reno's community-versus-downtown-casinos conflict antedated the MGM Grand and the slow-growth movement of the 1970s by at least a decade.

Location was not the only front in this emerging struggle; so was funding. In Reno the room tax proved to be an ideal approach because it cost voters nothing, since tourists would provide the revenue. The convention center was also "camouflaged," as Allen later pointed out, by being pitched to the public by the Fair and Recreation Board as an arena and civic theater—a good venue to watch local basketball teams and other events.

Leaders promised the community they would impose strict spending limits and allocate all excess revenue for local parks and recreation departments. Money would also go to the board, which the hotels liked because they could now pay less in dues to the chamber of commerce. Thanks to all the internecine warfare, the Centennial Coliseum did not open until 1965, six years after Las Vegas's convention center debuted. In anticipation of the opening, investors bought up land in the area to build casino resorts and commercial developments to serve those visitors and residents who would be patronizing the multipurpose coliseum (which was renamed the Reno-Sparks Convention Center in 1982). In 1964 local businessman and rancher Ralph Casazza opened Shopper's Square on the family's property, which later helped pave the way for the march of development down Virginia Street southward to the new Park Lane Mall in 1967 and the Meadowood Mall in 1979.[21]

These events helped reinforce the decline of downtown's central business district (CBD). Initially, business groups were positive. Jordan Crouch, senior vice president of First National Bank, viewed the spike as a good sign: "This will focus attention on Reno as a business location, which was ignored up to a few years ago." Crouch felt that "this nice orderly growth would encourage more business investment in the city." It did, but a lot of it was in the suburbs, especially southward down Virginia Street toward the convention center and, after the 1960s, farther out along the US 395 corridor toward Washoe Lake and Carson City. As residential developments sprang up in south Reno and in county areas, the stores followed, further draining the CBD of customers, much like the pattern in Las Vegas and cities across the country.[22]

As in Las Vegas, constructing a modern jetport went hand in hand with building a convention center. The site of the original 1920s airport in Reno (Blanchfield Airport), near Plumas Street on much of today's Washoe County Golf Course, was abandoned for a better site. When the Boeing Air Transport Company got the contract to deliver mail in the region, company vice president Eddie Hubbard in 1928 selected a site on 120 acres (part of today's Reno-Tahoe International Airport) southeast of downtown. The facility, which the company named for Hubbard, opened the following year. In 1937 United Airlines acquired Hubbard Field, and in later years the carrier bought more land to extend runways and expand flight operations. In 1953 United began leasing the facility to the City of Reno. A few years later the municipality purchased the now-570-acre airport for $914,000, with plans to build a modern terminal in time for the Squaw Valley Winter Olympics. The city used the old field in the interim, because relatively few tourists flew into town. Indeed, there were only fifteen scheduled flights daily at Hubbard in 1953 and just twenty-eight in 1963.[23]

But the dawn of the jet age (the first commercial passenger jets landed in Reno in 1964) changed all that. The city soon relegated the old field and its little "shack" of a terminal to the scrap heap of history. The new terminal opened for passengers in late 1959. It was formally dedicated on February 15, 1960, on the eve of the Winter Olympics, for which the newly named Reno International Airport served as gateway. The construction of this new facility definitely gave momentum to the effort by Clark County commissioners to build a spacious new jetport south of Las Vegas, a proposal that voters approved less than a month after Reno dedicated its new terminal.[24]

Though modern, the new Reno passenger building was far from perfect. In 1968 Western Airlines and another carrier announced they were increasing jet service to Reno and asked the chamber of commerce's Air Service Committee to lobby city officials for "improved service from better parking to cleaner washrooms." Specifically, the airlines wanted a paved lot nearer the baggage area, an enlarged baggage area, and space for buses. Municipal leaders could hardly refuse. So, once satisfied with the city manager's response, Western Airlines launched daily jet service to Reno in 1968 from Sacramento, Los Angeles, and Ontario. Nonstop service expanded to Chicago in 1970, which was vital to later resort development. The new terminal served the city well during the Olympics and into the 1970s, when new resorts opened and airline traffic increased.[25]

The area's other airport, Reno Stead, northwest of town, became a support facility. This field had opened in 1942, built by the US Army Air Corps for the war. Stead later functioned as a small air force base, with the Nevada Air National Guard helping to make room for this by moving its facility to the city airport in 1954. Nine years later, however, the Pentagon ordered the base closed, along with twenty-five others as part of Defense Department budget cuts. This was a disappointment for Reno, because it occurred just as the Defense Department was pouring more money into Nellis Air Force Base in southern Nevada, making it a primary training center for NATO crews and allowing Las Vegas to diversify its economy with a large defense sector. Of course, Reno-Stead did not close for good. In 1966 the military transferred the former base to the City of Reno, and it began operating as a municipal airport. By the 1970s it served as a base for civil aviation, including helicopters, and was home to the Reno Air Races, an annual event that drew thousands of tourists to the area. Earlier in 1968 Lear Industries purchased thirty-five hundred acres on the base for an industrial park where the company could test a steam car and other products it was developing.[26]

In the 1950s and '60s business and political leaders also worked to improve car and bus access to Reno from its major customer base, California. For years the city had relied on the two-lane US 40 to deliver gamblers from the Bay Area and Sacramento. In the 1950s Pappy Smith lobbied Nevada's congressional delegation to get US 40 expanded to four lanes across the Sierra and from Donner Summit down to Virginia Street. East of Reno the highway resumed its original two-lane width across the sparsely populated Great Basin.[27]

Despite this better road, Reno's weather continued to discourage tourism, especially in winter, when temperatures could be brutally cold. On New Year's Eve 1965, for instance, the mercury on Virginia Street plunged below zero, and this was not a rare occurrence. Northern Nevada's frigid weather, while a boon to skiers, only served to divert visitors to places like Las Vegas. Only the most diehard Reno loyalists braved such conditions in winter. Reno promoters, however, were up to the challenge—even with the chamber's small budgets. One of Jud Allen's best moves early in his tenure as head of Reno's chamber of commerce was to hire the Holiday Hotel's director of publicity and promotion, Don Burke, to a similar position with the chamber. Allen had created a promotion committee composed of the publicity directors from some of Reno's best-known properties. Together, they had devised a plan to attract more visitors from the Bay Area by establishing an outpost in San Francisco, a Reno publicity and travel office located in a storefront on Market Street. This resembled an action taken by the New England states, which in the 1960s began renting storefronts in Manhattan's Rockefeller Center to draw New Yorkers to the quaint environs of the Berkshires and beyond.[28]

Burke, a creative and aggressive promoter, was the ideal choice to head the new office. In 1963 he devised one of his best promotions for luring Bay Area residents to Reno by chartering what he dubbed the "Fun Train" from the Southern Pacific. This weekend excursion train ran only during the winter months, "when automobile travel was hazardous." Its success prolonged its life for decades more. From 1963 to 2014 this "15-car block party" carried hundreds of tourists across the snowy Sierra. The seven hours whizzed by, thanks to Burke's ingenious contributions, which included the use of formal dining cars, a piano bar car, a dome car through the Sierra, a stripped-down car for dancing, strolling musicians, Elvis impersonators, and any other innovation he could think of to make the trip as enjoyable as the two-night stay in Reno. Burke and the chamber even equipped the so-called Dance Car with an orchestra on occasion to warm up the tourists in a way similar to what the Hacienda Hotel's "airline" did for Las Vegas–bound passengers in the 1950s. The first Fun Train to Reno brought four hundred people to the station near Virginia Street. As Jud Allen recalled, "It was the off-season, and the train brought in more gamblers than already existed in town." In later years Burke and the chamber supplemented this coup with the Reno Drive-up Package and airline Fun Flights. Even after the RSCVA began to siphon much of this revenue from the chamber, these promotions continued to help fill hotel rooms during Reno's "dead season," winter. In time, large conventions helped supplement these efforts during the cold months, just as big meetings helped fill Las Vegas hotel rooms during its normally dead period: during the week.[29]

Access was crucial to the development of both metropolitan areas, because they sat in a largely isolated state, separated from their huge California market by soaring mountains in the north and mountains plus desert in the south. For midcentury Reno, the train, plane, car, and bus were all crucial to its future as a tourist center. Interstate 80 promised to be a godsend for Reno, but it took a long time to get there. The new freeway, like the jetport, was vital to the city's continued growth at a time when long-distance train travel was in decline nationally. Both projects were crucial to Harrah's expansion and snaring MGM, Circus Circus, Del Webb, and other large companies.

But, once again, controversy flared—in this case, over Interstate 80's path through town—just as it had over almost every important undertaking in the city's modern era. Several routes were considered. According to Reno's other newspaper, the *Nevada State Journal,* and its editor Paul Leonard, initially two routes were under study: Third Street by the railroad tracks and a northern bypass that would have swept past the city, north of the university campus, which Nevada's congressman Walter Baring preferred. But the *Gazette* steadfastly advocated the Third Street route. The state highway department, however, wanted the Seventh to Eighth Street corridor for Interstate 80, because, according to Allen, westbound "travelers would be enticed to stop off at a casino rather than continuing on to the West Coast." Public sentiment, however, opposed this idea. When the highway department's plan finally came up for discussion at a public meeting, an overflow crowd protested that the road was too close to St. Mary's Hospital.[30]

In an effort to resolve this community conflict, the department hired consultants who considered five proposed routes. Two bypassed the city, and three bisected it. The Regional Planning Council and Reno City Council preferred the latter option along Third Street, because federal money would be available to lower the railroad tracks—a project that ultimately cost the city more than two hundred million dollars when it was finally undertaken in the early 2000s. The United Freeway Association, an out-of-state group, pushed for a complete bypass of the city, which won the support of Congressman Baring, who asserted that Third Street would "cut Reno in half"—a feat that the street-grade railroad tracks had already accomplished. Baring backed an investigation of the "selfish interests" pushing the Third Street route. Another group of consultants and more hearings only delayed construction longer. Ultimately, Seventh Street became the route, partly because the protest movement ran out of energy, leaving Baring without enough allies to keep fighting.

As historian William Rowley has noted, the final routing did not hurt the city core, because the city was not bypassed, nor was the freeway brought too close to Fourth Street, the site of today's Eldorado Hotel–Silver Legacy–Circus Circus hotel complex. However, the road did divide downtown from the university and the neighborhoods around it. In addition, the planning process was a long one, thanks to the usual divisiveness within the community. As a result, Interstate 80 did not open in Reno until 1974, eight years after Interstate 15 reached the Las Vegas Strip. In Las Vegas the freeway's routing did not cut through downtown or the Strip in a way that divided vital parts from each other. Instead, the freeway mostly separated the black Westside from the tourist parts of town, which was just fine with white officials.[31]

The 1960s witnessed not only Reno's efforts to obtain an interstate highway, a modern jetport, and a convention center, but also the first plans to improve downtown. By the late 1960s Reno officials were prepared to take any steps necessary to take Reno to the next new level for the millions of tourists they expected to draw in future years. With more airport expansion on the horizon and Interstate 80 gradually approaching, the city council was determined to exploit Reno's improved accessibility by stimulating the tourist sector. Two initiatives were crucial: Project RENOvation and expanding the red-line zone for unrestricted or unlimited gaming.

In the late 1960s a group of mostly downtown businessmen organized Reno Unlimited, which pushed the idea of revitalizing downtown by beautifying the Truckee River area and undertaking other projects—perhaps even converting Virginia Street into a pedestrian mall—to attract more tourists downtown. To this end the organization formally endorsed Project RENOvation and raised more than $100,000 to fund studies of the downtown area, which included identifying problems and their solutions. The city also contributed to the fund, along with casinos and other businesses. Together, they hired a San Francisco consulting firm, which surveyed visitors and, not surprisingly, recommended devising a plan for downtown that would provide more land for casinos to expand. Part of the solution lay in the city expanding its red-line zone for unrestricted gaming licenses, which represented a radical departure from traditional policy. It should be noted that since 1931, both Reno and Las Vegas had granted restricted gaming licenses (permitting just a few slot machines or maybe another game or two) to food stores, bars, restaurants, pharmacies, and even gas stations all over town. But both cities historically confined casinos with unrestricted gaming licenses to a few designated blocks downtown, so large gaming palaces would not invade residential and commercial areas. Part of Project RENOvation's vision for downtown also included public-private partnerships, including bond issues to fund public works to improve the area. Progrowth Reno activists in the late 1960s intended to use new casino resorts to invigorate downtown and help pay for it. To this end city and Project RENOvation leaders debated the wisdom of placing their $1.2 million Project RENOvation bond issue on the 1970 primary ballot when the school district pushed a $14 million bond issue to build new schools, the state had its own bond issue for parks, and the city supported another one for airport, street, and sewer improvements.[32]

Project RENOvation trustee Allen Dunn pleaded with councilmen to approve the ballot question, contending that the private sector had already pledged money and beautifying the Truckee River area was essential, because many private investors were holding back to see if the city government truly supported the enterprise. "If this project goes through," he predicted, "these investors will come in and tear down old buildings." As a result of these improvements, he contended, Reno's tax base would be greatly increased and voters would be satisfied to see that "over the long haul this will be the best $1.2 million the city has ever spent."[33]

But not everyone was convinced. City councilman John Chism openly expressed concern about too many bond issues on the ballot, and Mayor Bankofier insisted that nothing should jeopardize the city's airport, street, and sewer bond questions. City manager Joseph Latimore reinforced the mayor's view, telling councilmen that "people who already have a sewer and airport have little incentive to turn out and vote." In the end, the council deferred action on the beautification effort, sending a clear message to investors that despite all of the rhetoric, city leaders were not yet firmly committed to supporting downtown improvements. But after much prodding from growth advocates, the councilmen reversed themselves and placed the $1.2 million Project RENOvation bond issue on the ballot.[34]

Many supporters of downtown beautification remained unconvinced it would pass. First, not all downtown business leaders supported the proposal, and the big casinos were slow to contribute any of their own money to the project, which drew the wrath of many in the community. Even the conservative and usually procasino *Reno Evening Gazette,* which favored downtown's improvement, urged that Harrah's, Harolds Club, and the rest of the private sector in the urban core put up serious money *before* the election, or else "many voters will oppose the public's share of this [bond issue] because they feel the hotels and stores downtown will benefit the most from improvements." The newspaper insisted that in order "to help the bond issue the private sector must be more visible in promising money" for Project RENOvation.[35]

This editorial proved to be prophetic. In September 1970 Reno voters rejected the bond issue, just as Bankofier and Latimore had feared. Renters supported it, but in a separate vote required by the city charter, property owners did not, although both groups approved the bonds for street, sewer, and airport improvements. Mayor Bankofier attributed Project RENOvation's bond failure to the fact that the measure required a property tax hike, while the street and airport improvement's bond money would largely come out of the city's regular budget. He noted glumly, "In any community where you want to start renovating it's an uphill battle," but, at the same time, "we certainly couldn't stop our progress in building more sewers and streets." Later in his career, chamber of commerce manager, city councilman, and failed mayoral candidate Jud Allen had a slightly different view. Like others, he recognized that Reno voters were frugal, but it went deeper. He felt they could not get past their own personal interests to support projects that benefited the greater city at large: "I found that to most citizens their neighborhoods are their community. They could care less what is happening elsewhere."[36]

In its assessment of Project RENOvation's failure at the polls, the *Reno Evening Gazette* reiterated its position that voters faulted the big hotels for not being visible enough with their support. The vote itself, however, indicates another problem. While renters supported all of the bond issues by a vote of almost two to one, property owners approved the street, sewer, and airport improvements by a narrower margin, showing how conservative this constituency really was. Although many Reno property owners were undoubtedly glad to see their city expand, they were less willing to help pay for it. Clearly, many property owners who already had sewers as well as curbed, guttered, lit, and paved streets were not willing to help finance these amenities for others. While Las Vegas city voters at times also balked at paying for some public works projects, this was much less common in the Strip city, where public works bond issues routinely passed.[37]

Reforming Reno's historic red-line policy was just as controversial as downtown redevelopment, but progress on this initiative was more rapid—probably because it did not involve spending millions of dollars in public funds. Reno's city council passed the original ordinance in 1947, strengthened by various revisions in the early 1950s, to restrict unlimited gaming licenses to just a few streets downtown. However, licenses for a *limited* number of slots and even a few other games of chance traditionally went to bars, clubs, and other types of business establishments all over town. This had been the case for limited licenses ever since Nevada relegalized wide-open gambling in 1931.

Although Reno, like Las Vegas, had been a wet town during Prohibition and a liberal divorce mecca for many years, there was a broad consensus in both cities that unrestricted gaming licenses should be confined to just a few streets downtown near the railroad station where wide-open gambling had originated. Gambling, Reno, and Las Vegas seem almost synonymous for many people today, so it seems odd that both cities would restrict the activity, but they did. Reno's romance with gambling dated from the late nineteenth and early twentieth centuries, but residents never fully embraced the industry—even in the immediate postwar era. As one Reno newspaper editorialized in 1946, "It is true that the glittering array of establishments ... which dominate one block on Virginia Street ... give the appearance that gambling is Reno's chief occupation." The column then pointed out that in Reno and Las Vegas, gaming had expanded "far beyond that visualized in 1931 by the sponsors of the wide-open gaming law." The newspaper insisted that Nevadans and Renoites were "interested in the development of small industries, farming, ranching, mining and a widespread retail business, the things that have kept the state sound for three-quarters of a century." The editorial concluded by asserting that Renoites did not want these industries "submerged ... by the gaming business."[38] So, elements within the city's population, even into the 1950s and '60s, rejected the notion that Reno's future depended upon the construction of more casinos.

In September 1951 Reno's chamber of commerce joined with downtown retail merchants and other nongaming business owners in the central business district in an effort to convince the city council to issue no more gaming and cabaret licenses on Virginia Street in order to halt the spread of casinos and bars. Numerous business owners, including the manager of the Joseph Magnin store, complained to city leaders about having gaming establishments on their block. To appease them, a number of casinos sought to lease their buildings and have them relocate, but downtown business owners resisted this option. Clearly, the CBD was the place where transit lines converged and most Renoites still shopped. Many residents and merchants there clearly regarded the gambling halls and clubs as a nuisance, where drunks, gamblers, and various undesirables tended to gather, especially at night. But conditions grew worse after dark, when assault, burglary, and mugging sometimes occurred as a patron or two resorted to crime to offset their losses. Joseph Magnin executives even made sure that a guarantee not to locate a casino on the same block as their store was in their lease. Clearly, the expanding presence of gambling in Reno's CBD resulted in an uneasy coexistence between casinos and many traditional businesses.[39] There was a similar feeling in Las Vegas, where businessman and mayor Oran Gragson fought efforts in the 1960s and early '70s to enlarge the red-line district downtown and perhaps expand unlimited gambling to other parts of the city. But in Reno as early as the 1950s, the pressure to allow more room for casinos became intense. Rising tourist numbers and the demand for more gambling space ultimately led city hall to issue more licenses for the new Holiday Hotel-Casino (1956) and many more places in ensuing decades, as gaming-tourism became Reno's major industry.

The downtown nongaming business sector was the key group supporting a red-line zone. In the late 1940s and early '50s it was the chamber of commerce and retail merchants association that routinely opposed the granting of new gaming licenses downtown. Mayor Bud Baker, who was swept into office in 1961 as part of Earl Wooster's good-government reform group, even suggested on one occasion that Reno could easily get along without any gambling. Many Renoites, along with some smaller club owners, believed that Reno's old red-line ordinance was mostly designed to protect big operators like the Smiths, Bill Harrah, Ernie Primm, and Charlie Mapes, who were perennially close to city hall. In contrast, chamber of commerce head Jud Allen felt the law chiefly served the interests of downtown's nongaming business community, especially the retail merchants. Whatever the truth, it is clear that casino gambling divided Reno's business community. Referring to Reno's midcentury decades, Allen explained that the city "never created a long-range program for tourism development back in the pioneer days of gaming . . . [because] zoning was very tight and downtown merchants were concerned over property rental costs if gaming was allowed to expand unrestricted throughout the city."[40]

This fear ultimately came to pass not only in Reno but most spectacularly in the Atlantic City boardwalk area, when the development of casino resorts in the years after 1977 quickly raised land values to the point where longtime stores and low-end apartments were either demolished or priced out of existence. The same was true of downtown Las Vegas, where the proliferation of large gambling halls and hotels ejected numerous stores and homes from the Fremont Street area. Because many Reno store owners did not own the building they occupied, this was a real fear in a city with a relatively small CBD. Allen even went so far as to assert that the "the majority of citizens in Reno always blamed downtown gaming interests for holding back the development of major hotels and [the] forming of a 'strip' on South Virginia Street" near the convention center. Although Allen may have overstated this point, his many years of residence in Reno and his access to the city's elite and media lend credence to his point of view.[41]

Reno's professional people also opposed the spread of gaming. As casinos increasingly took over downtown Virginia Street, representatives of the Medico-Dental Building at 161 North Virginia, on the west side of the thoroughfare between First and Second Streets, complained that their building now sat on the only block left between Commercial Row and the river that was "free on both sides of night spots and devoted to substantial business establishments." Doctors and dentists, like their counterparts in other American downtowns, wanted to be located in a sea of stores and office buildings, not in the midst of a gambling den.[42] This was the problem for downtown gaming in midcentury Reno and Las Vegas. In the 1950s dense casino gaming, with more and larger operations than those in the early 1930s and '40s, began to proliferate in the heart of both cities, and nongaming businesses resented it—just as their nineteenth-century predecessors had resented the bawdy theaters and twenty-four-hour bars that supported prostitution and all-night revelry along the waterfront piers and near the railroad stations in Seattle, New York, Boston, St. Louis, and other large cities.

While 1930s businessmen and residents tolerated vice as a means of keeping taxes low and helping to partially insulate the state from the effects of the Great Depression, in the postwar era they did not want to see casinos take over downtown and permanently dominate their city's economy. As the *Nevada State Journal* summarized the sentiment in 1949, "Nevada's . . . future growth is no more dependent upon gambling than it is upon commercial fishing or the raising of citrus fruits. The whole thing—the neon lights, the carnival atmosphere and click of dice and chips—is incidental to the broad scheme of things." In fact, the *Journal* went so far as to declare that although it was true that "thousands of tourists are attracted here and to Las Vegas by wide-open gambling, . . . most of them would come anyway as we have other attractions just as interesting if not as spectacular."[43] Lake Tahoe, the snowcapped Sierra, Pyramid Lake, and other natural attractions probably would have made Reno a tourist mecca once the place had been properly marketed and developed. But Americans' postwar fascination with Nevada-style gambling and with Las Vegas only boosted Reno's tourist economy downtown. By the 1960s it was obvious that gaming had replaced divorce as Reno's major tourist draw, and the town's red-line district had to be enlarged to accommodate future development.

Nevertheless, Mayor Bankofier, like fellow businessman and Las Vegas mayor Oran Gragson, was cautious about expanding the red line downtown to allow more large casinos. But conditions dramatically changed in 1969 once Governor Paul Laxalt signed Nevada's new corporate gaming law. As the *Reno Evening Gazette* reported, "Since early last spring pressure has mounted from some quarters to relax the boundary containing heavy gambling downtown." Bankofier remained steadfast for a while, insisting that any action on the matter by the city council be deferred until all proposals were discussed and the final report on Project RENOvation was completed. In the end, after months of discussion, Reno's city council voted to abolish the red-line ordinance on May 11, 1970, effective January 1, 1971.[44] Unrestricted gaming licenses would now be issued for casinos anywhere in the city—provided they were attached to a hotel of at least one hundred rooms.

The backlash came swiftly. Critics complained that the new law effectively extended the old red line to the municipal limits, even allowing casinos into the suburbs not far from where families lived. Supporters countered that the ordinance required casinos seeking unrestricted gaming licenses to build a hotel of one hundred or more rooms, which tended to favor big operators and corporations. Under the old law one could get an unrestricted gaming license without building a hotel. But Reno, like Las Vegas, wanted more large hotels downtown rather than just small clubs to accommodate the expected influx of tourists in the 1970s and '80s. Supporters argued that Reno had given itself needed flexibility should a corporation want to build a gaming resort near the airport, by the convention center, along the approaching Interstate 80, or at the base of the Sierra in the western suburbs.

Critics charged that the new law would hurt the city's gaming industry, because no one could build a casino anywhere in town without a one-hundred-room hotel. They did not consider this a liberalization of policy, as the city council asserted, but regarded it as even more restrictive than the old law. This position was ably presented by attorney Byron Meredith, who represented the downtown Colony Club in its efforts to secure an unrestricted gaming license. He maintained there should be no need to build an expensive hotel and argued for putting the red-line ordinance to a public vote at the next election. Meredith told city councilmen that "people come to Reno to gamble. They don't come merely to find a hotel room. . . . You're not getting rid of the red line; you're just running it to the city limits . . . with this new ordinance." He insisted that even now, "little motels" in Reno were not filling up. Meredith then intimated that the big hotels supported the new law as a way of blocking the licensing of small clubs downtown that might siphon customers from Harrah's and other large operations.[45]

Opponents used every conceivable argument to repeal the ordinance. Fred Aoyama, who was part of an effort to recall Mayor Bankofier and two city councilmen, called the ordinance "discriminatory." Aoyama reasoned that a one-hundred-room hotel in 1971 cost at least one million dollars, and this would not let Reno grow, because it discouraged smaller investors from expanding downtown's gaming industry. Even more cynical was gaming executive Pete Cladianos, who asserted that the new ordinance changed nothing. The old ordinance, he charged, had held back Reno's growth for forty years, and he predicted its successor would do the same. Cladianos demanded that a public referendum decide the new law's fate. This idea was rejected by Bankofier and the city council, who opposed amending the new ordinance to award an unlimited gaming license to any operator who spent one million dollars to build a swanky new club that would benefit downtown. Instead, city leaders wanted to use their power to approve unrestricted gaming licenses as a tool to encourage the construction of more large hotels downtown to reinforce Reno's tourist economy. But the larger question was whether longtime residents not immediately tied to the gaming industry wanted their city to become another Las Vegas. For a while there was general enthusiasm about the city's prospects for growth, but much of this sentiment later gave way to concern about uncontrolled growth and the ceding of downtown Reno to tourists and casino interests.[46]

Nevertheless, red-line reform, more leisure time, an expanding national economy, and the increased popularity of gambling all resulted in the transformation of Reno-Sparks into a true metropolitan area. A new convention center, a modern jetport, and better highway connections all helped to enhance Reno's image in the 1960s. Preliminary estimates in May 1970 put Washoe County's population at 119,953. Sparks's 23,000 residents nearly tripled the 1950 figure, and Carson City's 15,624 figure in 1970 was more than triple its 1960 (5,100) number. Reno grew the most of all in absolute numbers; it had 32,497 people in 1950, 51,470 in 1960, and 72,863 in 1970. The city gained more than 20,000 people just in the 1960s, despite the phaseout of Stead Air Force Base in 1964.[47]

Of course, the growth of gambling and population forced local governments to spend more money. In October 1969 the Washoe County commissioners met to discuss land acquisitions for more or expanded county parks as well as public golf facilities and the local fairgrounds.[48] At the same time, Reno had virtually no bus service for its rising number of low-income commuters after Pioneer Bus Lines, a private carrier, went bankrupt. To the south, car-reliant Las Vegas was not much better off with Las Vegas Transit, which suffered through several strikes and myriad passenger complaints about service.

Education also tugged at the Reno area's coffers. In 1969 the Washoe County Teacher's Association, responding to large spikes in the cost of living, demanded a $700 cost-of-living increase per teacher. But an even larger expense was the cost for constructing more buildings. By 1969 Reno resembled Las Vegas, with its lack of schools and teachers to handle the mushrooming number of students. Population growth ultimately forced the Washoe County School District (WCSD) to seek another bond issue in 1969 to fund more facilities. The district's last bond issue had been $10 million in 1965. In 1968 an outside consultant predicted that by 1980 the district would need up to $4.5 million for the new schools, and that was a conservative figure, given the fact that the local student population was growing at an annual rate of 5 percent. As school superintendent Marvin Picollo observed, "We don't want to have to put students on double sessions or people won't move here, and this will be bad for the community as a whole." Reno had faced the prospects of double sessions in the 1950s due to the postwar baby boom. But thanks to the education reforms pushed by Las Vegas assemblywoman Maude Frazier, Governor Charles Russell, and others, Nevada had established a sales tax and used it, together with other funding sources, to help finance new schools in the area. However, the 1960s and '70s brought new challenges for the school district, just as they did for its counterpart in southern Nevada, where Las Vegas's growing population combined with the baby boom to overload classrooms.[49]

Picollo knew that school expansion would require an increase in property taxes—something he dreaded taking to the voters. As he explained at one public meeting, the 5.23 percent increase in student enrollment over the previous year (an increase to 27,424 from 26,059) represented the "highest percentage increase for any year during the previous five."[50] Enrollment had actually dropped in 1966 because of the Defense Department's phaseout of nearby Stead Air Force Base, which had resulted in an exodus of families, but Reno's overall growth and increased gaming easily offset that loss in the late 1960s. In 1968 the district hired more teachers to reduce class size, but the student surge in 1969 created a space crunch that put the WCSD 300 students over its enrollment estimate. Even though the WCSD opened Procter Hug High School in 1967 to serve students in the northern part of the metropolitan area, by the mid-1970s another high school was needed. The local construction industry eagerly awaited these projects, because, despite continued population growth, in September 1969 Washoe County building permits and construction dropped sharply due to tight money and high interest rates. These events presaged the arrival of a lengthy recession that plagued America for most of the 1970s.[51]

As early as 1968, long before the advent of the MGM Grand Hotel and the big new resorts of the late 1970s, Reno residents had to pay higher taxes to fund new schools and other government services for the metropolitan area's increased population, which came mainly from the growth of its tourist industry. In March 1968 the Reno area's property tax rate reached five dollars per one hundred dollars of assessed valuation, the maximum property tax rate allowed under the Nevada Constitution, to help raise the two million dollars necessary to fund local schools. As Reno's financial director, Delbert Heidrich, noted, the higher taxes also resulted from a "general increase in costs, much needed street improvements, and traffic safety controls." But the rise in taxes drew the wrath of conservative property owners as well as the *Reno Evening Gazette,* which objected vigorously to the increase in sales, gasoline, and property taxes. "The city, the county, [and] the school district," it declared, "should not assume that they have first claim to the income or property of any individual or any business firm or any property owner." Here was just one side of the antigrowth movement. Underlying the growing complaints of other citizens about snarled traffic, worsening air pollution, and water shortages were the costs involved in extending infrastructure and services to more and more people.[52]

Exacerbating these problems was gaming's growing presence downtown and its inordinate influence at city hall. While Renoites accepted gaming and divorce as part of their postwar economy, they scoffed at those who perceived these activities as their city's dominant industries, much less its future. It was in the 1950s and '60s, when Nevada-style gambling became increasingly popular and neon-fronted clubs increasingly took over downtown, that residents became even more concerned about the CBD's increasingly honky-tonk atmosphere. But Reno voters opposed higher taxes and growing urban problems as much as they disliked increased gaming-tourism. They literally wanted Reno to remain a small city and not become another boomtown like Las Vegas, which by the 1960 census had passed Reno in population (64,405 to 51,470) to officially become Nevada's largest city. This growing band of citizens preferred a policy that Boulder City still devoutly embraces today, limited growth, in which the amount of new business licenses and housing permits is strictly limited by government.[53]

In an effort to satisfy critics and secure more control of growth-related problems, Reno-Sparks leaders, like their counterparts in the Las Vegas valley, advocated consolidating many government services in the metropolitan area. There were good reasons for doing so. For example, when the new Washoe County Courthouse opened in 1964, its jail capacity was only 163, and Reno's held only 106. Neither was enough by itself, because the number of prisoners always ballooned "during the tourist season." By the early 1970s there were calls to consolidate the jails of Reno and Sparks and build a large new facility as a money-saving measure, as well as pursuing the same efficient approach for other municipal operations.[54]

Consolidation of the cities' jails was a reform that required consideration, as did other regional approaches to urban problems. Actually, a very limited form of regional government already existed in the metropolitan area. In October 1971 Reno, Sparks, and Washoe County leaders had signed an interlocal agreement approved by the State of Nevada to form the Washoe Council of Governments to serve as "the planning and development clearinghouse agency" for the greater metropolitan area. This new agency struggled with several issues in its early years, which tested its viability. For example, as Reno and Sparks quarreled repeatedly over the expansion of their jointly run sewage treatment plant, the *Nevada State Journal* suggested reorganizing the Washoe Council of Governments, because the city's and county's current members were juggling too many committee assignments and were not consulting enough with expert staff. The Regional Planning Commission also faced problems, as Reno and Sparks began to resent county domination of that body. In the Las Vegas valley there was not much better cooperation between the cities and county, although there was less disagreement over streets, highways, and sewage treatment than there was in the North.[55]

In 1977 Mayor Menicucci began voicing support for some consolidation of city and county government services as a way of saving money. At this same time, Las Vegas mayor William Briare, just like his predecessor Oran Gragson, supported consolidation of whole governments in southern Nevada's metropolis. Like Briare, Menicucci was an insurance man who recognized the added expense and administrative red tape caused by having two or three jails, multiple fire departments, and separate bureaucracies for processing licenses for contractors, repair companies, and other businesses operating across municipal boundaries. So, noting that voters made it clear they wanted a reduction in government spending and with a mayoral election looming, in January 1979 Menicucci asked the Washoe Council of Governments to endorse consolidation of the governments of Reno, Sparks, and Washoe County to save money. Carson City and Ormsby County (which ultimately dissolved as a county in favor of the city) had done this in 1969. But Reno-area officials would not be as open-minded as their neighbors in the state capital.[56]

Menicucci made his pitch just two months after voters in Las Vegas's unincorporated townships soundly defeated consolidation with that city in November 1978. These events transpired during the Iranian oil embargo, which had raised the price of gasoline and jet fuel to the point where it curtailed tourist spending. Menicucci argued that with municipal and county revenues down, efficient government was more vital than ever before in the metropolitan area. Nevertheless, the Washoe Council of Governments politely rejected his proposal, suggesting instead that representatives of the three governments discuss the proposition further before putting it on the ballot. In the end, rival leaders and the public were lukewarm to consolidating services. Only much later in 2000, with the Reno-Sparks area mired in a major recession, did the county (the Truckee Meadows Fire Protection District) and city finally come together and consolidate their fire services. Twelve years later, though, Washoe County commissioners even pulled out of that agreement over what three commissioners considered to be excessive union benefits. But even though consolidation of services, much less whole governments, faced stiff opposition in both metropolitan areas, regional government bodies provided a slightly more popular option. Still, it took time. It was not until the 1980s in southern Nevada and the 1990s in northern Nevada that the regional approach to metropolitan problems began to run more smoothly.[57]

In contrast to these conflicts, there was little disagreement about how to handle racial minorities. Here consensus largely ruled—at least among white residents. For years Jim Crow held sway in Reno, just as it did in Las Vegas and other American cities. Until the Civil Rights Act of 1964 Reno's downtown clubs and some businesses were even more racially segregated than Las Vegas and quite militant about it. In Las Vegas the get-tough strategy of the local chapter of the National Association for the Advancement of Colored People (NAACP) succeeded earlier than its counterpart in Reno when, four years before passage of Lyndon Johnson's sweeping civil rights act, *most* casino resorts on the Strip and downtown agreed to allow black customers in. In Reno, however, progress on the open-accommodations front was slower. Jud Allen recalled an executive from one hotel contacting him about a black couple who stayed at the place over the weekend on a chamber of commerce "Fun Flight Package." The hotel's position was clear: "If you can't screen who you sell to, then we don't want to be part of your program." But the fallout from racial protests in Selma, Montgomery, Birmingham, and elsewhere eventually reached Nevada, as NAACP chapters in Reno and Las Vegas became more aggressive in their quest for minority rights. There were several sit-ins at businesses in downtown Reno, including one in June 1960 at Arch Drug featuring, among others, Charles Kellar, counsel for the Nevada NAACP, and Eddie Scott, future president of the Reno branch of the NAACP.[58] But despite these and other actions, virtually all of Reno's hotel-casino operators successfully resisted open accommodations and fair employment practices for African Americans, Native Americans, and Asian Americans until after passage of the federal Civil Rights Act of 1964.

Local political leaders were complicit in dragging their feet on minority rights, as they were in Las Vegas and many other places across the nation. In May 1962 the Reno City Council advised the local branch of the NAACP that although it opposed casinos discriminating against minorities on the basis of color, it could not pull a gaming license simply for that reason. In Reno and in Las Vegas even major black headliners could not sleep at the hotels where they performed. In the 1940s, '50s, and '60s, Reno's racial minorities responded by establishing their own gambling clubs in the rundown eastern edge of the downtown area, primarily in the Lake-Evans blocks east of Virginia Street. Most of these places did not close until Harrah's and other major casinos downtown, under intense federal pressure, finally opened their doors to minority customers. Nevertheless, racial problems continued well into the 1970s, long after national and state civil rights acts went into effect. As late as September 1975 the city's newspapers continued to print stories about charges brought against Reno police officers for harassing and beating minority residents, and conditions were not much better in Las Vegas.[59]

Nevada civil rights activists fought Jim Crow on a variety of fronts. In the 1960s and early '70s Reno resembled Las Vegas and most American cities with its racially segregated neighborhoods. Restrictive covenants in deeds that denied home ownership to black and Native American residents existed in most neighborhoods. This practice helped confine black residents to two enclaves: one in northeast Reno and the other in "Black Springs," north of the city, on US 95. In midcentury Reno and Las Vegas black communities formed not in the inner city, but on the urban periphery. For many years after the Warren Court began ruling in favor of minority rights, Reno and Las Vegas continued to be the scene of discriminatory practices. It was not until the late 1960s that Nevada legislators passed a law permitting victims to file civil rights suits under state law against employers and businesses practicing discrimination. Then in 1971 Governor Mike O'Callaghan, an early champion of civil rights in Nevada, signed a state fair housing bill, which began the process of ending residential segregation in Nevada, and most important in its two metropolitan areas. In the early 1970s court-mandated school busing also went a long way toward ending segregation in the Washoe and Clark County School Districts. Also helping to ease tensions and provide some help for Reno's minority workers was the Economic Opportunity Board of Washoe County, whose programs provided manpower training and other support for the area's poor.[60]

Reno's treatment of minorities had to change, because in later decades they would account for an increasing share of the city's population. In 1970 African Americans constituted 2.2 percent of Reno's population (2.4 percent in Sparks); in 1980 the figures were 2.7 percent (1.4 percent) and in 1990 2.9 percent (2.4 percent). While the Native American population remained below 2 percent in both cities for this thirty-year period, Hispanic numbers grew steadily, from 5.1 percent in Reno (5.7 percent in Sparks) in 1980 to 11.1 percent (8.6 percent in Sparks) in 1990. The number of Asian–Pacific Islander residents in Reno also grew, from .08 percent (.05 percent in Sparks) in 1970 to 4.9 percent (4.5 percent) in 1990. By the 2010 census African Americans composed 2.1 percent of the Metropolitan Statistical Area's (MSA) population, Native Americans 1.4 percent, Hispanics 22.1 percent,

TABLE 1.1
Resident Minorities, Reno Area
Percentage of Population

Year	African Americans		Latinos		Asian–Pacific Islanders	
	Reno	Sparks	Reno	Sparks	Reno	Sparks
1970	2.2	2.4	No data	No data	.08	.05
1980	2.7	1.4	5.1	5.7	2.2	2.6
1990	2.9	2.4	11.1	8.6	4.9	4.5

and Asian–Pacific Islanders 5.6 percent. These trends typified those in Las Vegas and many other western cities.[61]

As the 1960s ended Reno was finally on its way to resolving the Jim Crow issues that had antagonized relations with minority residents and visitors from the Bay Area market, whose population consisted increasingly of African Americans, Hispanics, and Asian Americans. The city also succeeded in building a convention center to position itself as a player in the West's expanding midlevel convention industry. Reno reinforced this initiative with a multimillion-dollar expansion and modernization of its airport. After 1960 the municipal airport was crucial to the area's effort to attract more tourists and convention visitors. Its modest success in doing so eventually established the foundation for the city to attract interest from some of the larger resort companies, encouraged by the legalization of corporate gaming in Nevada. By the early 1970s the stage was now set for MGM, Del Webb, Circus Circus, and others to consider building large casino resorts in the municipality. Reno promoters were optimistic about the city's future in 1970, and the decade did not disappoint them.

Chapter Two

LAS VEGAS AREA

Laying the Foundation, 1945–1975

DURING THE LATE 1940S AND EARLY '50S the wartime boom on Fremont Street and along the Los Angeles Highway never really ended; it only intensified. The opening of the neon-fronted Golden Nugget in 1946 was a precursor of bigger things to come. The place was just a big gambling hall until Steve Wynn got control in 1973. He added a hotel tower in 1977 and a second one in 1984. But in 1950 gambling halls and not hotels dominated Fremont Street. The Pioneer Club, the Boulder Club, the Las Vegas Club, and virtually every other place on the street were designed more for daytime and evening gamblers than for overnight guests. The Eldorado Club on the first floor of the old 1932 Hotel Apache could obviously handle overnight guests. But in 1951 Benny Binion bought the place and reopened it as Binion's Horseshoe Casino. Binion's later dethroned Harolds Club as the most famous gambling hall in the West, especially after Binion held his first World Series of Poker there in 1970. The Hotel Apache hung on a while longer, but the 1941 El Cortez Hotel farther down Fremont Street was almost as grand as Reno's El Cortez, and just as busy. Still, it was hardly sumptuous, nor was the Sal Sagev Hotel (later the Golden Gate) near the railroad station. Like most downtown hotels, they were comfortable, but reflected the maverick, Old West image Las Vegas was trying to portray at the time. The city's casino district, while beckoning, was hardly a place that most modern travelers would want to stay for more than a few nights, although the arrival of the Fremont Hotel in 1956 and Del Webb's twenty-six-story Mint Hotel and Casino tower in 1962 above its namesake club helped to divert some tourists from the Strip.[1]

As postwar America increasingly embraced the new car culture, it was the motor courts on Fifth Street and along the Boulder Highway that appealed to auto tourists. More important, however, was the growing "strip" of casino resorts on the Los Angeles Highway, with all of their parking, dining, gambling, entertainment, and outdoor attractions. This bubble of growth to the south along with the continued operation of the Basic Magnesium factory, by 1954 a privately owned chemical complex producing titanium, manganese, and a range of other chemical products, helped create the first faint indications of the metropolitan area to come. But there was also growth north and east of Las Vegas. The World War II gunnery school, shut down in 1946 and reopened three years later for the Cold War, became Nellis Air Force Base in 1950. The Korean War, other hostilities, and later Vietnam converted it into a major tactical base where the newest fighter jets and their pilots trained. The 1951 opening of the Nevada Proving Grounds for nuclear testing invigorated the northwest sector of Las Vegas's valley, as scientists, support staff, and supply trucks increasingly plied the two-lane road connecting Las Vegas to Camp Mercury. By 1953 Henderson and North Las Vegas were both incorporated cities. In 1960 the US Census Bureau finally designated Las Vegas as a Standard Metropolitan Statistical Area (SMSA), reflecting the fact that federal officials now considered Las Vegas to be more than just a small city.[2]

In the postwar decades the valley's two major gambling centers, the city of Las Vegas and Strip, though competitors, often coordinated their efforts to promote the area's tourist growth. At this time, the Mob and Mob-related operators had a large presence downtown and on the Strip, and they quietly worked with non-Mob gamers to promote the area's growth. The Mob's presence was crucial to the valley's development. It was the Mob's access to Jimmy Hoffa and the Teamsters' Central States Pension Fund and to other sources of capital that financed the construction of the many resorts the early Las Vegas Strip needed to maintain its momentum before corporate funding became available in the 1970s. It was in the interest of Mob managers and former Mob figures such as the Flamingo's Gus Greenbaum, the Desert Inn's Moe Dalitz, and the Dunes' Major Riddle to cooperate with city and county leaders to get the federal highways and other projects needed to fill their casinos and spur more rounds of expansion.

A new airport was an early item on the postwar agenda. In 1947 Senator Pat McCarran advised city and county leaders to cede the old Western Air Express Airport northeast of town to the air force and construct a new facility for the airlines somewhere else. Las Vegas and Clark County

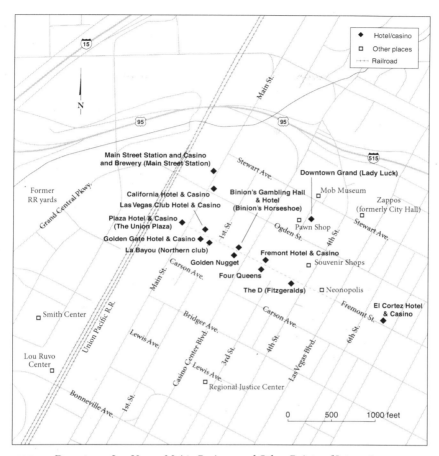

MAP 2.1. Downtown Las Vegas: Major Casinos and Other Points of Interest, ca. 2013

commissioners agreed to build a new civilian airport near the old Alamo airstrip, just east of the Los Angeles Highway, a few miles south of the Fabulous Flamingo. The new airport opened in 1948 and delivered the still relatively small number of regularly scheduled and chartered flights to the Strip and Glitter Gulch for more than a decade.[3]

At roughly the same time, voters in the cities and county agreed to buy out the Union Pacific Railroad's water sources and infrastructure by creating the Las Vegas Valley Water District, which the state formally established in 1947 and local voters approved in the following year. After the Union Pacific Railroad sold its wells, pumps, and pipe infrastructure to the district, the latter began delivering water to the Las Vegas area in 1954. The district, which was run by the Clark County commissioners, used its bonding and fee power to build the lines from the old Basic Magnesium Plant in Henderson that would in September 1955 deliver the first Lake Mead water to Las Vegas, the Strip, and their emerging suburbs twenty miles west of the lake. Just as important was the city and county working together to create the Fair and Recreation Board in 1957 (later the Las Vegas Convention and Visitors Authority [LVCVA]) to construct a major convention center on donated land behind the Riviera Hotel. The facility, which opened in 1959, encouraged Reno and Sparks to form their own Fair and Recreation Board that same year and build the Centennial Coliseum to fill their hotel rooms during the week with convention delegates.[4]

Improved access to Las Vegas was also a concern. Passage of the Interstate Highway Act of 1956 triggered local routing debates, as it did in Reno. But there was less conflict in southern Nevada. Las Vegas and Clark County commissioners cooperated to choose the optimal route, just west of the Strip and downtown, where few of the bulldozed homes were owned by Anglos, as the road made its way through the city and into North Las Vegas. The racist routing of Interstate 15 through the predominantly African American Westside duplicated the approach in Nashville, Chicago, and other metropolitan areas around the nation. Although dedicated in March 1966 and opened a few weeks later to Sahara Avenue, Interstate 15 did not reach downtown until 1970 and did not pass through North Las Vegas and out of the metropolitan area until the following year.[5]

By 1960 the Strip resorts did more business than Glitter Gulch, and the race was on to see which area would take the permanent lead. For the most part, however, the city and county cooperated with each other. The appearance of the town's new Nevada Southern college campus (later UNLV) in 1957 south of the city a few miles behind the Flamingo stirred no animosity, because most of the key government buildings and operations for both governments were downtown in the county seat, where they would remain. Regents picked the Maryland Parkway site in the Strip-city suburbs after the Union Pacific backed out of a land deal that would have put the school's campus in the city. This occurred after an employee leaked the secret negotiations to the press.[6]

So, as Las Vegans entered the 1960s, they looked back on a decade of rapid growth on the Strip as well as downtown and anticipated more of it in the future. Throughout much of the last half of the twentieth century the Las Vegas area played catch-up, trying to build enough hotel rooms to accommodate its increasing number of visitors. In September 1960 Las Vegans looked forward to construction of the Sahara's new tower and the hundreds of vitally needed rooms it would bring on line. Later that fall Fremont Hotel officials announced plans to double their resort's room capacity just three years after its opening. One local editor applauded this response, declaring that for too long, the city's gaming establishments had done little or nothing in response to the Strip's dramatic expansion.[7]

Over the course of the next decade a seemingly endless series of building projects dotted the valley. The local media portrayed 1963 as still another big growth year, thanks to the "enlarged scope of work" at the test site and to the city's convention business setting new records. As one editorial gleefully proclaimed, "Las Vegas seems to know no limitation," with eight major hotel-casino expansions expected to be completed by year's end. Then in 1966 the Four Queens on Fremont Street and Caesars Palace, Jay Sarno's thirty-million-dollar tribute to ancient Rome, both opened. Helping to fuel this expansion were conventions that annually pumped more than twenty-five million dollars into the local economy. In 1967 work began on the twenty-million-dollar Frontier Hotel, successor to the New Frontier, which had replaced the original Hotel Last Frontier in 1955.[8]

The Frontier's new owner in 1967 played a vital part in the Strip's development. Howard Hughes's surprising return to Las Vegas on Thanksgiving Eve 1966 augured the impending arrival of corporate gaming in 1969, a legislative reform that would set the stage for the Strip's transformation in the 1990s. In 1967 Hughes spent one hundred million dollars to acquire the Sands, Desert Inn, Frontier, and Castaways hotels as well as KLAS-TV Channel 8 (the city's CBS affiliate), the North Las Vegas Air Terminal, and two local airlines. At the same time, his rival Kirk Kerkorian announced plans to hire noted architect Martin Stern Jr. and spend eighty million dollars to build the International Hotel (later the Las Vegas Hilton and the LVH) next to the convention center and across the street from the twelve-million-dollar Landmark Hotel, which Hughes bought and finished in 1969. The International was Las Vegas's first truly large resort, considered by many to be the area's first megaresort. Several years later, after selling the Flamingo and the International to Hilton, Kerkorian hired Stern again to design the MGM Grand, the locale's second megaresort, which opened in 1973.[9]

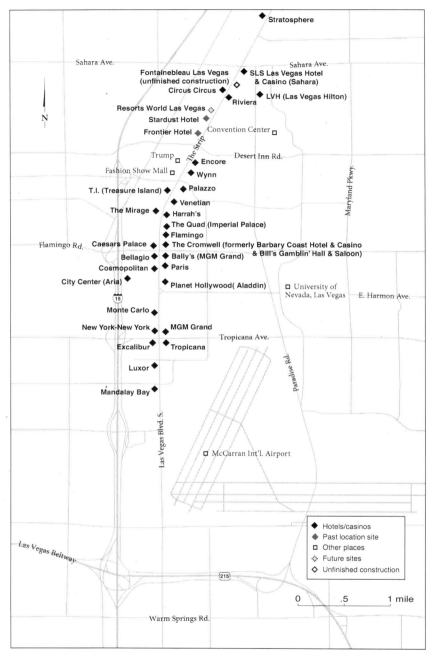

MAP 2.2. Las Vegas Strip

The growth of the resort sector only swelled the number of residents. By 1967 1,000 people per month moved to the valley. Estimates put the metropolitan area's population at 269,000 by July 1 of that year, and McCarran Airport passenger totals rose from 2.3 million in 1966 to 2.7 million in 1967. To serve the growing metropolis, the new five-million-dollar Foley Federal Building opened downtown on Las Vegas Boulevard. Two city parking garages, the Southern Nevada Water Project, and expansions at Nevada Southern University (NSU) campus, Nellis, and the nuclear test site rounded out the highlights of another banner year for the Las Vegas area. As the *Review-Journal* proclaimed in its New Year's Day 1968 issue, "Las Vegas has parlayed America's leisure time and growing desire for fun and entertainment into a multi-million-dollar industry that is the state's greatest economic asset."[10]

In addition to resort projects, defense spending contributed further to the metropolitan growth. In January 1961 local newspapers predicted that the arrival of new F-111 jets at Nellis would only enhance the base's strategic importance in the Cold War, making it the number-one "tactical air force base" in the country. This was a key prerequisite to safeguarding the facility from future budget cuts or the fate that the Reno-Stead base experienced. The test site also poured more jobs and money into the local economy. Thanks to the new Kiwi Program to determine the feasibility of using nuclear-powered rockets in space, the Atomic Energy Commission in 1960 pumped another fifty million dollars in funding to the facility's budget. Everyone knew this money would ripple across the metropolitan area in the form of more jobs, more supply orders, and more incremental profits for local businesses. In 1961 the Kennedy administration drafted plans to widen the test-site road to four lanes, a project that delighted city and county officials. In May 1962 US senator Alan Bible assured Las Vegas leaders that funds to enlarge the road to Mercury and the test site were in the new twenty-five-million-dollar supplemental bill for atomic energy and not in the federal highway budget, where they could be more easily cut. By January 1966 the expanded highway was open, with a speed limit of seventy miles per hour, so test-site workers could commute more quickly to their jobs, a convenience that only encouraged more employees to live with their families in the Las Vegas valley.[11]

The continued expansion of Las Vegas's defense and resort sectors spurred building across the metropolitan area. In just 1967 alone home construction rose 30 percent over the previous year. This growth, however, put a strain on local governments. As one editorial warned, "Our rapid expansion and development will bring new troubles and create new crises in many fields—city government, education, law enforcement and transportation. But we seem better prepared to face these problems than at any time in the past. Our overriding problem—water—does not seem as impossible to conquer as in the past." This was because Nevada's two Democratic US senators, Alan Bible and Howard Cannon, worked hard to convince then vice president Lyndon Johnson and other administration officials to approve federal loan guarantees to allow the water district to build a large-diameter pipeline that would permit Las Vegas to take Nevada's full share of Lake Mead water under the Colorado River Compact of 1922. Everyone knew that once the water problem was eased, Las Vegas's other problems would seem less formidable.[12]

Local water concerns had begun with the new decade. In August 1960 consultants for the Las Vegas Valley Water District urged authorities to move quickly to accommodate the more than six hundred thousand people it projected to live in the metropolitan area by 2000. But the district was more than six hundred thousand people short in its estimate. Water officials eventually had to take drastic action to conserve water until they could build more capacity to accommodate growth. In 1955 Las Vegans had to grapple with an issue that would begin to confront Renoites in the late 1960s: whether to install water meters. The meters were necessary to reduce waste and permit more growth. While many Las Vegans grumbled, the water district started installing them later that year, and the first metered billing began in November 1956. As historian William Rowley has noted, in Reno the threat of metered water only boosted support for managed-growth advocates in the 1970s.[13]

Rapid growth only exacerbated the situation. Residents soon realized the seriousness of the supply problem. In that same year the metropolitan area's lack of water forced officials to block the construction of a big apartment complex behind the Sahara Hotel for lack of water. Nervous state and local politicians demanded that state engineer Ed Muth review the situation. But Muth agreed with the district's need for a tax to raise the money necessary to fund the infrastructure required for supplying the Sahara Avenue development as well as for other growth-related building projects in the metropolitan area. He also denied permits to drill new wells in Paradise Valley south of the city line, because the water district

Laying the Foundation 49

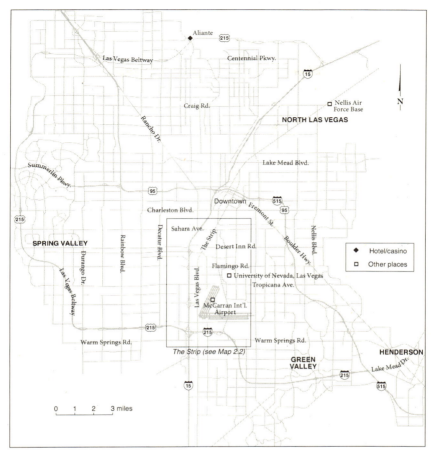

MAP 2.3. Las Vegas Metropolitan Area

was already overcommitted with promises to accommodate growth and the supply of water available underground was unknown. In 1961 the district estimated that it would take twenty million dollars just to install more pumping equipment and build a new transmission line from Lake Mead to Paradise Valley. The water district consequently asked for a huge rate hike and requested a bond issue to pay its share of the cost, while Senators Bible and Cannon worked to secure federal funding for a large pipeline from Lake Mead that would deliver Nevada's full share of Lake Mead water. Residents had no choice if they wanted their metropolitan area to grow. Later in November 1962 local newspapers urged voter approval of a bond issue to help the Las Vegas Valley Water District expand the valley's water supply. A few days later the measure passed, partly thanks to one editorial's warning that "defeat of the bonds would strike the area with a water shortage next summer and cripple new construction at the height of the Las Vegas population explosion."[14]

Water was merely one challenge posed by Las Vegas's frantic growth; traffic was another. In 1961 local newspapers emphasized how residential development on the city's near west side had poured more traffic onto Vegas Drive, Decatur Boulevard, and Bonanza, making driving more difficult. The only solution was to build wider and better roads. Part of the solution to traffic jams was the installation of a traffic-light synchronization system, which Reno, Las Vegas, and Clark County all began work on in the late 1970s. Another part of the solution was to build more roads. Clark County commissioners could barely keep up with the breakneck pace of growth on the Strip and in its suburbs. In 1964 county officials announced plans to widen Desert Inn and Flamingo Roads that served the Strip city's mushrooming suburbs. They also planned to eliminate the dips on Maryland Parkway that slowed the flow of traffic at the Flamingo Wash. Work focused in these areas, because into the 1960s there was still little growth far west of the Strip; only a few arteries, like West Charleston, went past Decatur Boulevard. Most of the population lived in the eastern part of the valley, between the Strip job zone and the Boulder Highway near Lake Mead, from which residents took their water and to which they sent their treated sewage. So, the east valley is where governments struggled to extend such major east-west arteries as Sahara Avenue, Desert Inn Road, Vegas Valley Drive, Flamingo Road, and Tropicana and Hacienda Avenues. Some north-south arteries were also extended. By the late 1960s, thanks to construction of Commercial Center, the Boulevard Mall, and other shopping centers, Maryland Parkway was widened and paved from the city to the McCarran Airport's fence at Russell Road.

All this construction only frayed tempers. The lengthy delays occasioned by the widening of Maryland Parkway made residents angry with Mayor Gragson and the city commission. In his 1967 campaign for city commission, candidate Jim Corey blasted city hall and his opponent, Reed Whipple, for cutting down so many trees on Maryland Parkway north of Sahara Avenue for a widening project. Thanks to this issue, Corey, a tavern owner, defeated the incumbent Whipple, a popular leader in the Mormon Church and banker. While Las Vegans enjoyed the benefits of living in a boomtown, they resented the inconvenience.[15] In 1966 one newspaper reported the widespread complaints about "the uncoordinated approach to construction involving streets." The presence of tracks only complicated matters. While the railroad tracks at street grade slowed traffic in downtown Reno, they snarled commuter traffic headed to Las Vegas's budding western suburbs, where "getting across the railroad right of way is the major obstacle in going to or coming from work."[16] At the same time, residents and commuters on the Strip had to cope with crews building Interstate 15, whose bulldozers and other heavy equipment blocked Sahara, Charleston, and other vital east-west thoroughfares for most of the decade. Unfortunately, the Interstate 15 freeway project took more than five years to complete between Sahara Avenue and North Las Vegas. Had the freeway opened earlier, it would have allowed many commuters to bypass surface streets to get to the Strip job zone, but construction delays were numerous. In one case the Nevada Department of Highways filed suit in 1966 against the Union Pacific, which demanded nine million dollars for its land near today's Spaghetti Bowl of freeways; the state valued the tract at two million dollars. The battle dragged on for months while commuters sat at red lights.

Just as aggravating was the growing presence of parking meters downtown. With population rising, customers could no longer find parking spaces near the businesses they were patronizing. The number of meters grew steadily into the late 1950s and early '60s, and so did public outrage. By November 1962 the Las Vegas City Commission received a flood of petitions signed by more than one thousand residents protesting twenty-four-hour parking meters. Nearly fifty years later Mayor Carolyn Goodman, who came to Las Vegas in 1964, recalled bringing rolls of quarters with her whenever she drove downtown. But in the 1960s the mass of local and tourist traffic, lured by the growing number of hotel-casinos in the CBD, forced the city to take action. Many downtown merchants voiced their support for meters, while others petitioned for their removal.[17]

In 1959 Las Vegas voters, much like their Reno counterparts, were convinced that city hall was too close to the city's local gaming community. To some extent, Las Vegas and Reno resembled the model described by historian Amy Bridges. In the 1940s and '50s the mayors and many councilmen of both casino cities were increasingly influenced by the club owners downtown. Unlike Reno, Las Vegas had commission government, which, despite its reform pretensions, failed to protect the city from the influence exerted by casino and development interests. Indeed, three-time mayor Ernie Cragin was accused of running a Democratic machine in the 1930s, and in the 1940s critics such as Charles Pipkin of the Las Vegas Taxpayers' Association publicly accused him of working too closely with the "Houssels machine" of downtown gaming operators. In 1951 voters elected former city engineer C. D. Baker mayor, but that did not really solve the problem. City managers still came and went amid the constant conflict at city hall. So in 1959 voters elected a fresh face as mayor, longtime businessman Oran Gragson, a political newcomer who owned an appliance store downtown.

Much like Barry Goldwater in Phoenix and numerous other reform-minded businessmen in other midcentury Sunbelt cities, Gragson vowed to clean up city government. To this end, Gragson forced out city manager A. H. Kennedy, who, as Las Vegas's onetime police chief, should have done more to break up a burglary ring operating within the city's police department. Gragson broke up the ring and fired the police chief in addition to sending the officer most responsible for the burglaries (which even included Gragson's store) to jail. In his 1959 campaign Gragson vowed to bring honesty and integrity to municipal government, using much of the same rhetoric as Earl Wooster's reform committee in Reno. Still, Gragson and the city commissioners represented the progrowth downtown business coalition that Carl Abbott, Thomas Baylis, and other urban scholars have traced in postwar Sunbelt cities.[18] Gragson was, however, also a coalition builder, like some of the Sunbelt mayors that Bridges described. Gragson attracted support from all major voting blocs through his honesty rather than his political ability to forge powerful alliances or to organize a small army of city workers to back his policies. Like Mayor Bud Baker in Reno, Gragson pushed for construction of a large convention center, an interstate highway, and a modern jetport. Like Baker, Gragson also believed in the use of zoning to guide growth. In the early 1970s he even opposed construction of the Meadows Mall, a huge indoor retail center on Valley View near Charleston Boulevard, because he thought there were already too many shopping centers in the neighborhood.[19]

The rapid growth of the Las Vegas area in the 1960s certainly tested Gragson's mettle and his ability to handle urban problems. In 1940, before Basic Magnesium and the Gunnery School opened, the city of Las Vegas had 8,422 people; in 1950 the number jumped to 24,624, in 1960 to 64,405, and ten years later it reached 125,787. Aside from the street projects and parking meter controversies this growth brought, Gragson, along with other government leaders, also had to expand the valley's water and sewer infrastructure as well as its wastewater treatment capacity to cope with growing visitor and resident populations. Reno-Sparks faced the same problem a decade later, when large companies began building resorts that overwhelmed the cities' jointly run wastewater treatment plant, an event that sparked a fierce conflict and litigation between the two municipalities. Lack of sewers also threatened new construction in various parts of the Las Vegas valley. In 1960, for instance, the city commission created a sanitary district to fund a 3.5-mile outflow sewer main from Cheyenne Avenue to Nellis Boulevard to transport the area's increased wastewater. Because of excessive gypsum in the soil, septic tanks could no longer handle the sewage. Local residents were unhappy to pay sudden assessments to finance this and other projects, but they recognized that eliminating septic tanks would raise overall property values in the area. They also knew that by extending the new main into their neighborhood, branch networks could be installed to promote even more development and simultaneously widen the local tax base.[20]

As population continued to rise in the 1960s, the city of Las Vegas's sewage treatment plant began to approach capacity. In early 1969 an engineering consulting firm urged the city to consider enlarging its wastewater plant, which also served North Las Vegas. It was only good policy, because Clark County's sewage treatment facility had been malfunctioning and Las Vegas would soon have to take some of its overflow. This would be difficult, because with all the recent growth in the city, the municipal plant was expected to reach capacity by 1971. The Strip city, however, was the main engine of growth at this time in the metropolitan area, so the county commissioners eventually took the actions necessary to treat the wastewater created by the burgeoning population of the Strip (Paradise and Winchester Townships), Spring Valley, and the other unincorporated townships in the valley.

After the City of Las Vegas failed to annex the Strip in 1951, county commissioners moved quickly to create a fire department and other agencies needed to keep the Strip resorts and the nascent suburban neighborhoods this job zone was creating under county control. Up to this time, county residents had relied on cesspools, septic tanks, and a few small treatment plants to handle wastewater. In 1954 a district court decree created what is today called the Clark County Water Reclamation District. In the next year county voters approved a bond issue to build sewer lines and a wastewater treatment plant serving the Strip and its immediate suburbs. The system began operating in 1956. In 1973 state legislators expanded the area served to include all of the unincorporated towns in Clark County, but the main focus of spending and construction was the ever-expanding Strip city. After a protracted battle with the Environmental Protection Agency (EPA) in the 1970s over the county's pollution of Lake Mead, a federal lake, and some of its tributaries in the Lake Mead National Recreation Area, Clark County began construction of its advanced wastewater treatment facility at its central plant east of the Boulder Highway in 1976, and it opened in 1982.[21]

As the metropolitan area spread outward across once distant washes, flood control also became an issue. Floods not only harassed residents trying to get to work but imperiled tourists as well. In September 1960 massive flooding on US 91, the highway connecting Las Vegas to its prime market in Southern California, only reinforced the view that the new Interstate 15 freeway could not come soon enough. Engineers knew that its modern design would help protect the city from loss of business, especially in summer when storms flooded the desert washes along the US 91 route to town. But valley-wide flooding was another matter. In the spring of 1960, after several major floods swept across roads throughout the expanding metropolitan area, Senator Howard Cannon, Las Vegas's former city attorney, pushed for help from the US Army Corps of Engineers. The latter came to Las Vegas, studied the problems, and ultimately proposed an expensive flood-control system that required substantial funding. But on April 10, 1962, Las Vegas–area voters rejected the eight-million-dollar bond issue for flood control.[22] Two factors were chiefly responsible: the lack of storms that spring and the abundance of other expensive projects, which seemed more critical to Las Vegas's growth at the time. In the end, the voters' action was fortuitous, because later studies in the 1980s demonstrated that the corps' system design was flawed.

The metropolitan area's surging population also pressured the newly created Clark County School District (CCSD). Unlike Reno, where new school bond issues raised public ire, in Las Vegas they were almost expected. More than forty thousand students enrolled in the area's K–12 schools in September 1962, with fifty thousand expected in 1963. As CCSD superintendent Leland Newcomer observed, "Right now in what we call the 'slow season' for enrollment [summer], we wake up every morning needing three complete school rooms and teachers to handle the 90 youngsters coming into the system." Newcomer predicted he would have to hire six hundred more teachers by September 1963 and projected an increased enrollment by 1964 of twenty thousand students—virtually the entire enrollment of Washoe County! Just to acquire sites for schools in 1962 cost the district $700,000, with Valley High School's land alone totaling $310,000. As Las Vegas and the Strip city exploded with new buildings, businesses, and population, the value of all lands soared far beyond Washoe County levels, driving up the amount and number of bond issues. As Newcomer observed, during the summer of 1963 the district could build a new elementary school every week and "still not meet the needs" of the metropolitan area.[23] But unlike their counterparts in the Reno area, southern Nevadans continued to encourage growth on the Strip and continued approving bond issues, apparently convinced that growth would ultimately pay for itself.

It took several years of building for the CCSD to catch up. Not until 1965 could Superintendent Newcomer report that only Western High School would be on double sessions. Three years earlier twelve thousand students had been on double sessions, but a $37 million bond issue passed in 1964 and rapid construction had eased the crisis even in the face of the surging population a year later. Newcomer happily announced that seven new elementary schools would open in 1965–66 and work would soon begin on a vocational technical center, later called Vo Tech. In 1965 there were fifty-four thousand students in Clark County regularly attending K–12, and the figure only rose with each new decade, until finally leveling off for a while in 2010.[24]

Capital improvements for education were not limited to K–12. Local college student, business, and political leaders pressured state and university officials to expand the Nevada Southern campus on Maryland Parkway. In 1961 the state purchased eighty acres west of the existing campus to bring the school to the edge of Paradise Road. The sale was necessary to acquire contiguous lands for expansion before land values rose any higher in response to growth on the Strip and along Flamingo Road and Tropicana Avenue. By the early 1960s it was obvious that Nevada Southern needed a larger campus. In 1962 Valley Bank executives E. Parry Thomas and Jerome Mack helped form a seven-member foundation to purchase land to expand the school's property. This was vital because the college was already running out of room just five years after opening its campus. As the metropolitan area's population steadily increased, school officials correctly predicted enrollments would rise for the rest of the century. In 1965 the Board of Regents finally made Nevada Southern a "university" with a hint of autonomy (full autonomy from the Reno campus came in 1966). As the

Las Vegas Review-Journal noted in 1964, "The hard luck sister of the University of Nevada at Reno did a hard year's growing up on its barren Maryland Parkway campus."[25] But the school now boasted fifteen hundred students, a testimony to the economic boom occurring just two miles west of the campus on the Strip. In 1964 NSU graduated its first senior class with bachelor's degrees. The regents' appointment of New Mexico's Donald Moyer as chancellor was also a significant step. As the *Review-Journal* observed, "The creating of dual chancellorships for Las Vegas and Reno was ... a significant move forward toward equal status between the two universities." This translated into more money, staff, and buildings. Thanks to federal and state grants, NSU was about to get a student dormitory (Tonopah Hall), a $1.5 million expansion to its library, and a $1 million science hall by the spring of 1966. All of these additions helped accommodate the increased enrollment that everyone expected.[26]

Other public facilities in the metropolitan area also needed expansion. In the summer of 1960 the new Clark County Courthouse prepared to open downtown with more courtrooms than its predecessor to handle the steadily increasing number of judges, trials, and lawyers created by the area's continued growth. Leaks and cracked walls delayed the building's operational status, but at least it was finished in time to ease the overcrowding caused by the growing caseload. The same was not true of Las Vegas's new city hall. Despite the expansion of the city's boundaries and population, frugal city commissioners were slow to heed Mayor Gragson's call for a modern facility. Municipal leaders finally took action in the late 1960s. In June 1969 the *Review-Journal* supported approval of an $8 million bond issue to build the new city hall. The newspaper explained to readers that the current building, erected in 1935 with New Deal funding, was literally "bursting at the seams with people." Although the city had rented space across the street, this fragmentation of department offices was, in the words of one editorial urging passage, "a confusing system to the public." A few days later voters agreed and passed the bond issue.[27]

The expansion of public hospital facilities was more gradual, because private hospitals such as Sunrise, Rose de Lima, and eventually others catered to an increasing number of patients. In October 1960, with the metropolitan area's population surging, thanks to increased activity at Nellis Air Force Base and on the Strip, county commissioners put a bond issue on the ballot to purchase a forty-acre parcel between Las Vegas and North Las

Vegas as the site for a new, greatly expanded Southern Nevada Memorial Hospital (today's University Medical Center—the only public hospital in the Las Vegas area). Ultimately, voters rejected this idea, preferring instead that the county keep the facility on its existing four-acre campus and expand the hospital in phases. Constantly beset by bond issues for more schools, better roads, and other public works projects vital to growth, Las Vegas–area voters did not regard a new hospital complex or flood control as vital priorities at that time.[28]

This was not the case, however, with the convention center. In 1967 the Clark County Fair and Recreation Board officially changed its name to the Las Vegas Convention and Visitors Authority, which sounded more like similar entities in other American cities, as Las Vegas began to compete for conventions on a national scale. The name change also erased the stigma attached to a flawed 1964 bond issue in which the Fair and Recreation Board tried to get control of Las Vegas Country Club lands, a move that only antagonized local newspapers and voters. Prior to the 1980s both convention authorities still had to get voter approval for each bond issue to expand their facilities, and success usually depended upon strong media support. In November 1968 the *Las Vegas Review-Journal* endorsed a new bond issue to expand the facility, because "it is consistent with the rate of economic growth in this area and it is an inevitable step in our effort to remain competitive in the convention market." Failure to support the bonds, the newspaper warned, "could retard the growth of Las Vegas as a convention city."[29]

Even more important than the convention center's expansion was the airport's. The key behind the rapid development of airline service to Las Vegas was the passenger jet's arrival. After a series of test flights in the mid-1950s over the skies of Renton, Washington, the Boeing 707 began serving airlines in 1957. The news only reinforced the efforts of Clark County commissioners to move forward with construction of a modern and enlarged McCarran Airport, with a new entrance and terminal on Paradise Road to replace the original one on US 91 (south of today's Mandalay Bay). To this end, they scheduled a bond election for March 1960, hoping, no doubt, that the sparkling new terminal in Reno might influence the vote. Local fiscal conservatives such as radio personality Joe Julian denounced the project as too costly. Julian insisted that commissioners meet the challenges posed by the jet age with "realistic planning." He also contended that the county commissioners should keep the airport at its present location on US 91 south of the Strip, "where most property owners wanted it to stay."[30]

The construction and expansion of both the convention center and the airport reflected the growing role of the emerging Strip city and the Clark County commissioners in helping to promote the metropolitan area's expansion. Both facilities were vital to drawing tourists and delegates to the hotels on the Strip and in the various municipalities. In particular, both facilities were crucial not only to the room expansion of Strip hotels, but also to their development of substantial convention facilities on their properties. This was especially true in the years after 1980, when the meeting industry became a more integral part of the resorts' business. Because each new room and expansion project multiplied the number of new jobs in the valley, the ripple effect of increased air travel and convention traffic helped expand the Strip city and the three incorporated cities farther outward.

In February 1960 the *Las Vegas Review-Journal* reported that county commissioners were concerned that passage of six million dollars in school bonds the previous October might endanger voter approval in March of an eight-million-dollar bond issue for the new jetport. But local newspapers came to the rescue and strongly endorsed approval, citing the fact that jets brought nearly double the passengers in one plane than their propeller-driven cousins had delivered, and Las Vegas therefore had to dramatically increase terminal capacity to handle the growing number of visitors and their luggage. The Las Vegas Chamber of Commerce also counseled the business community and public to support the new airport with its longer runways and larger tarmacs, because jet service would mean more jobs and business for the metropolitan area. In the end, Clark County voters once again supported the growth agenda and approved the bond issue.[31]

There was also progress on other fronts to increase the number of airline passengers. In the fall of 1960 Senator Cannon testified before the Civil Aeronautics Board in favor of allotting more airline routes to Las Vegas and Reno. Cannon never believed the CAB had given Las Vegas enough airline connections. In 1978 he used his position as chair of the Senate Subcommittee on Aviation to push legislation to abolish the CAB and finally deregulate the airline industry. Even with CAB restraints, Las Vegas air traffic grew constantly in the late 1950s into the 1960s. In 1960 Clark County commissioners, acting as the airport commissioners, approved plans to build a modern jetport on Paradise Road. After all, 1960 was the year when the airport landed its one millionth passenger, and everyone knew the number would only grow. In 1948, the new postwar airport's first year of operation, barely one hundred regularly scheduled flights had arrived. By 1960 *daily* departures frequently exceeded that number. But the new McCarran jetport took time to build. Construction snafus and other problems delayed completion until March 1963, when the facility finally opened for flights.[32]

As in Reno, the cost of growth was substantial for local residents. Not only were there numerous bond issues to pay off, but taxes also rose. In June 1963 voters in all Nevada counties rejected hiking the state sales tax from 2 percent to 3 percent to fund schools and other services related to growth. Sentiment in Clark County as well as Washoe also opposed establishing a state income tax and instead favored raising the gaming tax to generate more revenue. Prior to the referendum, Governor Grant Sawyer and Lieutenant Governor Paul Laxalt had endorsed the sales tax increase to help fund schools.[33]

Property taxes also went up, especially in Clark County. As Las Vegas's built-up area expanded, Clark County assessor James Bilbray Sr. raised the assessed value of vacant land by 50 percent. He noted that any higher increase would "harm the economy" by driving speculators away. Predictably, the increases brought a chorus of complaints from investors. Bilbray responded that current homes were being assessed at one-third of their market value. Vacant land had to produce more revenue for state and county coffers to help offset the cost of expanding services and roads in the metropolitan area. Some businessmen and landowners complained that Bilbray had not reassessed many of the big hotels for six years or more. Eventually, the Nevada Tax Commission looked into Bilbray's actions and sided with him, recognizing that Las Vegas's growth had forced him to increase the tax rate.[34]

In 1964 Walt Casey, president of the Las Vegas Chamber of Commerce, conceded that according to county law, assessing retail properties at 35 percent of market value was legal. But he warned that overestimating market values to collect more revenue could wipe out smaller businesses. The *Las Vegas Review-Journal*, however, sided with the tax commission and urged residents to accept the tax increase. Bilbray certainly understood that for "the politically powerful casino center and downtown business district" reassessment was a hot potato, so, as the newspaper explained, he wisely opened his books to allow the "unbiased" state team to verify his estimates. As the newspaper observed, the process had been transparent and the reassessment of downtown property was crucial to generating enough revenue to fund government services during a boom that every businessperson hoped would continue.[35]

Growth-related expenses afflicted not only county officials but the city as well. To expand its tax base, the City of Las Vegas continued to annex subdivisions on its periphery where residents were willing to join in return for services. But not all of these places were relatively affluent. In 1964, for instance, the city annexed Vegas Heights. City planning director Don Saylor developed a blueprint for neighborhood land use, and the city formed an assessment district to fund improvements. But Vegas Heights was a low- to moderate-income neighborhood whose property owners objected to paying assessments for improvements and preferred a citywide assessment. In the end, the city sought money from the Department of Housing and Urban Development (HUD) to finance the upgrades in order to save money but get the neighborhood into the city.[36]

As all three cities in the Las Vegas valley and the county's unincorporated areas began to fill with homes and businesses that needed efficient government, some officials proposed creating regional commissions and other structures to address metropolitan needs. In 1964 Clark County commissioner and future Las Vegas mayor Bill Briare failed to convince local officeholders to create a "League of Elected City and County Officials" to meet monthly to discuss "valley-wide" problems. North Las Vegas city manager Clay Lynch, however, did agree that the traditional approach—creating special boards to address specific problems—was unwieldy because there were too many boards. Lynch and North Las Vegas officials were particularly concerned about floods, since the county flood-control bond issue had failed two years earlier. But Lynch and his counterparts in Henderson and the county did not support Briare's proposal, so the valley remained politically fragmented, although some entities such as the Clark County Regional Planning Council helped bring a measure of cooperation. The Las Vegas valley clearly needed an institution like the Washoe Council of Governments in the Reno area, but Briare envisioned a more ambitious solution: full-scale metropolitan government.[37]

In the early 1960s Briare first raised the possibility of consolidating Las Vegas with the county's unincorporated townships (which included the Strip) and with North Las Vegas, Henderson, and possibly even Boulder

City. Various business leaders pushed the reform to save money on licenses and also on taxes and fees by eliminating needless duplication of police, fire, licensing, and other services. State lawmakers in 1971 passed legislation establishing commissions to study the issue. But the 1973 creation of the Metropolitan Police Department, in which the City of Las Vegas Police Department and Clark County Sheriff's Office merged, was the only reform that resulted from this effort. Attempts to form a metropolitan fire department failed due to strong opposition from county commissioners, the three cities, suburban voters, and even firemen. After failing in 1946 and again in 1951 to annex the Strip, Las Vegas tried again in 1978, led now by Mayor Bill Briare. In a referendum regarding whether Las Vegas should annex the county's unincorporated townships and some other lands, county voters in the emerging Strip city overwhelmingly refused to join Las Vegas. As a result, regional government agencies became the preferred way of dealing with metropolitan problems such as flood control, highways, and planning. But conflicts still occurred in the fragmented metropolis.[38]

Obviously, the Las Vegas metropolitan area owed much of its growth to the Strip's amazing development; by 2011 its resorts alone employed more than 103,000 workers and contained almost ninety thousand hotel rooms for the half million or more people visiting each week. But, as noted, the Strip was also the core of its own city. By vigorously opposing the efforts of various Las Vegas mayors to annex the unincorporated townships of Paradise and Winchester, which included the Strip and the lands immediately around it, county commissioners retained control of the central part of the valley from east to west and much of the land to the south and southwest. They also denied the City of Las Vegas hundreds of millions of dollars in revenue from Strip property taxes, gaming taxes, and other levies. The value of keeping the Strip city and the miles of land it encompassed in their jurisdiction awarded Clark County commissioners the bonding power, revenues, and other resources they needed to build the street networks, utility infrastructure, police and fire stations, parks, libraries, and other amenities to promote the growth of suburbs, office parks, and retail centers outward in all directions from the expanding line of major resorts on Las Vegas Boulevard South. However, by failing to capture control of the Strip and its burgeoning suburbs, the City of Las Vegas was in a weaker position to operate as the central city within its metropolitan area. Las Vegas battled with the City of North Las Vegas over funding issues, much as Reno did with Sparks.

In 1964, for instance, Las Vegas and its neighbor could not agree on how to divide the costs of widening Owens Avenue or building an underpass to carry traffic below the Union Pacific tracks. This widening project resulted somewhat from the general improvement of North Las Vegas as well as from population gains during the 1960s. Indeed, the little city that grew up on Las Vegas's eastern edge, the place Las Vegas refused to annex for decades, became a large city in the late twentieth century and effectively blocked the city of Las Vegas's ability to grow to the east and northeast, just as the Strip city did to the south.[39]

Due to strong leadership from people such as city manager Clay Lynch and Mayor William Taylor and thanks to the metropolitan area's overall growth including Nellis Air Force Base, North Las Vegas, once "little more than a poorly kept backyard of Las Vegas," experienced "a flood of new residents" in the years after 1950. A 1964 bond issue of $1.6 million had paved, curbed, flagged, and lit more than thirteen miles of streets. In May 1963 voters approved $8.6 million in capital improvements to extend water mains and drill two major wells while also installing a sewer interceptor line with laterals down Losee Road. The city also built Civic Center Drive through desert wasteland to connect with two of its major arteries, Twenty-Fifth and McDaniel Streets. Planners hoped to build a new civic hall at the location, which would hopefully encourage formation of a business district nearby. Plans also called for a "Losee Industrial District," where warehousing, chrome plating, machine prefabricating, and wrecking firms later served the entire metropolitan area. By 1964 the city had also master-planned five of eleven projected neighborhood parks. North Las Vegas also began assembling parcels of land for the Cartier Avenue Urban Renewal Project, which, along with slum clearance, would eliminate some of the city's blighted appearance.[40]

Additionally, the city planned to break ground in 1965 for a new city hall and fire substation as well as a new sewage treatment plant to reclaim water for parks and golf courses. North Las Vegas also began planning for the first phase of an ambitious project to create a 1,000-acre "desert recreational area" north of Craig Road. Under Lynch's proactive leadership, the municipality started to overhaul and expand its zoning regulations to accommodate its 1965 master plan, which addressed water supply, sanitation, streets, flood control, and a range of other issues. In January 1965 North Las Vegas began construction of its $1.8 million Civic Center, hosting the city hall, main library, and central parking garage. Work also continued on the Rose Garden Urban Renewal Project and began on the 110-acre Cartier Avenue redevelopment project. Lynch also obtained $143,000 in federal funds for the North Las Vegas library—Nevada's full share of federal library money for that year. All this occurred as crews began work building the Nellis Industrial Park, whose $2.8 million price tag represented "the largest district investment in the state's history."[41]

While North Las Vegas preoccupied itself with public works and planning to try to improve its image, the new city of Henderson also struggled to maintain an appropriate level of services in the face of constant growth. Water was an early problem. In the mid-1950s the city was chronically short of water. In 1940–41, when the federal government built the massive Basic Magnesium Plant to supply magnesium ingots to Southern California's airplane factories, the plant got an excellent water line from Lake Mead as well as a sewer system for the factory and the little Basic Townsite. When Basic Magnesium, Inc. (BMI), bought the complex from the State of Nevada in 1952, it got these systems. So, when Henderson formally became a city in 1953, it had to deal with the company for its water. The Las Vegas Valley Water District considered BMI to be the principal supplier of water for the new city. In 1954 BMI sold Henderson the water and sewer lines within the city's borders. But urban growth and high per capita usage pressured the city's little system, and water pressure remained low throughout the decade. This in turn made it hard for residents to supply their evaporative coolers in summer while also threatening the fire department's ability to douse major blazes. Sewer service was also inadequate, and in 1955 city voters had to support a bond issue for the improvements to both the city's water and its sewer systems.

In later years Henderson worked with the Las Vegas Valley Water District to plug most of its lands into the valley's water grid to improve service to existing neighborhoods and new subdivisions. The city ultimately had to spend even more money to create a sewer district that could expand fast enough to keep the county commissioners and their sanitation district from invading the city's northern border along Sunset Road. The city also struggled to extend streets. While assessment was the main form of financing, Henderson could not develop too quickly without adequate road connections. Finally, in 1957 the Nevada Department of Highways built the cutoff to Henderson from US 91 (the route of today's St. Rose Parkway), thereby allowing motorists to bypass the Strip and Las Vegas, but there were still not enough roads for commuters to the Strip job zone. Until the 1970s and '80s when more roads and surface streets began linking Henderson directly to the Strip job zone, the city lacked the tax base to fund many of the municipal services residents needed. Moreover, the failure of BMI to join the city only exacerbated the problem. Even today, this huge complex of chemical factories, with its millions of dollars in property and yearly profits, remains a county island in the midst of the city, because taxes are much lower in the county than in Henderson. The real growth and improvement of this municipality did not come until the 1980s, when the Strip city's suburbs finally grew over to Henderson's northern and western borders and Hank Greenspun's American Nevada Corporation began developing Green Valley. As thousands of people each year moved into the expanding city, Henderson finally had a tax base large enough to fund infrastructural and other improvements.[42]

Las Vegas continued its efforts to capture outlying suburbs spawned by the growing popularity of casino gambling. As in Reno, Mayor Gragson and other nongaming businessmen were concerned that unrestricted gaming-license establishments remain within the red-line zone downtown. This was part of Gragson's stated effort to promote "managed growth"—an increasingly popular buzzword in municipal circles during the late 1960s and '70s. As noted, the policy even led him to oppose construction of the Meadows Mall in the western suburbs on Valley View Boulevard and the US 95 expressway. His action, however, only antagonized local landowners, who saw the mall increasing population, home building, and land values. Angry residents charged Gragson with trying to use his power as mayor to limit suburban shopping in order to protect the CBD, where his own appliance store sat. In the end, the mall was built.

Gragson stood firm, however, on the red-line ordinance, which restricted gambling to certain blocks near the railroad station. This policy dated from the 1930s, a decade earlier than Reno's original ordinance. As mentioned earlier, in 1955 and in 1963 Reno city fathers voted to extend their red line, first to the west side of Virginia Street and later to Sierra Street, to allow Ernest Primm to enjoy the benefits of an unrestricted gaming license for his Primadonna Hotel. But in 1970, after much controversy and debate, the city council, rather than bending its red-line ordinance any further, abolished it and allowed unrestricted gaming anywhere in the city if the casino was attached to a one-hundred-room or larger hotel. In Las Vegas Mayor Oran Gragson fought the efforts of outgoing city commissioner George Franklin to expand the red-line zone, and the mayor's stand was generally supported by the local media and residents. In 1961 Las Vegas city commissioners had rejected a licensee who wanted to establish a race book on Fremont Street. Several years earlier the state had prohibited race books in casinos, and Las Vegas officials responded by banning them on Fremont Street to upgrade the area. The city commission supported regulations that confined unrestricted gambling to a red-line zone and limited the number of race books to one for every 12,500 people in the population. Such restrictions, however, were much less prevalent on the county-controlled Strip, where a more liberal approach toward gambling was practiced. Even in 1978, when advocates and opponents debated the value of allowing the city to annex the Strip and its suburbs, county residents complained that the city's zoning laws were much more stringent than the county's.[43]

Nevertheless, growth advocates as well as investors wanting to expand Fremont Street's casino core with more hotels periodically challenged the city's red-line policy. In April 1975 outgoing commissioner Franklin again pushed to abolish the red-line ordinance that confined unrestricted gaming licenses to six blocks downtown and to a few blocks on the Westside. In 1971 Franklin had dropped a similar proposal. At the time, the determined opposition of downtown gaming interests and Mayor Gragson had blocked Franklin's proposal for fear that small casinos and slot arcades would spread everywhere and discourage the construction of large hotels downtown. But four years later he renewed his charge that the red line had never benefited the city, but just served the downtown "gaming kingpins" who wanted to preserve their monopoly, an argument similar to the ones voiced by critics in Reno. Franklin went on to suggest that space for gaming was so limited downtown that men such as Thomas Hull (El Rancho Vegas), R. E. Griffith and William J. Moore (the Hotel Last Frontier), and Billy Wilkerson (the Flamingo) had been forced to create the Strip. They had built their resorts in the county because there was no red line, not just because taxes were lower. Franklin reasoned that if the city abolished its red line, gaming establishments would increase and so would revenues. He felt this was the best way to compete for resorts with the Strip. Franklin also could not understand why downtown had to be the place where the city confined gambling. The anti-red-line forces eventually made some headway in the mid-1970s when the city granted a gaming license for Bob Stupak's Vegas World (today's site of the Stratosphere) on Las Vegas Boulevard, two blocks north of Sahara Avenue.[44]

Somewhat related to the city's devotion to maintaining the red line was its at-least-stated desire for "orderly growth" or "managed growth." In his successful 1963 bid for reelection, Mayor Oran Gragson, after reviewing how many streetlights, traffic lights, and linear feet of sewerage were installed during his first term, touted his commitment to "orderly growth." This was roughly the time when it became a major issue in Reno. So, both cities, with their railroad heritage, traditional transportation-based economies, dense building patterns, and sense of community, embraced orderly growth in the 1960s and '70s.[45]

Local media also reflected the belief of city leaders and many residents that Las Vegas cherished this goal. In August 1960 a *Review-Journal* column noted that although Las Vegas had undergone significant population growth since the war, sprawl had been limited. As late as 1969 the *Review-Journal* continued to nurse the idea that the city of Las Vegas was successfully managing growth. In 1969 an editorial boldly asserted, "Las Vegas is in control of its growth while Los Angeles is trapped in pell-mell expansion." The column went on to claim, "We have smog controls ... while Los Angeles, piling industry atop industry, is in trouble." The writer then insisted that Las Vegas could stop "smog contributors," and he assured readers that "relief was forthcoming," while Los Angeles, with its temperature inversions, "is caught up in the coils of megalomania." This testifies to the fact that at least some Las Vegans suffered from the same delusion that their city somehow had growth under control, which it did not. In the Strip city but also in North Las Vegas and Henderson, building had long been by variance rather than adhering to a formal plan, and control of the valley's air pollution was still a dream that would not be realized until the 1980s or even later. Moreover, the Strip city's continued leapfrog expansion outward posed a serious challenge to the city of Las Vegas and its CBD. As one contemporary source noted in 1965, "The downtown businesses, once our retail hub, are fighting to hold on in the face of shopping complexes in outlying areas."[46]

In Reno the managed-growth debate was more complicated, because it involved the potential costs associated with enlarging the metropolitan water supply, expanding the sewage treatment plant, metering water use, higher utility costs, rising crime, the need for more schools, and myriad other factors. While both the City of Las Vegas and Clark County employed some zoning to determine land use for industry, commerce, residential areas, and casino resorts, managed growth was more of an illusion. In fact, both governments sought as much development as possible, and leaders championed one bond issue after another to build more schools, increase water supply, construct a new airport, and do a thousand other things necessary to facilitate expansion in the 1960s.

Of course, the sixties posed other challenges. While Las Vegas struggled to accommodate population growth and urban sprawl, it also grappled with race relation issues. A largely Jim Crow city since the late 1930s, Las Vegas would not have succeeded in the 1970s and afterward had it not reformed its treatment of minority customers and residents. The first battleground was public places, where segregation reigned supreme. The story has been told before and will not be repeated in detail here, but clearly, the Las Vegas chapter of the NAACP had an advantage over its Reno counterpart, because southern Nevada's area black population was considerably larger. This was largely due to the Strip city's growing number of large resorts with their many low-paying custodial-type jobs. In 1960 the Las Vegas metropolitan area had eleven thousand black residents compared to a few thousand in Reno. This allowed NAACP chapter president and local dentist James McMillan to recruit several thousand protesters for his threatened march down the Strip in March 1960. McMillan and other civil rights leaders demanded that hotel-casinos on the Strip and downtown open their guest rooms, casinos, showrooms, restaurants, and pools to all minorities. Most of the hotel owners on the Strip and in the city, worried about the effects of violent protests on tourism, complied. With Governor Grant Sawyer and *Las Vegas Sun* editor Hank Greenspun urging them to meet with local civil rights leaders, most owners eventually accepted the so-called Moulin Rouge Agreement and reluctantly opened most hotels and casinos to minorities. Some, however, eventually took action against their black employees who demanded that *all* public places in the metropolitan area be desegregated. By January 1961 it was obvious that, despite the agreement to desegregate most public places in the Las Vegas area, the battle was not yet won.[47]

While open accommodations for minorities existed at most resorts by early 1960, for several years afterward there was little progress on other fronts. The same was true of Reno, where casinos remained closed to minority customers. Storey County's James Slattery, along with other conservatives, tied up a fair employment practices bill in the 1961 state senate and did it again in 1963. Victory finally came in 1965, thanks partly to

Lyndon Johnson's Civil Rights Act of 1964 and the threat of federal court action. The resorts in both metropolitan areas and their unions publicly agreed to open up better-paying jobs to minorities, but soon resorted to foot-dragging for as long as they could. In response, NAACP attorneys, led by Charles Kellar, sued in federal court and eventually broke the logjam. A federal consent decree in 1971 finally made higher-paying hotel-casino positions in the Las Vegas area available to minority men.

But gender discrimination continued to flourish. Women of all colors, including whites, had to wait until later in that decade for their chance. A 1981 federal consent decree further helped them. In 1958 Las Vegas city commissioners had passed an ordinance prohibiting women dealers and reaffirmed it in 1970. However, the commissioners rescinded the ban a year later at the request of Sam Boyd and other casino operators, who wanted to employ women dealers at their new Union Plaza Hotel. In that same year Governor Mike O'Callaghan pushed a state open-housing bill through the legislature that finally allowed minorities to live anywhere in the metropolitan zone. Residential segregation had begotten school segregation, a practice that finally began to end when Clark County school superintendent and future governor Kenny Guinn, under pressure from the courts, implemented the Sixth Grade Busing Plan in 1972, which integrated classes in most parts of the metropolitan area.[48]

By 1975 Las Vegas, like Reno, had put the worst aspects of its Jim Crow days behind it and actively courted minority customers, just as millions of African Americans and others were finally moving above the poverty line and could afford a gambling vacation. In the 1960s and early '70s, the city and Strip counted other achievements. Las Vegas–area leaders decided to move its airport in 1960 to a more spacious site capable of accommodating jets. Work also began on the Southern Nevada Water Project to provide enough supply for up to several million residents and tourists, although, as will be shown, as early as 1989 frantic growth threatened to create a new water crisis. The school district also kept pace with population growth, especially in the new Strip city, whose growth rate exceeded those of Las Vegas, Henderson, and North Las Vegas. New schools, roads, and plans to expand the convention center, along with the debut of sumptuous new resorts such as Caesars Palace, the International, and MGM Grand, positioned Las Vegas, and especially the Strip, to become a leading American tourist destination in the years to come.

Chapter Three

RENO AREA

The Growth Wave Rises and Recedes, 1970–1990

RENO ENTERED THE 1970S in an optimistic mood. Thanks to its efforts and those of Las Vegas, Nevada-style gaming was becoming increasingly popular. More Americans than ever before were traveling on vacation to the Silver State, and it was no longer primarily a California market. Thanks to growing affluence, jet service, the democratization of the credit card, and other factors, it was now easier for people to travel long distances. Reno's political and gaming leaders prepared to accommodate them. They understood that their city was woefully short of modern hotels, and the 1970 abolition of the city's historic red-line ordinance was an effort to incentivize more construction. On the other hand, some citizens were concerned about uncontrolled growth and, like their counterparts in other postwar western cities, emphasized the need for more planning.

Just a year or so after Reno's new red-line ordinance went into effect, some county planners pushed the idea of better managing the city's growth, a position with which many residents agreed. The origins of Reno's blue-ribbon task force program on growth and development resulted from a 1972 HUD-sponsored conference in Portland, Oregon, attended by the Regional Planning Commission and other Washoe County representatives. At about this time, Portland officials and other Oregonians were considering major zoning legislation to control growth in the metropolitan area and in other parts of the state where sprawl threatened fragile ecosystems and natural beauty. Portland was the center for new planning approaches to the West's rapid growth and was the obvious choice for the two-day conference. Having returned from the conference inspired, members of the Regional Planning Commission, in league with the newly created Washoe Council of Governments, convinced city and county officials to act. The latter created a task force composed of blue-ribbon panels filled with prominent citizens from Reno, Sparks, and the county to study ten key issues: water supply, air pollution, housing, codes, design, physical restraints, the economics of growth, public finance, optimum size, and planning.[1]

These ten panels heard testimony from experts and the public and eventually drafted reports that identified problems and suggested policy approaches. Water was a key priority, because shortages became a constant concern for the Reno metropolitan area by the late 1960s. Experts estimated that 220,000 people was the maximum population the Truckee Meadows could accommodate under the most ideal circumstances without drying out parts of the riverbed. The Truckee was the city's primary source of water, while outlying valleys relied on wells. But wastewater was becoming an issue, even as early as the 1960s. Everyone agreed that pollution thrived at the jointly operated Reno-Sparks Sewage Treatment Plant, which was in dire need of expansion. Engineers advised the task force that only strict water conservation measures would allow Reno to accommodate more people and permit additional growth. Otherwise, officials would have to undertake an expensive effort to bring water from distant sources. But, as the blue-ribbon panel on water warned in its report, "a high use in this area represents business, industrial, tourist and parkland uses, and major reductions would dramatically alter the character and flavor of the community."[2] None of this was good news for the casino industry.

The panel also rejected the idea of relying on septic tanks as a means of avoiding expensive bond issues to expand the metropolitan area's sewer network and build a new or vastly enlarged sewage treatment plant. Indeed, panel members emphasized that the danger of too many septic tanks in an expanding urban area was their tendency to pollute underground wells, although members did recommend investigating the feasibility of establishing a metropolitan water district. They knew that more than twenty years earlier, Las Vegas–area residents had voted overwhelmingly to create the Las Vegas Valley Water District to buy out the railroad's feeble water system, which, along with wells, had served the community since 1905. Reno panel members recognized the importance of this move. Creation of a water district allowed officials to levy fees and issue bonds to extend the water system throughout the Las Vegas valley and help construct enough straws from Lake Mead to support the dream of a metropolis with a million or more residents—a dream that came true in the 1990s.

Members of Reno's water panel also understood the valuable role such districts had played in promoting urban development in California and elsewhere in the West. Beyond the obvious advantages of such an authority's bonding capacity, the task force recognized "the need for coordinated land, water and sewer planning for the entire Truckee River system." This included enlarging the Reno-Sparks Joint Treatment Plant to accommodate sewer lines that would be needed in neighborhoods near the river and underground wells where septic tanks could not be used.[3] So, for the first time, Reno-area community leaders addressed the obstacles posed by water that would have to be overcome if the city hoped to become a substantial metropolitan area later in the century.

Officials in Reno, Sparks, and Washoe County began to appreciate the idea that development throughout the entire Truckee River Basin "should be coordinated." To this end, another blue-ribbon panel studied air pollution, which became an increasing concern in a city that hugged the scenic western Sierra and where residents preferred smelling the mountain fir trees instead of the gasoline and diesel fumes emitted by the growing number of trucks and cars in town. This group warned how "single family residential sprawl contributes to air pollution by automobile use." Casino dealers, pit bosses, and cocktail waitresses tended to have better-paying jobs, especially before the 1980s, when the Internal Revenue Service began cracking down on undeclared tip income in Nevada. These workers could afford cars and large houses in newer suburban subdivisions. The blue-ribbon panel recommended more "planned unit development," along with increased reliance on public transportation, to reduce air pollution in the Truckee Meadows, which resembled Portland's decision to encourage infilling as well as the construction of more multioccupancy dwellings near its urban core. Of course, the blue-ribbon panel realized this type of housing would be more appealing to custodial and other low-income resort employees, but tourist industry workers with high-paying jobs were still more likely to own at least one car and reside in a single-family home.[4]

To reduce air pollution further in the Truckee Meadows, the panel recommended finishing Interstate 80 as well as the "north-south" freeway (today's US 395/580), to connect Interstate 80 with the airport and eventually with Carson City. The group also supported the Project RENOvation idea of creating the "Virginia Street Mall," a tree-shaded pedestrian walkway stretching from Interstate 80 to the city's financial district near the

Truckee River, which would eliminate thru traffic and parking (except for hotel cab stands) around the casino core. Members also urged the appointment of a county traffic engineer and insisted that street construction "be coordinated" with that official and an independent traffic-planning group. In addition, the blue-ribbon panel called for an end to "the shortage of east-west through streets and the implementation of a synchronized traffic light system much like the one that Clark County had begun to implement."[5] The group's insistence on the greater use of bicycles and carpooling echoed a familiar refrain voiced throughout urban America. Finally, panel members called upon city officials to convince the Southern Pacific to try to run most of its long freight trains through Reno at off-peak hours, although they stopped short of demanding an expensive lowering of the tracks.

But many in town wished they had. The presence of a railroad in the middle of downtown created mounting problems in the twentieth century. In 1868 when the Central Pacific platted Reno, the grid of streets straddled the tracks, with part of the town on the north side and most to the south. In contrast, Senator William Clark's Las Vegas Townsite, which included Fremont Street, lay completely east of his railroad line. So, the trains never crossed the city's main commercial artery, although the passenger station at the head of Fremont Street abruptly halted the road's western direction before it reached the tracks. In 1900 there was still just a smattering of structures and people north of the station in Reno, just as there was in the McWilliams Townsite west of Senator Clark's yards a few years later. By 1910 the tracks and other railroad structures virtually isolated the old Westside, which conveniently became a segregated black neighborhood in the 1940s. By the 1980s and '90s, most of the street crossings in Las Vegas had either been put above or below grade, and by 2000 the railroad-yard lands had been transferred to the city, which soon ripped them out and cleared the land for building.

But Reno never got the main rail yards for western Nevada. Wadsworth had them until 1902, when the Central Pacific announced that a new town, which became Sparks, three miles east of Reno, would become the repair center for the company's western Nevada division. Nevertheless, the mainline tracks still crossed Virginia Street at grade *and* virtually all of downtown Reno's other north-south thoroughfares as they were built in the twentieth century. Pedestrian fatalities became such a problem that the railroad in 1902 began work on an underground crossing of the tracks, which many pedestrians ignored. By 1930, with the university growing and so many residences north of the tracks, it was obvious the tracks needed to be raised or lowered. Though first recommended by Reno's city engineer in 1938 as a possible New Deal project to improve downtown, a series of mayors opposed spending city money on the improvement, because they felt the cost was not worth the benefit. With so many railroad-grade crossings in midcentury American towns, they did not consider it to be enough of a nuisance. In the 1960s Congressman Walter Baring, who could have worked with Senators Bible and Cannon to get federal funds for the project, had actually opposed lowering the tracks because he thought the trains added to Reno's small-town charm. But in 1973 the Blue Ribbon Panel on Growth and Development noted ominously that both the river and the railroad had become "serious barriers to north-south traffic flow."[6]

Yet even in the 1970's, Mayor Carl Bogart could not justify the expense compared to what the city would get for it, nor could his immediate successors. This was true until the late 1970s, when the casino-building boom increased population and made the city a more significant tourist attraction. However, the downtown casino industry and city leaders who relied on tourists for a steady source of revenue were concerned about the effect a multiyear reconstruction project would have on business and traffic. As a result of these concerns and the railroad's sluggish response to funding part of the project, more years dragged on with nothing being done. This occurred even though it was becoming increasingly obvious that Reno had to do something. In a January 1979 editorial, the *Evening Gazette* reported that one hundred thousand cars and trucks daily traversed the tracks in Reno's CBD. The newspaper estimated that twenty-four trains completely stopped downtown traffic for ninety minutes everyday. So, Reno's growth made lowering the railroad grade more of a priority. The few streets boasting overpasses were also subject to traffic jams, because drivers tried to avoid Virginia Street and parallel roads.[7]

As the *Gazette* reported, the trains caused backups "along the main downtown streets especially cramped Virginia Street," blocking "north-south and east-west traffic flows." Aside from the threat to public safety and the danger of chemical explosions downtown, the idle cars only worsened the city's air pollution. The constant danger from accidents and blocked fire trucks and other emergency vehicles was compounded further by the effect on tourists, because the railroad station was just east of Virginia Street, where many of the big casino hotels built their parking garages. The *Gazette* concluded by warning that the barrier posed by trains threatened the city's future. As the newspaper put it, "At a time when the city is redeveloping its downtown into a modern bright quadrangle of lights and entertainment, those tracks continue to draw their long dark shadow through the center." Despite these problems, the blue-ribbon panel knew that neither the struggling Southern Pacific nor voters would be anxious to spend the millions necessary to raise or lower the tracks. So, the panel's final report sidestepped the issue, postponing action for sometime in the future.[8]

A separate blue-ribbon panel addressed housing issues, a popular subject with the local media. In the 1970s William Harrah and a growing number of gaming operators in Reno-Sparks announced plans for resort expansion or new construction. After noting that "because of the large numbers of professionals and retired persons in Reno, the housing market contains a large number of single-family dwellings," one local newspaper congratulated city officials for approving several low-cost rental developments, a move that the air-pollution panel had also championed. The column explained how the rising cost of real estate in the metropolitan area had "priced conventional housing out of the reach of most casino employees." This highlighted another growth-related problem that government leaders and the private sector had to address. The metropolitan area expected the arrival of five thousand new casino workers over the next few years, but only 2,155 rental units were on the drawing board—11,000 units short of the projected need. Reno faced a definite housing crisis. Because the average casino employee's salary in Reno was $660 per month, of which roughly one-quarter was spent on housing, the newspaper concluded that $215 would not buy anyone a good house or even a decent apartment.[9] Of course, salaries rose because of the high rates of inflation besieging American workers in the late 1970s, but Reno still faced a housing crisis worsened by the expansion of its casino resorts.

The blue-ribbon panel's report on local housing recognized that home ownership was becoming possible for only a small percentage of the growing population. It also recognized that the private sector needed to build fewer two- and three-bedroom homes and more affordable rental apartment complexes and mobile home parks. Even the demand for public housing far exceeded the supply. But, as the task force conceded, it was "difficult to establish mobile home parks near most local existing residential areas." This was also the case with low-income and public housing developments because of their tendency to depress nearby real estate values. The panel also worried that a large influx of gaming and hotel workers would trigger other unwanted consequences. As the group's report noted, "Heavy housing demand can bypass close-in properties and encourage leapfrog, sprawl development with [the] concurrent need for excessive auto use" that contributed to traffic jams and air pollution.[10]

What the panel feared in 1974 came true in 1978 when the MGM and the other large resorts opened and, with all of their new low-income employees, triggered the expected housing crisis. By June 1978 the lack of rental apartments had reached the point where the *Nevada State Journal* published an editorial opposing the effort by some developers to convert rental apartments to $120,000 condominiums by adding fire walls and other building-code upgrades. The newspaper argued that the city was in dire need of affordable housing for low-income workers and their families and applauded the decision by the Reno and Sparks City Councils to deny sewer allocations to developers building condominiums. The editors also endorsed action to limit the number of condominium conversions in both cities and pointed to Palo Alto as a model. That city's ordinances permitted condo conversions of rental apartments only when the latter's vacancy rate hit a specified percentage, which it never did. With the Sahara, Circus Circus, and the Mapes Money Tree all opening the next day, on June 30, the *Journal* urged both Reno and Sparks to adopt Palo Alto's philosophy.[11]

Task force members also emphasized that while Reno's casino core was being transformed by construction, the new buildings should be aesthetically appealing in their design and that more consideration should be given to historic preservation. This was a major point. As historian Alicia Barber has noted about the reconstruction of downtown Reno in the 1970s and '80s, Del Webb, Fitzgeralds, and other operators had assembled enough land for their casino resorts by purchasing dozens of lots that for decades had hosted Reno's built past, including bars, clubs, shops, apartments, and other midcentury businesses. But in the 1970s, '80s, and '90s, this vintage cityscape was demolished to clear land for modern new resorts catering to late-century tourists and gamblers. Beginning in the late 1960s into the early 1980s and beyond, Harrah's towers (1969, 1981), Fitzgeralds (1976), the Sahara (1978), Circus Circus (1978), the Onslow (1982), and many other high-rise structures destroyed parts of blocks and even entire blocks of the former city and dwarfed in scale the buildings that remained. In the process, much of downtown Reno's historic charm was obliterated.[12]

This process resembled the one in downtown Houston, where many of that city's charming old buildings and businesses yielded to modern skyscrapers, which, like Reno's big casino hotels, often had no windows or doors for an entire block. Much of the pedestrian-oriented streetscape one would expect to find in San Francisco, Chicago, or Manhattan was gone, but in Houston the buildings at least served the needs of major oil companies and corporations that employed local residents rather than tourists. In Reno, however, these structures served the needs of casinos and only promoted the cession of downtown to visitors rather than residents. Indeed, since the advent of casino gambling in American cities, casinos, when numerous, have disrupted the traditional urban fabric. Take, for instance, Atlantic City, where the construction of large casino resorts after 1978 not only destroyed beachfront hotels, apartments, and other businesses in the community, but also drained neighborhood taverns of their customers, who now preferred to drink in the resorts' sports books and bars.

As Bryant Simon has observed, unlike their counterparts in Las Vegas, where the virgin desert provided a virtual blank slate upon which Strip casino operators could build their gaming palaces, "Donald Trump and other New Jersey casino owners couldn't move from the city or take over the sidewalks, so they built over them and around them." Aside from creating a wall between city residents and their boardwalk, the casinos, quite deliberately, looked away from the city and the sea and toward the streets leading to the highway from which cars and chartered buses delivered an endless stream of customers. None of the first wave of casino hotels in Atlantic City had stores on the boardwalk or places to sit outside and sip a drink. The casino hotels formed a barrier between their customers and the boardwalk. Built away from the boardwalk, Harrah's Marina was designed so that "customers had no place to look out at the bay, the ocean or at the Atlantic City skyline except from the parking deck's first floor." The same pattern held in Reno, where there were virtually no windows at Circus Circus or the Sahara looking out at the street and where nearby convenience stores, souvenir emporiums, and pawn shops, all geared to serving visitors, gobbled up pedestrians outside the hotels. The deliberate design limited the amount of people headed over to the river past J. C. Penney's, Woolworths, Lerner's, and Ardan's (all of which closed up for lack of patronage by 1991) or to downtown restaurants and other attractions that typically flourished in *normal* American cities.[13]

Clearly, the design-committee members, like many of the other task force panels, were frustrated by the problems they encountered, most of which resulted from the rapid urbanization of an increasingly casino-filled city. But committee members trudged forward. Convinced that what Reno needed was slower growth and a more diversified economy, the panel on aesthetic design recommended a variety of useful suggestions to improve the urban fabric. In addition to suggesting moving more utility lines underground and forcing downtown businesses to plant more landscaping, it urged construction of an integrated sewer system that would coordinate wastewater flow and sewage treatment from Reno, Sparks, and outlying communities in Washoe County. But the panel stopped short of advocating the consolidation of more urban services, much less whole governments, an idea that at the time was under serious consideration in the Las Vegas valley.

Beyond housing, traffic, and pollution, growth itself was a major concern, as it was in Portland and dozens of other cities across the West. Reno's blue-ribbon panel examining physical growth warned officials that rapid urbanization was "speeding up water runoff, eliminating ponds... [and] lowering the water table," while also straining "street and highway facilities" and other services. Even though the panel agreed that southern Washoe County's lands could accommodate a half-million people if necessary, it concluded that "weather and climate can impose restrictions and can easily influence planning and development decisions." This was particularly true, given the long winters and temperature inversions that traditionally plagued the Truckee Meadows.[14]

The panel also cautioned that development on floodplains, such as the lands between the Truckee River, the MGM Grand, and the airport runways, "should be restricted," and high-density housing "should be isolated from airport and highway noise areas." In the 1980s and '90s, highway officials addressed this concern by erecting barrier walls along the sides of US 395 to mitigate highway noise, leaving lands bordering the elevated freeway available for development. But the panel's largest issue was clearly unrestrained growth. In ominous language members warned that the current 4.5 percent rate of population growth in Washoe County was "excessive and must be slowed." The solution to reducing this annual average growth rate was to restrict jobs not only in gaming but also in warehousing and manufacturing. So, this panel, as well as the other ones, was looking not just to slow down the expansion of tourism and gambling, but to slow down growth in general by restricting it—even in the nongaming sectors of the metropolitan economy.[15]

Why? To preserve the quality of life. As the panel noted in its report, "A very rapid rate of growth will lead to a parallel rapid rate of growth, which would lower the community's quality of life." At this time and afterward, the Las Vegas area was experiencing a much greater rate of growth than Washoe, but no similar movement arose in Clark County. In Las Vegas, Henderson, North Las Vegas, and the county, politicians, businessmen, and voters regarded growth as the key prerequisite to improving the quality of life. This, however, was not the case in Reno. As the blue-ribbon panel on growth observed, the Reno area had "still not experienced many of the problems which have grown to serious proportions in numerous communities in California," but the fear was that if rapid population growth continued in the Truckee Meadows, "these problems would be hard to avoid." The best way to avoid them, noted panel chair and UNR economics professor William Eadington, was to limit population growth to 3 percent annually by restricting the rate of job growth in gaming, warehousing, and manufacturing. But the minority report, filed by progrowth businessman Wayne Dennis, emphasized the benefits of increased population and gaming revenues, which "must be encouraged." Clearly, then, not everyone in the city or on the committee viewed the 1978 debut of the MGM Grand and the impending arrival of the Sahara, Circus Circus, and other properties as vital to Reno's future. Indeed, the blue-ribbon panel even had the temerity to suggest placing a countywide proposition on some future ballot, giving voters the option of insisting that annual growth be limited to 3 percent.[16]

The majority of the panel's members also recommended that any "proposed new commercial or industrial project [that] would directly employ more than twenty-five employees" should produce an "impact statement," which would estimate the likely population increase as well as "economic, social and ecological effects of the project." This certainly would have raised eyebrows among investors. According to the final report, approval or disapproval of the project would be based on its "compatibility with long-term growth objectives." This was certainly not occurring in Las Vegas or to the north in the Boise area, which was in the early stages of securing a computer industry that would help boost the old potato town's metropolitan population past 430,000 by century's end. Nor was this the kind of thinking that governed the growth process in Phoenix, Dallas, or Houston. Instead, Reno community leaders and residents seemed to relate more to the experience of places such as Portland, Livermore, and other cities in Northern California. Reno's blue-ribbon panels reflected what historian Carl Abbott has called the "antigrowth activists" and "quality-of-life liberals" in the modern urban West as opposed to antigrowth minority activists in Dallas and other Sunbelt cities, who opposed the bulldozing of their neighborhoods by business elites to create new sites for convention centers, interstate highways, and urban renaissance areas. In Reno, Portland, and other managed-growth cities, it was often the scientists, university professors, and nongaming businesspeople as well as salaried employees who "view[ed] their cities more as residential environments than as economic machines."[17] Reno residents, for instance, supported the new thirty-six-acre warehouse that J. C. Penney's built in the city in 1979, a large project that used Nevada's 1949 Freeport Law to create dozens of permanent jobs, property tax revenues, and truck-related businesses in the city. Renoites just didn't want more large resorts that required substantial public expenditures.

So, the Reno panel pressed the case for "managed growth," much to the delight of many residents. This group included future mayor Barbara Bennett, "who read the entire [ten-volume] report—not once but many times," and was inspired by the task force's findings to run for office to try to enact them. The task force's major recommendation was as follows: "The governing bodies of Reno, Sparks and Washoe County, in cooperation with all residents of the area, should make every effort to slow our rate of growth." The reasons underlying this view were numerous. Growth was not free; it cost a lot of money. Growth also made citizen participation more difficult; it was easier for big developers and corporate executives to influence public policy. Growth did not always benefit the community; not all businesses were compatible. On this issue Reno contrasted greatly with the Strip city, where county politicians and resort executives saw growth paying for itself in the long run by expanding the tax base. More population meant more taxpayers to fund the up-front costs of new streets, schools, and infrastructure.

Most Strip-city residents also preferred more development, supporting most bond elections and candidates for office with growth agendas. The Reno panel, on the other hand, ignored this and instead pointed to Tucson—whose plan for growth was its master plan—as a city that Reno should emulate.[18]

Reno's blue-ribbon panels worked for almost two years and produced their final reports in 1974, roughly two years before MGM announced plans to build its $115 million resort near the airport. The panels' reports became more significant as the MGM Grand prepared to open in May 1978, so the city's newspapers republished all or large portions of the reports then. In her 1989 reminiscence managed/slow-growth mayor Barbara Bennett (1979–83) succinctly summarized her position as well as those of many citizens at the time. She quoted planner Robert Eckert, who wrote a lengthy editorial in 1975 that said: "We are in an area where the population is going to exceed a quarter of a million; winter months will feature constant smog and carbon dioxide health hazards; most of the influx of persons will be low-paid gaming industry employees unable to afford housing in swanky new subdivisions." As a result, he predicted, "High-density apartments will spring up everywhere" in Reno. He also observed somewhat prophetically that "property taxes would soar" for police and fire protection, water rates would triple, and the crime rate would rise. This is what Bennett and the public saw as the real threat to Reno. MGM was merely the beginning of "the development community's" agenda for Reno. Bennett and her allies, however, recognized that the city's geographical position up against the Carson Range, with only a few snowy peaks and a portion of Lake Tahoe to rely upon for water, was not the best location for even a small metropolis. "It has always been my argument," Bennett declared, that "this community is fragile and it can only stand so much development"; the new MGM Grand was just too much for Bennett and many of her supporters.[19]

But the city's development community, consisting of builders, bankers, real estate agents, the building-trade unions, and other groups that stood to gain from growth, welcomed MGM to town. On November 10, 1975, the company announced it would construct a large resort in Reno on the site of a 110-acre gravel pit. Initially, the corporation did not make it clear where it intended to build. Its executives had negotiated earlier with the Redfield Estate for 210 acres on South Virginia Street; then the company announced it had leased a tract in west Reno, where it planned to erect a one-thousand-room hotel near Interstate 80. In the end, MGM chose a spot near the airport along the route of the proposed 395/580 freeway, which in 2012 finally connected Carson City with Interstate 80 in Reno. At the time, no one questioned the effects this large resort would exert on the city. If they had, recalled regional planning director Dick Allen, "They would have been ridden out of town on a rail."[20]

Following MGM's announcement, six other casino projects were approved, "setting off the biggest building boom in the city's history," in the words of former city councilwoman Pat Lewis. A critic of the process, Lewis recalled how the MGM "was rushed through" the planning process by city leaders. She noted that the "MGM was saying 'you really have to rush this thing through. We got a lot of bucks in this and we need some quick answers now.'" Lewis, who then sat on the council, credited MGM for its shrewd strategy, which worked well for the corporation. In contrast, the developers who built the Meadowood Mall on DeLucci Lane a few years earlier saw the Reno City Council delay action on their proposal for more than a year. In that case, according to Lewis, "the developer was required to participate in providing roads and traffic signalization."[21]

In contrast, MGM never faced such hurdles and won quick approval, just as it had earlier in Clark County. In fact, regulation was so lax that contractors utilizing the "fast-track" method of construction installed thousands of feet of electrical wire in the building that later blueprints never utilized—a fact not made public until after the MGM fire of 1980.[22] In Reno the construction and approvals process for the new MGM also moved ahead with great speed. Lewis remembered that the city council was "impressed by what I call the silk suit boys." Rather than subject Alvin Benedict and other MGM executives to a realistic appraisal of the problems created by their resort, city officials meekly deferred to virtually all of their wishes. Why did they do so? As Lewis recalled, MGM was considered "a biggie; it was like having the president or somebody who's your hero come to town." There was little or no concern about growth issues. In 1975 the reaction to MGM was much like what one would expect in the laissez-faire, growth-hungry atmosphere of Clark County. As former Washoe County Commission chair Dick Allen remembered, "The chamber of commerce felt the city could . . . keep growth problems under control."[23]

Former Reno city manager Joseph Latimore had a different view. He had come to Reno in 1960 to serve in the newly vacated city manager position.

From 1960 to 1974 Latimore helped make the government more efficient by modernizing administration and saving the taxpayers money. He left in 1974, just before the historic meeting with MGM executives took place. In fact, Latimore recalled that he did not even know MGM was coming until after the public announcement. Despite the city council's obviously secret negotiations with company executives, Latimore nonetheless disagreed with Lewis, insisting that Reno at the time needed MGM more than it needed Reno. "The city," he insisted, "was looking for a way to boost the economy," and MGM was the answer, given the area's relative failure to attract other major industries. Reno city councilman Clyde Biglieri concurred, explaining that in 1974–75, Reno's economy was at a modern low for jobs in the construction sector. There had been a "dramatic drop" between 1973 and 1974 for new commercial and residential building permits. MGM and the other new resort projects it encouraged provided the momentum that Reno desperately needed. The city's construction industry began to pick up in the mid-1970s and early '80s. But unlike Las Vegas, Reno could not sustain the boom once tourism leveled off.[24]

Not surprisingly, Reno promoter Jud Allen also disagreed with Lewis and MGM's critics. He saw gaming and tourism as crucial to the area's economic future. In his 1997 book-length reminiscence, Allen reminded readers that in 1969, downtown businessmen had joined to form "Reno Unlimited" to help fund a study for the revitalization of downtown. The consultant subsequently concluded that to satisfy growing consumer demand, Reno needed to add at least 485 hotel rooms per year. This recommendation had to have been on the minds of city councilmen in May 1970 when they voted to abolish Reno's red line and grant an unrestricted gaming license to any casino with a hotel of 100 or more rooms. As Allen recalled, Reno barely kept pace with that figure, even with the Sahara Reno, MGM Grand, Circus Circus, the Comstock, Harrah's new tower, the Colonial Inn, and John Ascuaga's Nugget in Sparks. Moreover, Biglieri insisted that if Reno had rejected the MGM Grand or delayed it, as Lewis and others wanted, there was "no doubt" in his mind that "the county and Sparks would have welcomed them." This, he concluded, would have been an economic disaster for the municipal government. "Had the [MGM] hotel-casino been located outside of Reno, the city would have still faced its impacts but missed out on the general revenues," much like the city of Las Vegas did with MGM and other large resorts in the Strip city south of the municipal border.[25]

Reno's leaders therefore did everything they could to bring MGM to their town. On May 19, 1976, city officials signed what later became a controversial agreement with the company to trade 14 acres of the old riverside sewer plant land near the gravel pit for 17 acres of land MGM owned elsewhere in town. This helped the corporation assemble the 114 acres it needed for the resort. Controversy arose later when this deal blocked Terminal Way, the chief north-south road to the airport's main entrance, from crossing MGM property to connect with Greg Street in Sparks. As the opening day for Kirk Kerkorian's resort approached, the story took the form of a political exposé. Indeed, the local media reported how the agreement helped MGM maintain its property rights by not extending a badly needed road through the resort's land. This action, critics charged, clearly showed that street improvements were not coordinated in the metropolitan area and that city officials routinely worked to please gaming interests to the neglect of the public—a fact that annoyed many residents. At issue was whether Greg Street should have been extended across the resort's property. The City of Sparks favored the road extension and engineers for the Regional Street and Highway Commission made it their priority, but Reno officials opposed the improvement, calling it "too expensive." The city council also opposed a land swap. But the *Nevada State Journal,* which had also favored Greg Street's extension, declared that Reno's city council "could easily have made dedication of land for the extension a condition for approving a land exchange agreement." Obviously, city officials badly wanted the MGM resort and did little to antagonize the resort's executives. In response, Reno's city councilmen defended their actions, claiming the land deal was a crucial prerequisite to getting MGM to build its resort inside the city and that Interstate 80 and the future north-south freeway (US 395/580) would better connect Sparks to the airport.[26]

As their hotel prepared to open in May 1978 and in an effort to defuse some of the public criticism the project had aroused, MGM executives reassured residents and the local media that the resort only confirmed Reno's rapid rise to prominence and assured them it would reinforce the area's appeal as a tourist center. MGM Board chair Fred Benninger was clear about why the company chose to build in Reno. Lower labor costs were a big factor that would help offset the lower gaming profits the company expected to earn in comparison to its Las Vegas resort. Although Reno experienced a construction slump in the early 1970s, Benninger insisted it was still one of the nation's fastest-growing cities. The metropolitan area was also home to "a large pool of experienced hotel and casino employees" that MGM could draw from. The "favorable attitude of local officials toward the project" also impressed MGM executives, if not residents and critics. Finally, the city's lack of growth-control measures was another reason, and one that probably led antigrowth activists in the area to redouble their efforts to block the powerful gaming industry from co-opting city and state officials any more than they already had.[27]

When it opened on May 3, 1978, the MGM's crystal chandeliers, coffered ceilings, and Hollywood theme throughout mirrored much of the grandeur of its Las Vegas cousin. The resort's debut was definitely a major event in Reno's history. Sensing a need to step up the company's favorable public relations campaign, however, executives came forward to tout the new place's potential benefits in press releases and interviews. Noting that the new hotel could host more than ten thousand delegates, sympathetic local newspapers trumpeted the fact that the MGM, all by itself, would almost double the metropolitan area's convention capacity. Everyone knew that conventions were crucial to filling Reno's hotels and casinos during the week. So, with more large resorts in the works and the airport's terminal expansion slated for completion in 1980, the resort community braced itself for a major boom. Aware that their new hotel was raising the kind of concerns in some quarters that the company never encountered in southern Nevada, MGM executives were quick to reassure residents about two major questions: first, the resort would not divert tourists and conventioneers from patronizing the downtown's hotels and clubs, and, second, the new property would greatly boost Reno's visitors, justifying expensive airport improvements. MGM's convention sales and marketing director Joseph Esposito directly addressed the growing fear that MGM would divert tourists and convention delegates from downtown. He told residents that the resort would seek national conventions and confidently predicted that with only 1,015 rooms at the hotel, "high-quality conventioneers" would go downtown, too. "We're not going after Harrah's business," he declared. "We go after all sizes of conventions, but our marketing is geared to the national level, because our facilities are so much bigger than others."[28]

He was right—much to the relief of Harrah's and other downtown executives. During the MGM's opening week, there was little siphoning of business from the casino core and no major exodus of dealers and other employees to the new resort. Actually, the MGM's debut helped fill the downtown's hotels with gamblers. As one Virginia Street employee explained, "Most gamblers liked a certain place and then visit[ed] other places; it's hard to change their habits." Many Reno regulars avoided the MGM altogether because they liked to play in the "gaming core" downtown. After the first few weeks, it was clear the resort would not hurt the city's other casinos; it would simply bring more tourists to town. Of course, Bill Harrah was taking no chances. Even before the MGM opened, he purchased land on the west side of town for "Harrah's World," a 4,000-room hotel-casino even grander than the MGM, but his plans never got very far due to his illness and eventual death in June 1978.

Esposito further advised that Reno's conventions would now be "bigger and richer," with more doctors and corporate executives coming to town than ever before. He predicted that MGM delegates would request accommodations ranging from economy to deluxe, and the resort would provide free shuttle service to downtown—a courtesy that hardly pleased local cab drivers. He pointed out that not every delegate would want to stay at the MGM; many would prefer the downtown atmosphere. At the same time, not everyone would patronize Harrah's or the Sahara; some would seek out less expensive places such as the Sundowner, the Holiday, and the Riverside.[29]

Esposito also reassured Reno's many slow-growth advocates that his resort, though large, would immediately boost the city's traditionally sluggish convention business, an event that would benefit many local businesses and the overall economy. He predicted that MGM would transform the Reno-Tahoe area into a "new convention destination in the country." Esposito emphasized that Reno's peak convention season was fall and winter, so MGM conventions could "be used to fill the valleys of Reno's peak-and-valley tourist business." The only major hurdle for MGM was to downplay Reno's traditional promotion of skiing, so conventioneers would not be frightened away by bad weather. Noting that tourism had become the third leading industry in the nation, Esposito asserted that his resort would exert a "multiplier effect" on Reno's economy and insisted that the proposed beautification of the Truckee River would allow Reno to fashion "a distinctive drawing card" for delegates as well as tourists. Esposito therefore embraced the proposals of groups such as Project RENOvation, observing, "All of these things are important for conventions."[30]

He pointed to the City by the Bay as an example of how Reno could develop into a destination where tourism provided the money for other improvements. "Look at San Francisco," he declared, where tourism "is becoming its number one business, and look at all the improvements going on there." He was right. In many cities such as San Francisco, tourism had replaced manufacturing and even commerce as the leading industry. Esposito noted that the conversion of the old Ghiradelli chocolate factory into a mall, the push to make Chinatown and Fisherman's Wharf hark back to the city's Gold Rush days, as well as efforts to glorify the city's bawdy nightclub legacy, taken together, boosted San Francisco's tourism profits in the 1960s and '70s. These attractions not only raised additional capital to build the Hyatt on Union Square, the Hilton, the Westbury, a large new tower on the St. Francis, and other hotel projects downtown, but also contributed mightily to the city's coffers and to the willingness of more corporations to build office towers there. For Esposito and his colleagues, San Francisco's experience offered convincing proof that tourism was the key to Reno's prosperity.[31]

Growth critics, including the *Nevada State Journal,* were less optimistic. Their concern that MGM would worsen many existing problems partially offset the euphoria of local boosters. Local journalist Burton Swope noted that MGM executives were sounding the familiar refrain of how the resort would enlarge the metropolitan area's tax base, but, as Swope noted, it would also increase the need for services immediately. Although the MGM's Fred Benninger conceded that the sewage treatment plant's expansion had to be undertaken soon, he reassured local skeptics that Reno's other problems could be solved over time by the increased tax revenues his new resort would generate. Critics countered that thousands of new MGM employees and their families would create an immediate need for more parks, streets, and garbage collection — all of which would hit the city's budget hard. They also pointed out that the Environmental Protection Agency would not allocate millions of dollars to expand the joint Reno-Sparks Sewage Treatment Plant until the cities developed a plan to minimize air pollution from the facility. As the *Nevada State Journal* noted, "Because the demand for services during a period of rapid growth outstrips revenues coming in to pay for them," the cities had to prioritize. Reinforcing this point was Jerry Hall, director of the Regional Street and Highway Commission, who declared that "we're behind in our road building because of a lack of funds [now], . . .

so more congestion is going to occur." He predicted that MGM and the new resorts soon opening would only exacerbate the housing crisis identified by the blue-ribbon housing panel in 1974. As the *Journal* explained, "The number of low-cost housing units in the Truckee Meadows has lagged far behind demand, while the price of houses has skyrocketed," leaving a short supply of affordable housing just as the MGM was opening.[32]

There was a similar problem at the airport, where major terminal expansion still under way in 1978 inconvenienced passengers and airlines. Indeed, that was the same year that airline deregulation took effect, and new airlines looking to establish jet service to Reno desperately needed gates. At this time, nine airlines were seeking CAB approval to serve Las Vegas and possibly Reno. At the same time, the city lacked enough space for downtown convention delegates. Mayor Menicucci and Reno-Sparks Convention and Visitors Authority board chair Bob Rush both agreed that the authority would have to undertake a substantial expansion of the Centennial Coliseum, but this only convinced critics in the Truckee Meadows that "rapid growth was occurring without the benefit of growth management."[33]

On a related front, longtime Reno columnist Bill Sternauer reported that many local residents resented the gaming community's excessive "influence on the city and its government." Sternauer quoted one citizen who complained at a public forum: "It's good that we have a chance to present our view, but the city won't listen to us peons. They just listen to Harrah's and the other rich people. Money, money, money is running this town." The man bemoaned the fact that there was little parking available and that sewage and traffic problems abounded, because "growth is just getting out of hand." And in a city already beset by casino-related crime, he pointed out that although the MGM "is beautiful and all, . . . it's going to bring in a lot of undesirables." Other residents, however, thought the resort would lure more wealthy residents to town, which Reno needed. But it was clear that many citizens were bitter about the gaming industry's pervasive influence at city hall. "They tell you to cut down on water usage," one Renoite complained, "but they let the big hotels be built."[34]

City hall critics seemed to be everywhere in the audience. Another speaker charged that "the city fathers have always been behind in their thinking. . . . We can blame the city council for most of our problems," such as pollution of the Truckee River. This was a valid observation. For years the council and Regional Planning Commission had been advised by their own engineers to clean up the river, but they never did. That night, however, MGM was still the favorite target of outraged citizens. As one Lemmon Valley resident told Sternauer, "Let MGM and the others stay in Las Vegas where they belong. Just tell people not to come to Reno. I liked it back in the old days like back in 1932–33 when horses walked in and out of bars on Virginia Street." Then, too, Reno's large number of former Golden State residents did little to hurt the managed-growth movement. As one California transplant put it, "I'm from a planned community where there are rules. Reno is just too money hungry." He went on to complain that Reno "is becoming too crowded. There is just no room." He noted that "Las Vegas is a big wide open desert, but there isn't as much room here" in Reno's smaller valley, which was hemmed in by hills and mountains. "That's why it's becoming dirty and there are water and sewage" problems.[35]

Las Vegas city residents did not have to contend with the effects of megaresorts on an expanding casino core, because they had the Strip city lying in the spacious desert flats just to their south, which handled these issues. So, Las Vegans were far less concerned about a casino threat downtown than were Renoites. But it is not altogether clear whether people in town or those living on Reno's ranch-land periphery would ever have accepted a strip of resorts, with all the growth it would bring. Property owners would have benefited initially from the sale of land for hotel-casinos and other businesses. But, given the growing popularity of slow growth among residents, there may well have been opposition to rapid, casino-driven urbanization that marred the area's scenic mountain views and displaced much of its ranching landscape in the rush to attract more tourists.

In one study UNR historical geographer Paul Starrs traced the growing local popularity of slow-growth policies to Reno residents' long-standing support of laissez-faire and to their suspicion of probusiness city politicians and especially to the "the rapid influx of new residents, many of them escaping crowding and urban problems in California, [who] created a population predisposed against expensive public projects to bring in more visitors." All of these factors, Starrs explained, "generated an anti-growth movement" with significant voter support by the 1980s.[36]

In April 1978 Mayor Menicucci appeared at a two-day engineers' seminar and suggested that critics of Reno's growth should restrain themselves. Menicucci concluded that the government needed expert help to update its old master plan and reminded the assembly that the city councilmen were not engineers themselves. Others saw the problem as Reno's laissez-faire approach to growth at any price. In response, managed-growth supporter and architect Ed Parsons told the mayor there were currently few professional planners in the area, "because we've driven them all out" by ignoring their recommendations. Parsons finished by declaring that Reno had "too many lawyers and too many high-powered businessmen running the town."[37]

Menicucci was particularly vulnerable to this criticism. It was obvious that he and other progrowth councilmen were supported by a group of businessmen with a development mind-set. As later mayor Barbara Bennett remembered, in 1979 Menicucci and progrowth councilmen Clyde Biglieri and Marcel Durant "all had very pro-growth records. They had approved the MGM, the Peppermill, the Sundowner, the Eldorado, the Sands, Circus Circus, and Harrah's addition. Some of these recommendations had been made against the approval of the Regional Planning Commission," whose members were concerned about the lack of water supply and sewage capacity to support the growth these projects would bring. Bennett noted that, despite the actions of these councilmen, the public was not in favor of runaway growth. Retribution came a few years later. In 1979 Biglieri and Durant failed to win reelection and Menicucci lost the mayoralty to Bennett, although the development lobby remained in charge of future city councils—just with new members. This was the confusing part of Reno politics after 1978: Reno voters elected slow-growth mayors citywide, but at the ward level they continued to elect a majority of city councilmen who were, at least covertly, supportive of casino-resort building projects when the development lobby pushed its agenda on them.[38]

Even in 1975 when MGM announced its plans, there was much public and press opposition, but the project went through. Clearly, this was not the kind of public reaction that greeted MGM and other hotel executives when they opened new resorts in the Las Vegas area, where more jobs and population were always welcome. In Reno, however, there was growing concern in the 1970s over how MGM and the other new hotels and expansions would affect the community. For example, at one public forum with residents in 1977, Washoe County School District officials warned that hotel construction would bring thousands more families to town. District leaders expected a 3 percent growth rate in 1978, but the projected increase by 1982 was 7 percent. This would require the construction of seventy-four new elementary school classrooms, thirty-eight middle school classrooms, and fifty-four high school classrooms, plus the need to acquire more and bigger school buses "to transport some 75 percent of all new students who will be living where no schools or already crowded schools exist." As a result, the district would be seeking a $48 million bond issue to pay for the services, an announcement that did little to comfort taxpayers at the meeting. School officials also advised residents that there were no funds to build a vocational school in the bond issue, but they mentioned that new low-income students might require a special reading program and that more teachers, social workers, and psychologists would have to be hired. As WCSD superintendent Marvin Picollo pointed out, "It's true that Clark County... has always been extremely supportive of bond issues—it [the CCSD] has never lost one [bond election]. But that doesn't mean that we can't lose one. This [$48 million bond issue] will be a whole other ballgame."[39]

Las Vegas's experience with growth only raised more concerns among Renoites. Former Clark County School District deputy superintendent Cliff Lawrence, by now the Carson City school superintendent, told the crowd that the CCSD was able to cope with growth by constructing schools quickly. "Anytime you have rapid growth and a fast turnover of students, you're going to have many social problems." This warning only reinforced the views being expressed by managed-growth advocates. As Lawrence explained, "If you have a youngster who is new to school and doesn't feel he quite fits in, you have problems." He further advised the crowd, "If you get a whole group of kids like that, it results in tremendous pressures." Lawrence then told the group that school construction in the area could get very expensive and concluded by telling them, "I think this area is on the verge of what we saw in Clark County." These were hardly reassuring words for many residents who openly wondered whether their town should even try to emulate Las Vegas—a sentiment that would have been sheer heresy in the 1950s and '60s.[40]

Sewage treatment was another troublesome issue. Reno's new wastewater plant was completed in 1966 and fully operational a year later. But just a few years after that, it was in dire need of expansion, thanks to Reno's casino boom and surging population. Indeed, from 1960 to 1970 just that city's population rose from 72,863 to more than 100,000. Five years later the city agreed to double the plant's capacity, but councilmen delayed taking action. In July 1973 the town's public works director, Warren Meacham, urged city councilmen to hire a design firm, but they ignored him. Then in May 1976 Reno voters rejected a $7.2 million bond issue to expand the plant, although the city continued issuing building permits in anticipation of the MGM and the arrival of other new resorts. Here was another problem. Not only were Reno activists concerned about new resorts threatening the area's quality of life, but frugal voters did not support the needed infrastructural expansion to handle the wastes generated by more tourists and a larger resident population. While Clark County commissioners were slow to build a modern wastewater treatment plant in the 1970s and had to be prodded by the EPA with threatened lawsuits, the argument was as much over high environmental standards at Lake Mead as over money. Las Vegas and Clark County voters did not reject vital bond issues necessary for resort and suburban expansion, because the area's tax base was rapidly expanding to pay for it and antigrowth sentiment was not widespread. Later in November 1976, Reno-area voters finally approved a $6 million bond issue to enlarge the plant, and work began in 1978.[41]

Slowly, a crisis arose even before 1976 because Reno was using more than 400,000 gallons per day of Sparks's share of treatment-plant capacity. All new housing or hotel projects needing more than 15,000 gallons of treatment water daily had to be approved by the Reno City Council, and that body kept approving them—despite warnings from the City of Sparks, the State of Nevada, and the EPA. In 1981 MGM's request to expand its hotel by one thousand rooms illustrated the problem. Mayor Bennett noted that the city lacked the sewage capacity to handle the MGM's additional tower and complimented the Regional Planning Commission for recognizing this and rejecting the proposal by a vote of seven to one. But Menicucci (who, despite his loss to Bennett in the mayoral election, still had two years left on the city council) and the other city council members ignored the evidence and voted to approve the MGM's tower. Even though Mayor Bennett pointed out that the hotel expansion would consume 92,800 gallons of sewage capacity that Reno did not have and force the construction of cheap housing for 1,400 new residents (housing that local builders did not want to build for lack of profits), the council ignored her. Why? Because, as Bennett put it, "the city council had already approved an early start for Harrah's [new tower]. In other words, they gave them approval to go ahead before they knew the sewer capacity would be available, and the same kind of situation arose again in the MGM thing."[42]

Bennett recalled that water was also an issue. After all, 1977–78 had been a drought year when Renoites cut back on lawn watering and put bricks in their toilets to conserve water. Obviously, they did not do it to give the MGM a new tower and future casino resorts a life. As Bennett recalled, when the city council considered MGM's proposal for a new tower addition, "I questioned the wisdom of . . . [it] because of the limited water supply." Sierra Pacific, the utility company that supplied power and water to the Reno metro area, had insisted there was a water shortage in 1981 and 1982. "Then all of a sudden they came back and softened it," Bennett complained. "They said the water supply was sufficient. But the state engineer's office said . . . that just the subdivision and condos that had already been approved [by the city council] *exceeded* Sierra Pacific's water availability at that time." Obviously, the development lobby was very active behind the scenes, pressuring not only elected officials, but even utility executives when it could. Unfortunately for gaming promoters, 1976–79 were drought years. So, the opening of the MGM, Circus Circus, the Sahara, and other large gaming resorts at this time, with their enormous demand for water, did little to dampen the fervor of antigrowth residents.[43]

Clearly, the Reno City Council's actions in approving so many new projects, given the city's lack of resources, were irresponsible, just as they had been in 1975 and into 1976, with development after development "breezing through" the council and the equally irresponsible Regional Planning Commission. These approvals occurred even though Reno shared its treatment plant with Sparks, and councilmen in both cities had promised not to permit construction of new residential, commercial, and gaming projects that would cause either city to exceed its allotted sewage capacity.[44]

So, in September 1976 Sparks sued Reno to stop issuing new building permits. The two cities had argued all summer about how much capacity Reno could use. Finally, on September 18, 1976, Washoe County District Court judge John Gabrielli extended a ban on new building permits for both cities, because any more construction would put the sewer plant beyond capacity. This ruling pleased the EPA and officials in the Nevada State Environmental Quality Division but created problems for both cities. Ultimately, they and the county raised fees for builders of new houses, apartments, and commercial structures and tapped other revenue sources to expand the metropolitan area's sewage treatment capacity to accommodate current needs and the future growth that everyone expected.[45]

Unfortunately for Reno growth advocates, just as the MGM opened, officials in northern Nevada's other big gaming area, Lake Tahoe, were implementing growth controls. In 1978 Douglas County commissioners were determined to limit growth at Lake Tahoe to four major hotels on the south shore to prevent pollution of the lake at the same time that California governor Jerry Brown was urging Nevada to join the Tahoe Regional Planning Agency. Even Senator Paul Laxalt opposed the proposed Harveys Inn to be built just north of Stateline's casino core on US 50. The concurrent growth of Carson City's suburbs, including plans for a new ten-story Ramada Inn in the northern suburbs, also raised concerns among some antigrowth activists in that area.[46]

Pro- and antigrowth forces in Reno, realizing that a small metropolitan area was forming in the Truckee Meadows, recognized the need for some regional government. In May 1978 one *Nevada State Journal* editorial endorsed merging the planning staffs of Reno and Sparks with the Regional Planning Commission as a way of implementing more coordination of planning through a metropolitan approach. While the newspaper, like many local officials, stopped short of urging one consolidated government, it did support the so-called Washoe Council of Governments, the 1970s institution that facilitated local government entities working more closely than ever before in providing a variety of services. The goal was to coordinate "and not fragment" the planning of "cross-valley streets" and other projects.[47]

According to Mayor Bennett, the 1947 law that created the Washoe County Regional Planning Commission and charged it with drawing up and enforcing a regional plan for the area gave the county commission "the final say . . . to make determinations for the city of Reno" as well as for Sparks. This became increasingly unacceptable to both cities in the 1970s. So, in May 1981, Reno pulled out of that body and formed its own city planning commission, whose members, much to Bennett's dismay, were controlled by the dominant progrowth group in the city council. Sparks also pulled out of the Regional Planning Commission shortly afterward, not wanting to give the county commissioners any more influence over what that city could do. The same lack of regional unity also ended the effective functioning of the largely advisory Washoe Council of Governments, which died a slow death in the 1980s. Only in 1989 was the Truckee Meadows Regional Planning Commission resurrected by legislative decree, after it became increasingly obvious that Reno, Sparks, and Washoe County had to work together. The cities had to cooperate, using the new 1979 Regional Transportation Commission of Washoe County, to run the Citifare bus system properly and plan roads that crossed through the cities and county. They also had to work together with the Truckee Meadows Water Authority (created in 2001) and similar regional entities.[48] As the Reno area grew into a metropolis somewhat later than Las Vegas, leaders recognized, as their southern Nevada counterparts had increasingly recognized in the 1960s and '70s, that regional cooperation was necessary to address problems such as planning, transportation, water, flood control, and other issues that transcended city boundaries.

In addition to all the conflict over controlled growth and regional cooperation, the national media further challenged the growth lobby's agenda by insisting that Reno's boom would soon end in bust. *Newsweek*, for example, predicted in 1978 that the debut of casino gambling in Atlantic City would divert thousands of eastern gamblers away from the "Biggest Little City in the World." Then, noting that six major casinos were being planned for the Truckee Meadows area, the magazine warned that Reno "might choke on its own success," suggesting that the traffic jams, housing shortages, and water-supply problems would only be aggravated by the MGM and other large resorts.[49]

But Atlantic City posed no early threat to Reno; indeed, tourism boomed in the late 1970s. This was not the case in Las Vegas, where tourism sagged, thanks to Atlantic City's competition and the national recession, forcing Strip executives to reduce expenses by closing gourmet rooms two nights a week in addition to other cost-cutting measures. Then in 1979, when MGM took steps to expand its Reno resort to accommodate more visitors, controversy flared once again after the city council's "secret meeting" with company executives brought quick approval for MGM's request to build a second tower (giving it 2,001 rooms) to further support its casino of one hundred thousand square feet. Critics wondered how the city's sewage treatment plant could handle the wastewater produced by this expansion. One local newspaper reasoned that if each hotel room required 140 gallons of daily sewer capacity, this expansion would strain not only sewer capacity but also other utility systems. It also charged that MGM executives and city officials were recklessly underestimating the new tower's impact upon Reno's infrastructure. True, MGM suggested building its own sewage treatment facility, but engineers warned that, if it failed, the pollution could foul the Truckee River, which skirted the property. In the end, city officials decided to spend the millions necessary to expand the capacity of the Reno-Sparks Joint Wastewater Treatment Plant, an expensive proposition. At roughly the same time, the rapid growth of Reno's northern and western suburbs also forced the city to seek federal help to provide better sewer service to the wastewater plant from that part of the metropolitan area.[50] These events only convinced managed-growth advocates that their worst fears were being realized and that action had to be taken.

But the casino boom was only starting in 1973 when Reno attorney Don Carano and partners built the Eldorado, the first casino hotel north of the railroad tracks on North Virginia Street, where today most of the big downtown casinos sit. Five years later came the MGM and three more big casino properties. Reno was obviously on a roll, and gaming executives, like local boosters, were optimistic about the city's future. Besides the MGM, one of the most important new resorts was the Sahara, built by the Del Webb Corporation. In an obvious reference to the MGM, Sahara vice president and general manager Doyle Mathia, declared, "The Reno core has for some time been thought to be the most desirable area. And nothing has happened to change our minds about that." Mathia went on to insist, "We're not worried about the impact of Atlantic City or any other area of the country that legalizes casino gambling."[51]

Thanks to the optimism generated by the Sahara, the MGM, and Circus Circus, in the 1970s and early to mid-1980s a series of new hotels appeared downtown to supplement the big three. In 1976 Lincoln Fitzgerald unveiled his sixteen-story hotel-casino south of the El Dorado. Farther south, the Onslow opened in 1978. Several blocks west of the Virginia Street core were the Sands (today the Sands Regency), which debuted in 1970; the Sundowner (1975); and the Comstock (1978). These new properties, along with the old clubs in and around Virginia Street's casino core, teamed with the MGM, Circus Circus, Harrah's, the Sahara, and Mape's Money Tree to provide a much-larger array of venues for gambling tourists than were available in midcentury Reno. But the sudden appearance of these new places, all of them high-rises, convinced even more Renoites that gaming was taking over downtown.

The 1980s only reinforced this sentiment. Even with managed-growth leaders such as Mayors Barbara Bennett and Pete Sferrazza in office, the Reno Ramada (1980), Riverboat (1988), and Virginian (1988) opened for business, and in 1985 the Peppermill, on Virginia Street, two miles south of downtown, began evolving into a major casino resort from its humble coffee-shop beginnings. Of course, there were cross-currents in this process, as some existing places went under. The Colony, Silver Spur, and Horseshoe all closed before later reopening and closing again. The Onslow, Riverside, and Holiday hotels each closed for a few years, as did the Mapes Money Tree (by then Eddie's Fabulous 50's) and the Mapes Hotel, both of which closed in 1982.[52]

For the most part, chamber of commerce general manager Jud Allen remained optimistic. He had been a fixture in Reno's promotional efforts since the late 1950s and was convinced that the MGM, Sahara, Circus Circus, and the others would only bring more business to town. In the early 1970s he told Reno's blue-ribbon panel on growth that in gambling's "pioneer days," which he defined as the late 1950s and '60s, the chamber of commerce created a brochure to attract "quality hotels..., but we found the investors had been 'turned off' by Reno back in the pioneer days, still wanting to go where the momentum was—Las Vegas—even though it appeared to be overbuilt." Allen made a key point about one factor that separated Reno from Las Vegas. Tourists often flock to a "hot spot" where Hollywood celebrities and other "cool" people go to party. One can argue that today, Vail, Aspen, Santa Fe, South Beach, Sun Valley, Cancun, Cabo San Lucas, and Las Vegas, among others, hold that distinction. Although the hot places gradually change over time, Las Vegas has remained a member of this club for more than six decades and still maintains its status, thanks to visionaries such as Steve Wynn. Reno lost its cachet as a maverick getaway and divorce capital after World War II and, despite the MGM's and Harrah's best efforts, never really recaptured its former allure.[53]

Still, in 1978 Allen was hopeful about a Reno renaissance because of the MGM, noting that the resort had done more to refocus national attention on Reno "than ten new 200-room hotels would have accomplished." The "lowest point in our history," he declared, had been in the 1960s, when *Time* and *Newsweek* had portrayed the Riverside's temporary closing as "the death of Reno." But MGM's arrival changed all that. Still, Allen cautioned that Reno had to handle the surge in growth created by MGM "through proper planning." He argued that it was "imperative that we resolve our sewer capacity and streets and highway [problems] as soon as possible," because these public works projects were crucial to "alleviating the housing shortage, traffic flow, air and water quality," and other problems related to the city's recent growth.[54]

Unlike Las Vegas and the Strip city, Reno's tax base was not large enough to handle all of the growth-related expenses required to accommodate the increase in tourists, convention delegates, and population. However, the need for more schools and roads and the sewage treatment controversy were just part of the problem; at the height of the boom in 1977, the city lost control of its airport. As jet traffic increased, the facility required costly expansion. Fortunately, there was federal funding for this. In September 1976 the Federal Aviation Administration (FAA) awarded a $1.3 million grant for phase 1 of runway expansion. The money helped pay for a new north-south runway just east of the main landing strip to handle the expected increase in air traffic from the debut of the MGM, Circus Circus, and other new resorts and expansions. None of these funds were for terminal expansion, although money was available for land and property acquisitions around the airport's "clear zones" in the interest of noise abatement. The City of Reno's Community Development Department eventually met with "relocation specialists," and the city applied for an additional $8.5 million to buy out even more home owners who complained about the noisy jets. It took more than five years to satisfy most of these residents.[55]

The city, however, did not move quickly enough to improve its airport. By the mid-1970s there were enough tourists and airline complaints about the city's failure to maintain and modernize the facility that state legislators in 1977 approved legislation transferring ownership to a quasi-public authority, the Airport Authority of Washoe County. This move infuriated Mayor Menicucci and other city officials. The 1977 law that established the authority created a seven-member Board of Trustees with four seats for Reno, one for Sparks, and two for Washoe County. The official reason in 1977 for creating the authority was that "with the development of multiple contiguous communities, what was once a municipal airport, in both name and fact, is now a regional airport." It was now serving the population "of a large geographical area and ever increasing numbers of tourists." The unofficial reason, however, was the growing number of complaints from airlines and even state legislators about the backward state of the facility. As the legislation noted, "Development of the modern airport requires the expenditure of vast sums of money for land acquisition and capital improvements not available to the City of Reno." Noting that the city was "unable to operate the airport effectively within the traditional framework of local government," the law created the authority, whose territory included Reno, Sparks, their suburbs, and the rest of Washoe County, whose bonding capacity, if needed, would be substantial. Shortly after the authority began operating in July 1978, board members authorized a massive terminal expansion to accommodate the increased number of flights resulting from the growing number of resorts.[56]

This course of events contrasted with the Las Vegas area, where Clark County commissioners controlled the airport. During World War II the City of Las Vegas owned the former Western Air Express airport northeast of town. During the war the city issued a lease to the US Army for gunnery-school operations, but the field never ceased being a municipal airport. However, once the Cold War intensified after 1946, the county and city commissioners, on the advice of Senator Pat McCarran and others, decided to relocate the commercial airport along US 91 on the Los Angeles side of town. They put the area's defense sector on the Utah Highway, or northern, side of town, since there was relatively little traffic from Mormon towns to Las Vegas's casinos. In 1948 the Defense Department began construction on what later became Nellis Air Force Base, and county commissioners purchased George Crockett's Alamo Field as the site for Las Vegas's new commercial airport. In this chain of events the City of Las Vegas willingly handed over control of the area's commercial airport to Clark County. As a result, there was none of the conflict and resentment that marked Reno's forced ouster by the state from control of the airport serving its metropolitan area. In the Las Vegas area the county commissioners, not a quasi-public authority, have controlled the airport since the 1940s.

Creation of the Airport Authority of Washoe County clearly reflected the fact that Reno, by the late 1970s, had become a metropolitan area composed of Sparks as well as Washoe County's far-flung suburban population. The county airport authority was a semiautonomous entity created by the state that was not part of any local government and did not use local property or sales tax revenue to fund its activities. Its main sources of revenue were airport fees, bonds, and government grants. The airport authority owned and operated the big airport as well as the smaller Reno-Stead facility, which served general aviation. The City of Reno's role was reduced to controlling a few seats on the authority's board of trustees. Operations continued normally. By 1979 the airport authority's sixty-million-dollar airport expansion project was already well under way—and just in time. The MGM's opening and the expected arrival of more hotels in the next few years plus the 1978 deregulation of the airline industry meant more planes and tourists for Reno. Municipal leaders, however, with the city's various infrastructural projects and other obligations, may not have been able to get voter support for airport expansion bonds at that time.[57]

In 1978 airline deregulation briefly resulted in Reno losing three of the six airlines that served the area under CAB mandate. But by 1988, the city's best year for service, the number grew, thanks partly to the expanding number of airlines in business. As the years passed the airport authority funded a series of improvements, including a parking garage, enlarged bus facilities, and a complete renovation of the terminal's interior. In 2005 the state legislature changed the agency's name to the Reno-Tahoe Airport Authority, which more clearly reflected the effort to market Reno in conjunction with the entire Sierra area, including Lake Tahoe. This law also increased the number of trustees on the board to nine, giving the RSCVA some representation.

The costs associated with building and maintaining a modern jetport, schools, roads, wastewater treatment facilities, and other growth-related infrastructure only fed the anti-MGM, antigrowth, anti-Menicucci sentiment in the late 1970s. By the time of the 1979 mayoral election, the movement had won the support of most Reno voters. But the roots of this movement really antedated the MGM and the 1970s. Even before the casino boom and the blue ribbon–panel reports of the 1970s, it was clear that many locals were not anxious to see Reno grow into a full-fledged metropolitan area like Las Vegas. A 1969 survey of Washoe County residents found that 72 percent of respondents thought the city should remain the same size or get smaller. In 1973, five years *before* the MGM's debut, 85 percent agreed with this view. So, the antigrowth, or managed-growth, movement was on the rise in 1970s Reno. Carl Abbott and other historians have noted that many western cities in this period were concerned about uncontrolled growth. In places such as Portland and Reno, the managed-growth factions gained control and implemented measures to discourage uncontrolled growth. In other places managed-growth advocates lost and pro-growth forces held sway. In 1970s Reno the appearance of the MGM and other large resorts and the resultant surge in population only reinforced the managed-growth movement. Although the total metropolitan (MSA) population was even higher, in 1960 Reno had 84,743 residents; ten years later the figure hit 121,068 and then 193,623 in 1980, one year into Barbara Bennett's term as mayor.[58] As Sierra Pacific raised public doubts about the local water supply's ability to sustain this growth and proposed installing water meters in every building, many residents viewed the measure as a subterfuge to reserve scarce water for the future casino resorts.

They were probably right. Even though the voting public elected Bennett mayor in 1979, the city council remained firmly committed to growth. The development community, according to Bennett, was well organized and the public was disorganized. Even at town hall meetings in the various neighborhoods, the city's progrowth businessmen always had a "well-orchestrated" presence, with plenty of representatives and always different people at different meetings, to represent their interests.[59]

Not only did the growth coalition continue to dominate the city council during Bennett's administration, but plans were afoot to create a "strip" of resorts south of town to replicate what was happening in Las Vegas. In southern Nevada the Strip of resorts came first and then the convention center. In Reno the process was simply reversed. Today, there is no "strip" of resorts near Reno's convention center, but not for lack of effort. As Mayor Bennett recalled, in the late 1970s and '80s, "the county had approved a lot of big projects out on the south end of town, and there were a lot of other developments that were going in—like Harrah's owned property out there. They were talking about this huge development out quite a ways [even into the county]. Then there was another talk about Hilton." She remembered that "when Meadowood [mall] and some of those buildings in the area went in, . . . property on ideal corner lots was all being saved for something." Much of this land had been zoned agricultural, and now it was all becoming commercial. As the mayor noted, "It was always my opinion that if gaming was permitted to go out there, that's what it would be used for: big casinos all the way out."[60]

Getting approval for construction, even in the face of Reno's water- and sewer-capacity shortages, was not a problem: the progrowth city council of 1977–81 approved every big project. As Bennett recalled, "There was a problem on the South Virginia strip cropping up more and more too, because there had been a lot of approvals granted out there. Fortunately, many of them [casino resorts and other developments] to this day have not been built. . . . You can't keep allocating waters that have already been given to someone else." These efforts frayed tempers at the south end of town. Mayor Bennett mentioned in her 1989 oral history that when she defeated Bruno Menicucci in 1979, she surprised many people by winning a lot of votes in affluent south Reno. But as Bennett explained, she got a lot of votes from those residents who "moved to the south end of town, because they wanted some open space around them; now they find that this growth is encroaching and the very quality of life reasons for which they moved out there to begin with are threatened."[61]

Although there was significant discord over whether to develop the city's southern periphery, most Renoites supported Bennett's efforts to jump-start an effort to redevelop downtown. A decade earlier Project RENOvation, backed by Mayor Bankofier and the city's casino industry, had failed due to its $1.2 million price tag and the casino industry's failure to promise to ante up and pay its share. But support for beautifying downtown never died. In Reno downtown redevelopment and economic growth always went hand in hand. In the 1970s, however, city officials had learned the hard way that placing controversial bond issues on the ballot to finance downtown redevelopment was not the best approach to raise funds for that activity. Even in growth-hungry Clark County, the Convention and Visitors Authority by the 1980s had begun to bypass voters and employ mechanisms already used in other US cities to fund expansion. For redevelopment agencies these powers included buying private property for resale, establishing sales tax–increment districts to finance redevelopment, and issuing bonds, as well as using other incentives to foster renovation of blighted properties. Both Mayor Bennett and Las Vegas mayor Bill Briare lobbied the state legislature to pass a law awarding Nevada's big cities these powers. Following state approval, the city created the Reno Redevelopment Agency in 1983, and succeeding mayors used it to revitalize the downtown area.

In 1983 new city manager Chris Cherches predicted that Reno would have a downtown mall, sidewalk cafés, and walkways along the Truckee by 1987 or 1988, but lack of money delayed progress. Still, public support for downtown revitalization continued, albeit latently. In early 1987 a group of activists formed the Biggest Little City Committee, chaired by former Harrah's vice president for marketing Mark Curtis. In February 1987 this group held a public meeting that drew three hundred people who shared their ideas about how the city might transform downtown. The committee subsequently worked with Mayor Sferrazza and the Reno Redevelopment Agency to fund one of its major improvements: the Raymond I. Smith Riverwalk. This project opened to the public in 1991 and featured Nevada wildlife reliefs and sculptures by artist John Battenburg as well as unique fountains and other features designed to enhance the walkway's beauty for pedestrians and bikers.[62]

Clearly, in 1980s Reno public support grew for beautifying downtown and slowing down the construction of new resorts—a sentiment largely absent in Las Vegas and virtually nonexistent in the Strip city. Slowly, growth advocates such as Allen, Menicucci, and Reno's gaming executives became the adversaries who had to be stopped. Mayor Bennett and her successor, Pete Sferrazza, became the public's choice to slow down the gaming sector's expansive tendencies in the 1980s. But as the Iran oil embargo and the worsening national recession began to threaten Reno's tourist industry, some wondered whether this new policy course was a good one, especially after the Mapes Hotel and the Money Tree both closed. In his 1983 mayoral campaign against Sferrazza, Jud Allen and his supporters argued that the managed-growth approach by city officials only discouraged resort investors and threatened to prolong the local recession. Nevertheless, Sferrazza defeated Allen and went on to win the next two mayoral elections. At roughly the same time, the casino boom of the 1970s came to an end. The continuing national recession was the chief culprit, along with a lack of investor enthusiasm. In addition, the city's managed-growth policy did little to encourage investors, especially when there were more profitable opportunities for resort development in California, Las Vegas, and other western places.

Chapter Four

LAS VEGAS AREA

Recession Turns to Boom, 1975–2007

IN THE MID- TO LATE 1970S Las Vegas faced serious challenges. The shah of Iran's ouster from power and the emergence of a militant Islamic regime, led by the Ayatollah Khomeini, resulted in an oil embargo that drove up the price of jet fuel and gasoline, which did little to help Las Vegas tourism. At the same time, a growing national recession, punctuated by sharply rising interest rates, cut into discretionary income, which hurt all resort cities. Even worse, the legalization of gambling in Atlantic City followed by the opening of Resorts International in 1978 with the promise of more luxury gaming resorts near the boardwalk, financed not only by television mogul Merv Griffin and New York developer Donald Trump but also by Las Vegas gaming leaders, created new challenges.[1]

In its early gaming years Atlantic City threatened Las Vegas, because it tapped a huge eastern market that long had been the sole preserve of Caesars Palace, the MGM, and the other Strip resorts. For years the Las Vegas area's only serious gaming rival had been Reno, and that competition declined as the Strip grew in popularity. By the early 1980s, however, the continuing effects of the recession and gas crisis were being felt in southern Nevada. Strip resorts adjusted as best they could. Showrooms featuring headliners cut their traditional dinner and midnight shows to one. As airlines cut the number of nonstop flights from the East Coast to McCarran, the resort makers began shelving their ambitious construction plans.

There were, however, some large expansions at this time, particularly at the Tropicana Hotel, which built two high-rise towers in 1977 and 1986. But from 1979 (the Imperial Palace and Barbary Coast) to 1989 (the Mirage), no new resorts appeared on the Strip. Of course, some places opened in the late 1970s, but they were part of the new movement to build casino resorts in the suburbs or just off the Strip to provide supplemental rooms during big conventions and peak tourist seasons. Frank Fertitta's Bingo Palace (today's Palace Station) in 1976 began the trend. Sam's Town (1979), the Gold Coast (1986), and Arizona Charlie's (1988) reinforced it, setting the stage for Coast and Station resorts to build more suburban hotels into the next century. The 1979 Maxim (today's Westin Las Vegas) was just off the Strip, as was Bob Stupak's Vegas World (1979), which evolved into the larger Stratosphere Hotel-Casino by 1996. Although downtown added the California Hotel (1975) off Fremont Street and the Sundance in 1980 (which became Fitzgeralds in 1987 and the D by 2012), they hardly compared in size or significance to major Strip resorts.

Not only were no large resorts built on the Strip between 1979 and 1989, but resort designers seemed to be losing their creative edge. The Marina and Imperial Palace seemed little more than warmed-over versions of existing Strip hotels. Their boxlike casinos and small shopping arcade, showroom, lounges, and court of gourmet rooms off the casino reflected a certain sameness. Even Martin Stern's MGM Grand (1973) seemed little more than a variation of the triform design he had used for the International (later the Las Vegas Hilton and the LVH) in 1969. Las Vegas desperately needed new ideas and especially a new formula that would lure more visitors.

At the same time, despite the recession and all the drags on tourism, the metropolitan area itself already contained the seeds for its explosive growth into the new century. The roots of modern Las Vegas lie in the mid-1960s and '70s, when visionary resort executives such as Jay Sarno and Kirk Kerkorian established a strong foundation for later growth. The 1966 debut of the Strip's first major hotel, Caesars Palace, followed by Circus Circus (1968), the International/Las Vegas Hilton (1969), the first MGM Grand/Bally's (1973), and other new hotels in the 1970s, helped trigger a huge influx of gaming- and service-industry workers, including the first major immigrant wave from Mexico and Central America.[2]

By 1980 Las Vegas had begun to draw more doctors, lawyers, and other white-collar professionals, who arrived to satisfy the increasing demand for services. Joining these newcomers were thousands of middle-income singles both in and out of the resort industry, as well as a growing number of affluent Californians anxious to leave the Golden State for a more affordable home in Las Vegas, where taxes and the overall cost of living were less. This migration only increased in the 1990s with the flood tide of new megaresorts that followed the Mirage (technically, "*The* Mirage"). As the valley's population surged past 1 million in 1995, Las Vegas reached a threshold that eventually brought Lowes, Home Depot, Whole Foods, and other major chains that Californians and other transplants had come to expect. Further swelling this number was a growing tide of retirees from the East, enticed by the slick marketing efforts of Del Webb and other builders catering to senior citizens. By the mid-1990s residents fifty-five and over accounted for more than 20 percent of the valley's population. They came not only for the year-round sunshine and low humidity but also for the shows, restaurants, cheap buffets, low-end card games, and courtesy bus service offered by a growing number of city and suburban resorts. Technological breakthroughs also made Las Vegas a more desirable choice for them and for the thousands of business owners, professionals, and investors who needed to maintain contact with their businesses back home and with financial markets. The personal computer, the fax machine, cable television, e-mail, the cell phone, the Internet, and other innovations finally helped to end southern Nevada's physical remoteness and, in the process, fuel the Strip city's dynamic growth.

The development of the Strip as its own informal city was becoming obvious by 1970. In that year Las Vegas claimed 125,787 residents; North Las Vegas had 36,216 and Henderson 15,595; the Strip townships counted 89,667. Ten years later Las Vegas boasted 164,674 people, North Las Vegas 42,739, and Henderson 24,363. But the population of the Strip city (including the unincorporated towns of Paradise, Winchester, Spring Valley, Enterprise, Whitney, and Sunrise Manor) had jumped to 220,450 by 1980 and kept pulling away from the central city into the twenty-first century.[3]

As already mentioned, prior to the 1970s development had occurred mostly east of the Strip job zone, between Paradise Road and the Boulder Highway. While the city of Las Vegas grew mostly eastward toward neighboring North Las Vegas, the Strip suburbs south of Sahara Avenue also grew mostly eastward. This pattern eventually began to change. The development of a new suburban frontier west of the Strip, and in the city west of Decatur Boulevard, began in the 1970s. As early as 1971 the Pardee Construction Company began drawing up plans for Spring Valley. Located roughly between West Flamingo and West Tropicana from Decatur to Rainbow

Boulevard, Spring Valley, one of the valley's first master-planned communities, attracted some population in the 1970s, but more growth came in the 1980s. The Collins Brothers Corporation announced its intention of building the Lakes, a two-square-mile community of single-family homes and town houses north of Spring Valley, near Sahara and Durango. This development began to boom in 1984 once Citibank received permission to operate in Nevada and began construction on its forty-million-dollar credit-card processing center nearby to serve the western states. Desert Shores, Peccole Ranch, and a number of other projects came quickly on the heels of this, as the Strip city's western suburbs began to emerge in the 1980s. High-end homes that more than rivaled those in the Las Vegas Country Club, Rancho Circle, and the Scotch 80s neighborhoods appeared after 1983, once longtime Las Vegas businessman Joe Blasco began to develop Spanish Trail along West Tropicana, from Rainbow Boulevard to Durango Drive. Marketed as a guard-gated golf course community designed to provide many of the amenities offered by Palm Springs, Scottsdale, and other western haunts of the well-to-do, Spanish Trail attracted numerous casino executives, doctors, lawyers, and affluent California transplants as well as dual residents to its custom homes.[4]

The 1980s also witnessed the development of southern Nevada's first extensive master-planned communities. On this front the Las Vegas metropolitan area was ahead of its northern counterpart, where master-planned developments progressed more slowly. One of the first such places was Green Valley, which sprouted along Henderson's western periphery. Between 1956 and 1971 *Las Vegas Sun* publisher Hank Greenspun purchased more than eight thousand acres of scattered tracts in the desert southeast of McCarran Airport. Greenspun recognized that if Las Vegas continued to grow as he thought it would, the Strip would create enough jobs to stretch the built-up area from the Strip city's eastern suburbs all the way to Henderson, so in 1974 he formed the American Nevada Corporation to subdivide these lands and attract builders. But his early efforts bore little fruit. In the late 1970s Green Valley was still a remote place with no easy connections to Interstate 15 and the Strip job zone. Moreover, local housing demand was still limited by Atlantic City's competition and a national recession. As Geoff Schumacher has noted, helped by Greenspun's then son-in-law Mark Fine, who convinced the publisher to lower some prices, sell smaller and more easily developed parcels to builders, and secure better road access to the area, Green Valley home sales began to soar in the early to mid-1980s. As the national economy steadily improved and the Mirage opened and a frantic building boom commenced down the south Strip, Green Valley filled in with new residents and villages.

Reinforcing the trend was voter approval of Clark County commissioner Bruce Woodbury's Question 10, which enabled the county to begin work on a circumferential beltway linking major portions of the metropolitan area. While the opening of the Desert Inn Super Arterial in 1996, the widening of US 95 to the Rainbow Curve (2007), and the continued widening of Interstate 15 eliminated many bottlenecks, construction of the Bruce Woodbury Beltway around the valley was crucial to the suburbanization of Las Vegas, Henderson, and the Strip city. The beltway's origins lay in the county commissioner's successful effort to devise the transportation funding referendum that voters approved in 1990. The funding formula called for a mix of taxes and fees to build the road.[5]

Everyone agreed to let the county build the road. But controversy flared early when the road's first segments opened in the southern portion of the valley through largely vacant county lands. As Las Vegas city councilman Matt Callister angrily pointed out, as late as 1996 taxpayers in his city had already paid twenty-one million dollars, or 38 percent of the fifty-six million dollars total raised, and had yet to see any part of the beltway reach Summerlin, where densely populated neighborhoods desperately needed access to the Strip job zone and other parts of the metropolitan area.

County commissioners had begun the beltway in the east to link with the US 95 freeway connecting Interstate 15 and downtown Las Vegas with Railroad Pass. The idea was to provide Henderson commuters (that city earlier had annexed most of the Green Valley area) with faster access to the Strip job zone by running the beltway through open land south of the Strip and its main suburbs. The commissioners assumed that, once past Las Vegas Boulevard, the high-speed, limited-access beltway, with on- and off-ramps conveniently located at Decatur, Jones, Rainbow, and Durango, would encourage the construction of numerous subdivisions and shopping centers in the empty southwest portion of the metropolitan area on county lands. They were right. Southern Highlands, Rhodes Ranch, and myriad other residential developments spawned office and retail centers, which greatly expanded the county's tax base. The road did not reach the city of Las Vegas until the later 1990s, which only enraged the mayor and city council. County commissioners had sought little or no federal funding and needed all the property tax revenues they could get, so the road's delayed entry into Las Vegas became just another issue in an already politically fragmented metropolis.

Green Valley, to the east, benefited from the early beltway even more than Southern Highlands to the west. The extension of the Beltway to US 95 gave Henderson (and especially Green Valley) residents direct access to Interstate 15 and its various Strip exits feeding the resort corridor's job zone. In addition, the creation of freeway interchanges at key streets stimulated the building in the late 1990s and early 2000s of Green Valley Ranch, the Sunset Station hotel-casino, the District, the Valley Auto Mall, the Galleria Mall, and other commercial complexes in the Green Valley Parkway–Warm Springs–Stephanie Street retail zone. At this time, Reno also encircled its metro area with a road that stimulated some commercial development. Circumferential McCarran Boulevard, though less expensive to build than the Las Vegas beltway, nonetheless awarded motorists a way of moving around their metropolitan area rather than using existing surface streets in the middle—an option that allowed suburbanites to avoid downtown.

Affluent suburban motorists were not the only Las Vegans benefited by Woodbury's Question 10. For those residents who could not afford a car, the creation of the Citizens Area Transit (CAT, now RTC) bus system in 1992 was a marked improvement over previous service. More buses and routes made it possible for low-income commuters to reach the growing number of service-industry jobs across the metropolitan area. CAT was a godsend to low-income workers, and it marked one of the few times in the Las Vegas area when the usually fragmented metropolis approach to problem solving yielded to a valley-wide solution. The Reno area, on the other hand, acted even sooner to provide needed bus service for its lower-income commuters. In 1978 the Regional Transportation Commission of Washoe County created the Citifare bus system after the old bus company serving Reno-Sparks went bankrupt.[6]

From the mid-1970s into the new century, an increasing number of retirees as well as doctors, dentists, and other professionals serving employees of the resorts and county businesses lived not only in the burgeoning Strip city but also in the newer suburban communities of Las Vegas, Henderson, and North Las Vegas. As the expanding number of resorts on Las

Vegas Boulevard South helped fill Spring Valley, Spanish Trail, Summerlin, Green Valley, Anthem, Aliante, and many other places with residents, the mushrooming Strip city began to overlap parts of the valley's incorporated municipalities. The county commissioners had the resources to connect all of these residential areas to the major job zone stretching from the airport (whose development they also controlled as "airport commissioners") to the resort corridor and the valley's major convention center. By constructing the beltway in the years after 1992 and pushing for creation of the US 95 freeway in the 1970s, '80s, and '90s, as well as the CAT bus system, the county commissioners played a major role in knitting the valley's disparate neighborhoods and its three cities together with the Strip city to promote the metropolitan area's continued prosperity and growth.

Road construction was just one solution to the area's transportation needs. Optimistic that the twenty-first century would bring millions more tourists to Las Vegas, Clark County commissioners in 1978 announced plans for McCarran 2000 to accommodate the 30 million passengers to Las Vegas expected by the millennium. Spearheading the effort was Robert Broadbent. After serving as Boulder City mayor, Broadbent joined the Clark County Commission in 1968. One of the board's most talented politicians ever, Broadbent worked quietly behind the scenes to thwart Las Vegas's effort to annex the Strip city and, until he left the board in 1981, strived to protect the county's ascendant role in managing the metropolitan area's growth. As airport director, Broadbent cooperated with the convention authority and Strip hotel executives to plan a major airport expansion that would accommodate millions more tourists and delegates.[7] This process exemplified the Strip city's power in action. Financed by bonds and a surcharge on each airline ticket, the county spent most of the 1980s and '90s enlarging the jetport. The completion of the C Gates in 1985 and the first phase of the D Gates in 1998 allowed Southwest and America West Airlines to make Las Vegas a hub for their operations. Over time these two carriers more than doubled the number of flights to and from the area. This brought even more business to the Strip, awarding it even better access to capital for expanding existing resorts and building new ones. In 1992 42 percent (and in 2007 46 percent) of all visitors to the Las Vegas valley arrived by jet.[8]

Even before the advent of major new hotels on the Strip, the local population began to soar. For most of the years between 1986 and 2006, Las Vegas was the fastest-growing metropolitan area in the nation. During the late 1990s and early 2000s, Henderson and North Las Vegas briefly held the title of fastest-growing US city or were among the top-five contenders. In 1999 Henderson passed Reno to become Nevada's second-largest city, and in 2012 North Las Vegas did the same to become the third largest. The central city also grew between 1980 and 2000. In these two decades the city of Las Vegas's population jumped from 164,674 to 478,434, while Henderson (24,368 and 175,381) and North Las Vegas (42,739 and 115,488) also experienced a huge increase in residents. The construction of new upscale subdivisions, as well as large master-planned communities, helped encourage this population surge by offering prospective newcomers an attractive environment in which to build a home and raise a family.[9]

No development epitomized this trend more than Summerlin, which rose on twenty-two thousand acres of rolling desert west of Las Vegas that Howard Hughes had acquired from the federal government in a land swap completed in 1953. Originally called Husite, it became Summerlin in 1990 when the Howard Hughes Corporation named it for the billionaire's maternal grandmother. Unlike their counterparts at American Nevada in Green Valley, Hughes executives had the advantage of being able to sell hundreds of acres to William Peccole and other developers to raise the funds needed to build infrastructure, parks, trails, and other amenities in advance of construction. Summerlin was even more densely master-planned than Green Valley. The Hughes Company did not try to build a house on every available lot, but left hundreds of acres available for playgrounds, community centers, and a vast network of pathways. The firm also built Summerlin Parkway, a ten-mile extension of US 95, which later connected to the 215 Beltway, providing valuable access to model homes. In 1988 Del Webb Construction (later Pulte Homes), the Hughes Company's early development partner, began construction of Sun City, and home building itself began in 1990. For most of the 1990s and early 2000s, Summerlin, with its eighteen elaborately planned villages, was America's new-homes sales leader. Lewis Homes built the Hills, a gated community just south of Sun City, where the first Summerlin home sold in 1991. The Pueblo quickly followed this. Southward down Rampart Boulevard, the Canyons and its TPC golf course came in the mid-1990s. Very quickly, restaurants, chain stores, and some resorts began to appear, as did fine schools. Indeed, in 1984 future Las Vegas mayor Carolyn Goodman opened her elite educational institution, the Meadows School, on a then-desert tract in what soon became Summerlin. As the metropolitan area's population soared, development into the new century was nonstop. By 2001 eighteen thousand homes had been built, and construction continued steadily onward until slowed somewhat by the Great Recession.[10]

These events did not go unnoticed in North Las Vegas, which was eager to shed its long-held reputation as a crime-ridden, low-income town. Recognizing the problem, city councilmen did not try to lure Pardee and other builders close to the existing city. Instead, they sought Bureau of Land Management (BLM) tracts on the municipality's northern periphery, where developers could construct a new North Las Vegas of middle- and upper-income residences. Pardee stimulated the initial interest in 1990 by erecting affordable homes north of Cheyenne Avenue. Later in the decade city officials pursued the acquisition of seventy-five hundred acres of federal land farther north for a master-planned community they envisioned competing with Summerlin and Green Valley. Following the 1998 passage of the Southern Nevada Public Lands Management Act, which forced the BLM to sell off some of this parcel at auction, city-approved developers were able to acquire this site.[11]

Henderson, itself a former blue-collar town, enjoyed the revenue boost it got from Green Valley's upper-middle-class development and sought to encourage more building in the open desert along its periphery to the south, west, and east. In the late 1990s, after twenty years of planning and financing efforts, the Bass brothers and other developers created Lake Las Vegas. They were helped in the early stages by House Speaker Jim Wright, who persuaded the Las Vegas gaming community to ease its opposition to the project. State leaders also supported the project, despite local pressures to conserve water. This golfing community, rivaling Spanish Trail's elegance, featured its own man-made lake. Multiple Jack Nicklaus–designed golf courses, two upscale hotels, and the MonteLago Village shops and restaurants began taking shape in the late 1990s and early 2000s. At the same time, Del Webb laid plans for its second retirement community in the valley, Sun City Anthem, at the extreme southern end of Eastern Avenue in Henderson. In 2000 Del Webb opened the larger master-planned community of Anthem, which just between 2002 and 2003 attracted more than six thousand new residents and families.[12]

As the metropolitan area spread outward, floods became a major concern. In the 1950s and 1960s local voters had rejected flood bonds to build a

US Army Corps of Engineers system, because the town was still pretty compact and not that many residents' property was affected by the occasional storms. By the mid-1980s, however, suburban expansion put thousands of people at risk. Earlier approaches to flood control had been piecemeal and undertaken by various local governments to protect vital buildings in their jurisdiction.

But after a disastrous series of floods and with still lingering memories of the so-called Caesars Palace flood of 1976, when the specter of cars piled up by floodwaters in the resort's parking lot reached virtually every American television set, the Clark County commissioners led the fight for comprehensive metropolitan flood control. Once again, the Strip city demonstrated its power. Located in the approximate center of the metropolitan area and riddled with washes and natural floodplains, the Strip city needed protection. By the 1980s it was vital that county commissioners lead the campaign to raise enough money to safeguard property owners, builders, and developers from the growing risk associated with floods—a risk increased by the Strip city's tendency to leapfrog outward across wash areas that, until recent years, had been untouched by development. A flood-control system was necessary, because the entire metropolitan area was exploding outward.

County commissioner Bruce Woodbury, who spearheaded the campaign to build a metropolitan beltway, worked with state assemblyman James McGaughey and others to secure state legislation to raise the local sales tax by one-quarter percent to fund flood control. Of course, there was opposition from skeptical taxpayers. But valley-wide flooding in the summer of 1984 from a continuous series of storms finally turned the tide of public opinion. In the end, despite opposition from some conservative taxpayers and after a half century of inaction regarding flood control, the county, with help from three municipalities, convinced both voters and state legislators to give it the bonding power to build this multibillion-dollar project. Following state and voter approval, the county in 1986 created the Clark County Regional Flood Control District (CCRFCD) to undertake a thirty-year plan to protect the valley from floods. Construction began shortly thereafter. Almost three hundred million dollars in federal funds helped build the US Army Corps of Engineers' Tropicana and Flamingo Washes Project; most of the rest was local money. It should be noted that because the Army Corps' 1960s plan for the valley was seriously flawed, CCRFCD engineers devised a completely different design that required the construction of hundreds of miles of concrete channels and more than one hundred detention basins to protect the metropolitan area. By 2014 the system was still under construction but had already proved its worth—having successfully diverted floodwaters from several major storms.[13]

The process in southern Nevada differed somewhat from events in the Reno area, where, after several disastrous floods earlier in the century, the Army Corps built a series of dams upriver from the city to divert and store river water if warm weather and a high Sierra snowpack threatened to cause flooding downstream. However, floods in the late twentieth and early twenty-first centuries exposed the city's continued vulnerability to flooding, which required expensive new approaches to divert the Truckee's rampaging waters.

The Las Vegas area needed to solve its flood-control problems, because the Strip was about to undergo a dramatic transformation that would substantially increase the annual number of visitors as well as the army of workers serving them. To meet this challenge in the 1990s and early 2000s, the Strip resorts grew vertically, while the Strip city's suburbs expanded horizontally. The opening of the Mirage in 1989 sparked the revolutionary changes on the Strip that created what Steve Wynn called the "New Las Vegas." While falling interest rates, Las Vegas's continued affordability relative to California, and the stock market boom of the 1990s all helped, the Strip's reinvention of Las Vegas in the 1990s drove the process. The Mirage truly was the first megaresort of the "New Las Vegas" era. The resort's daring approach to attracting visitors led the way: with Siegfried and Roy's white tigers in the front, Atlantic bottled-nosed dolphins in the back, and a shark tank in the lobby, Wynn pioneered the use of special attractions to lure tourists into his casino. At the same time, he also pedestrianized the Strip with his erupting Volcano before an enlarged sidewalk that gave tourists a place to gawk. True, there had always been tourists walking on some parts of the Strip where the major resorts were, but most of the sidewalks were only one flag wide, because the resorts had nothing much outside to gawk at. Wynn changed all that with the Volcano in 1989, creating the transition from what architect Alan Hess has called "carscape" to "pedestrianscape." Four years later Wynn reinforced the trend when he staged a nightly pirate show outside his newest resort, Treasure Island, and in 1998 he unveiled the "Dancing Waters" in front of Bellagio—and again at Wynn Las Vegas in 2005 with his pine-tree mountain in front. In the early 2000s the county, with help of abutting businesses, widened virtually all of the sidewalks in the Strip area. Now, even at midnight, the Strip's sidewalks looked like Manhattan's at high noon.[14]

The new building projects on the south Strip came quickly. Wynn's special attractions as well as his other innovations forced his competition to try to surpass him. The Mirage Revolution of the 1990s not only inspired a line of dynamic megaresorts southward down the Strip, but also created thousands of new jobs that brought additional waves of white-collar, blue-collar, lower-income, and minority workers to the valley. This migration, in turn, helped feed the burgeoning demand for homes and apartments in Green Valley, Summerlin, and other communities.

Wynn's spectacular performance forced other resort makers to take action. After losing many of its customers and even some of its high rollers to the Mirage, Caesars Palace executives tore out their resort's northern parking lots to make room for what became the first phase of the Forum Shops. This Roman-style, enclosed shopping mall boasted many of the high-end stores one would normally expect to find on New York's Park Avenue, on Rodeo Drive, or in London, Paris, or some other chic European shopping venue. Caesars spent millions to build an attraction right on the Mirage's property line that would lure former customers back while also creating new ones. The effort was a major success. Within a year of the center's April 1992 opening, Caesars World began planning for further expansion, complete with gourmet restaurants and a mall show featuring the computerized sinking of ancient Atlantis to match Wynn's Volcano and his new pirate battle at Treasure Island. Caesars even brought in Wolfgang Puck, Las Vegas's first national celebrity chef, who opened Spago in the Forum Shops. This marked the beginning of the Strip's effort to lure celebrity chefs from around the world to the Strip, where they could serve their renowned cuisine in a tastefully appointed setting to a devoted public.[15]

Kirk Kerkorian initially contributed to the Mirage Revolution with a new MGM Grand Hotel, more sumptuous than its predecessor. After the disastrous November 1980 fire at the old MGM Grand that killed eighty-five people, Kerkorian reopened that resort before selling it to Bally's four years later. After a two-year absence from Las Vegas mandated by his deal with Bally's, Kerkorian returned to the Strip cash rich and looking for a site to build a grand successor. After pursuing various options, he finally chose the northeast corner of the Strip and Tropicana. To that end, he purchased the Marina Hotel and the Tropicana golf course behind it that extended eastward to Koval Lane. In December 1993 Kerkorian opened his new MGM Grand. With more than five thousand rooms and its own theme park, the new resort became the largest hotel in the world. Kerkorian then bought the northwest corner of the Strip and Tropicana across the street and with partners built the New York–New York Hotel-Casino. Epitomizing what has been called Disneyfied architecture and featuring dozens of Manhattan icons juxtaposed together in sizes out of all proportion to their actual scale, the resort was a $460 million tribute to Steve Wynn's revolution while also keeping him conveniently off MGM's corner.

Within three years of this hotel opening, Kerkorian moved next to buy Wynn's resorts, exploiting several factors, including a decline in the value of Mirage Resorts' stock value, growing stockholder concerns over costs, and Wynn's own frustration with having to please Wall Street analysts. In early 2000 Kerkorian made a $6.7 billion bid for Wynn's properties. Although Wynn was hardly pleased with Kerkorian's offer, he eventually took the deal. This now gave Wynn the money to go down the street and buy the Desert Inn Hotel, including its country club and golf course, which gave him the last big piece of real estate on the Strip.[16]

The deal gave Kerkorian more resorts, including Bellagio's high-roller list, which was worth its weight in gold. Profits from Wynn's former resorts helped pay off a large part of the purchase price and positioned what now became MGM Mirage to eventually make a successful bid for the Mandalay Bay Resort Group. The latter deal, consummated in 2004, made MGM Mirage (whose largest shareholders were Kerkorian and his Tracinda Corporation) the largest resort owner on the Strip.[17]

Mandalay Bay Resorts had its roots in Jay Sarno's flawed notion that gamblers would enjoy doubling down under a safety net with acrobats, trapeze artists, and other circus acts performing above them. He was wrong. Within a few months of its 1968 debut, the Circus Circus casino was in financial straits. A $23 million loan from the Teamsters Union allowed Sarno to construct a hotel behind the casino in the early 1970s. But cash-flow problems continued, and his alleged connections to organized crime figures hardly helped. Finally, in 1974, northern Nevada gaming executives William Bennett and William Pennington came to the rescue, purchasing the struggling resort and, employing the successful model pioneered by

Warren and Judy Bayley at the 1950s Hacienda, converting it into a place for families.[18]

Circus Circus quickly became a financial success, and over time Bennett went corporate, creating Circus Circus Enterprises, which opened a 725-room Circus Circus Hotel in Reno in 1978. This property established a firm presence for casino resorts in the zone north of the railroad tracks, especially after Circus Circus teamed with Don Carano's Eldorado and Silver Legacy to create the largest casino-resort complex in the Reno area. Pennington himself served as manager of Circus Circus, Reno, for ten years until his retirement, leaving Bennett to oversee the Las Vegas operations. The company expanded in Las Vegas by purchasing land along the Strip's west side, south of Tropicana Avenue. In an effort to draw more family business, the firm built the Excalibur. When it opened in 1990, this resort, with its oversize turrets and castle, represented Las Vegas's latest nod to Disneyfied architecture. Three years later the company opened the Luxor, just south of Excalibur. When it debuted in the fall of 1993 with its distinctive Cheops-glass-covered pyramid and point of light, Luxor set a new standard of elegance for the company. Luxor was an exquisite example of Spectacle architecture that would later help to inspire the designers of Paris–Las Vegas and the Venetian (technically, "*The* Venetian").[19]

In the late 1990s the company completed its trifecta when it began construction on an even more upscale resort that rose immediately south of the Luxor on the site of the old Hacienda, whose New Year's Eve 1996 implosion cleared the way for Mandalay Bay. Construction on this forty-four-story hotel continued for three years before it opened to the public in March 1999. With its wave pool, its Four Seasons Hotel embedded in the top five floors of the tower, its Shark Reef attraction, and its high-end restaurants, including Red Square, the $950 million resort marked another major addition to the south Strip. In 1999, in an effort to reflect the company's new upscale image, Circus Circus Enterprises moved its corporate headquarters into Mandalay Bay itself and changed its name to the Mandalay Resort Group. In that same year Bennett left the company after a power struggle. Taking his buyout money, he bought the Sahara at the extreme north end of the Strip. There, he spent the rest of his life in a spirited but ultimately futile effort to revive that aging property.[20]

Two additional players helped remake the Strip in the 1990s: Hilton Hotels and trade-show mogul Sheldon Adelson. The Hilton Corporation had entered the Las Vegas market after Nevada enacted its 1969 corporate gaming law, purchasing Kirk Kerkorian's International in 1971 and his Flamingo in 1972. In the 1990s Hilton's spin-off gaming company, Park Place Entertainment, had enlarged the hotel firm's presence on the Strip by purchasing Caesars Palace, Bally's, and eventually the Aladdin (today's Planet Hollywood). Hilton was not famous for erecting distinctive buildings. Most of its domestic and international hotels embodied standard architectural forms. But in 1996, when it purchased Bally's Entertainment, Hilton inherited an ongoing plan to build a Parisian hotel directly south of Bally's to match the distinctive architecture that was slowly transforming the south Strip into a must-see attraction. By the mid-1990s it had been years since Hilton had even built a new hotel, so executives spent months planning for the project. But when the $785 million Paris resort finally opened in May 1999, it made another contribution to the growing line of Spectacle architecture that adorned the south Strip. With its faux Arc de Triomphe and its half-size Eiffel Tower shining nightly in Bellagio's Lake Como across the street, Hilton's latest resort provided an architectural touché to Wynn's Bellagio.[21]

Sheldon Adelson's response to the Strip's changing cityscape was perhaps the most dramatic of all. Following his sale of Comdex, the computer trade show that made him a billionaire, Adelson bought the Sands Hotel and imploded it in 1996 to make room for his $1.5 billion version of Renaissance Venice. The theme was an ingenious choice, and he implemented it to the hilt, hiring noted architect Rem Koolhaas and designer Bob Hlusak to create artwork for the structure. When it opened in 1999, critics raved about the building's magnificence—from the front desk featuring a painted "bird's-eye view" of Venice to the dazzling Grand Gallery with its Armillary Sphere and multicolored marble floor leading visitors to the casino and up the escalator to an ersatz version of the Doge's Palace. The palace was Adelson's colorful gateway to the Grand Canal Shoppes, with its sixty-five-foot frescoed ceiling of gold-framed reproductions of works by Titian, Tintoretto, Veronese, and other masters. Added to this were scaled-down versions of the 1517 Campanile Bell Tower, Saint Mark's Square, the Rialto Bridge, and other Venice landmarks connected by a canal system, whose waters carried tourist-filled gondolas upon which singing gondoliers serenaded their guests as they sailed past the shops and under the street scene's bridges.[22]

By century's end Las Vegas had been reinvented, primarily on the Strip, by a new generation of resort makers who took the place a giant step forward from its Mob days when late-modern, low-slung resorts catering architecturally to America's midcentury car culture attracted tourists with their Rat Pack headliners, lounge acts, lush landscaping, and kidney-shaped swimming pools. The "New Las Vegas" not only featured spectacular architecture, all-suite resorts, and high-end shopping but also dozens of celebrity-chef-driven restaurants, as well as nightclubs (and later dayclubs) that completely transformed the town's appeal. By the early 1990s the Mirage, and soon all of the megaresorts it inspired, were making more money in their nongaming departments than in the casino—a far cry from the Mob era. Gone were the starlight dance floors where live hotel orchestras entertained nattily attired guests. Supplanting the old midcentury nightclubs were the House of Blues, Jet, Tabu, xs, Pure, and Tao, complete with their pulsating lights, celebrity hosts, and hip music tracks. These charismatic watering holes and an endless series of others only reinforced Las Vegas's all-night-party reputation.

In an effort to further promote Las Vegas's modern image and move passengers more quickly between resorts, the city and county supported construction of a privately owned, 3.9-mile monorail system running between the Sahara and MGM Grand hotels. Following the Seattle Century 21 Exposition in 1962, there had been several bids from companies seeking to build a sleek monorail system on the Strip. But there was little progress, mainly due to the expense and the area's 1960s car culture. As the Strip grew and traffic congestion worsened, monorail service became more practical. Former county commissioner and airport director Robert Broadbent pushed for construction of the monorail that today bears his name. In the late 1990s Broadbent was successful in convincing county commissioners to go forward with the project. The twenty-first-century version of the idea created an initial buzz. The vehicles and signals closely resembled those developed for Disney theme parks. After several delays phase 1 opened in 2004 to large crowds of tourists and locals who patronized it for a while. But, less than a year after the monorail's debut, mechanical problems, revenue shortfalls, and other factors led the system's operator, Transit Systems Management, to turn control over to the Las Vegas Monorail Company. Despite a vigorous advertising effort, ridership continued to fall below expectations for a variety of reasons. The first was the Sahara hotel's closure, an unforeseen event when the system was being planned in the early 2000s. The more crucial flaw, however, lay in the choice of route. Because resort company monorails already connected Mandalay Bay with Excalibur, the Monte Carlo with Bellagio, and the Mirage with Treasure Island, the new monorail ran behind those resorts located on the east side of the Strip. From there, however, it was a city block's walk to the Strip—something that many visitors did not relish. There had been talk of running the monorail down the Strip's center median, just as earlier proposals in the 1960s called for, but the big resorts, as well as the taxi companies, were cool to that idea.

By 2013 it was obvious that if construction of the next phase was undertaken, it would be to connect the system to McCarran Airport from the MGM and not to link the Strip with Fremont Street's casinos in the city—another manifestation of the Strip city's power within the metropolitan area. The early euphoria over plans to build the monorail and then extend it to Las Vegas and the main arteries of that city to benefit commuters caught the attention of Reno's leaders, who gave the idea of building a monorail in their metro area some consideration. There was talk of extending service from downtown out to the convention center, to the airport, and over to Sparks, but in the end there was not enough money or enthusiasm to undertake the project. Moreover, the declining ridership on the Las Vegas system by 2005 did little to revive support for one in Reno.[23]

Aside from the monorail, most of the new projects undertaken on or near the Strip in the 1990s and early 2000s were successful and only promoted more innovative thinking. Of course, change was not limited to the Strip. The city of Las Vegas's casino core on Fremont Street had to battle the Strip's surging popularity to claim its share of the profits. Downtown redevelopment was part of the transformation. Reno had launched its own redevelopment effort earlier in 1983 under Mayor Barbara Bennett, when the state established the Reno Redevelopment Agency to direct the process of transforming downtown into a more inviting area for residents as well as visitors. Also in that year the city created the first redevelopment district (the Reno Project Area), which encompassed much of downtown. In Las Vegas the process began a few years later in 1986, when the city under then mayor William Briare convinced the state to create the Las Vegas Redevelopment Agency, and during the administrations of Ron Lurie (1987–91) and Jan Jones (1991–99), when municipal officials approved $90 million in early spending to revitalize the CBD.

The initial projects were the Minami Tower and Bob Snow's Main Street Station. The city first cleared out a six-acre site on Las Vegas Boulevard filled with small businesses by using its power of eminent domain. But progress was glacially slow. On Las Vegas Boulevard South between Bridger and Clark Streets, Japanese developer Masao Nangaku, after acquiring city redevelopment funds for his projected thirty-five-story Minami Tower in 1989, failed to get financing and left the city with little more than a big hole in the ground for its efforts. The Koll Real Estate Group in Florida then abandoned its 470,000-square-foot City Center project in 1994. But Mayor Jones demonstrated real leadership in 1996, convincing city councilmen not to turn the site into a park or leave it empty. Instead, she argued for ceding the land to the federal government to build what became the Lloyd George Federal Courthouse. Jones convinced city councilmen that the courthouse was a crucial prerequisite to establishing a "legal corridor" downtown, which it largely did. In 2002 the building opened, the first federal building in the nation to embody the post–Oklahoma City bombing's strict security standards for construction. The facility quickly became an addition to the area that contributed momentum to the city's downtown revitalization efforts.[24]

Bob Snow's Main Street Station project, in which he renovated an existing hotel (Major Riddle's defunct Holiday Inn International) into a San Francisco gaslight-era resort, sucked up another $18.4 million in redevelopment funds. The city bet heavily on Snow, whose Church Street Station, a hip-hop complex of nightclubs housed in a restored Orlando railroad station, had been a success in the 1970s and '80s. But his Las Vegas project on North Main Street, a dark block north of the action on Fremont Street, proved to be a fiasco, closing just a few months after it opened in 1991. The Boyd Group ultimately bought the place in 1993, spent another $45 million renovating it, and reopened it in 1996. Once linked to the company's popular California Hotel, a hot spot for Hawaiian tourists across the road, Main Street Station finally succeeded.

While the Boyd Group ultimately rescued the city from a major debacle at Main Street Station, there was no rescuing the city from the Neonopolis disaster. The Neonopolis Mall, a $100 million retail, dining, and entertainment center constructed just east of the Fremont Street Experience, opened in 2002 to much fanfare. But poor management and lack of foot traffic made the complex a virtual failure from the start. The Jones administration sank $32 million into the project, including $15 million to build a large multideck parking garage for customers. Oscar Goodman's administration hoped the facility would eventually connect the tourist-filled Fremont Street Experience with the new Fremont East Entertainment District. But as former mayor Jan Jones glumly noted, the failure to build the Fremont Street Experience far enough east to reach Las Vegas Boulevard left Neonopolis in a no-man's-land, because few tourists ventured past the end of the electronic canopy. But some do now and more will—if Goodman's new Fremont Street East district succeeds.[25]

The Lurie and Jones administrations also worked to get control of the old Union Pacific Railroad yards behind the (Union) Plaza Hotel to develop those strategic lands. Jones dreamed of building a sports complex on the site to draw more residents and tourists to downtown. While the city negotiated to buy the land, Jones in 1996 worked with Polyphase Sports and Entertainment, a group of Dallas investors, to draw up plans for the $750 million domed stadium that could seat up to 110,000 fans—a project similar to Jerry Jones's 2009 Cowboys Stadium in suburban Arlington, Texas. But the plans fell through for a variety of reasons, and no large stadium was ever built downtown, although Oscar and Carolyn Goodman (who succeeded her husband as Las Vegas mayor in 2011) never completely gave up hope of building an arena there to perhaps host a National Basketball Association (NBA) or National Hockey League (NHL) franchise.[26]

Mayor Jones's crowning achievement was the Fremont Street Experience, Jon Jerde's barrel-vaulted electronic canopy ninety feet above the street that stretched several city blocks and converted Fremont Street into a pedestrian mall with bands, entertainers, and shopping kiosks. At night the Viva Vision canopy transformed briefly into a theater on the hour when the casinos dimmed their neon in unison to entertain visitors with a high-tech light show. Gaming executives were willing to sacrifice some gambling profits for ten minutes each hour to entice more tourists from the Strip to downtown. When it opened in late 1995, the attraction was an immediate success, dramatically increasing business in the city's casino core.[27]

But there was also development farther out. Along Las Vegas Boulevard two blocks north of the Sahara, Bob Stupak in the mid-1990s slowly transformed his 1979 Vegas World eyesore into the soaring Stratosphere Hotel-Casino. Although he eventually ran out of capital and had to let others finish the project, Stupak created an iconic resort in the city's south end, something the blighted "Naked City" neighborhood badly needed to supplement the aging motels, wedding chapels, souvenir shops, and slot arcades that lined its streets. At 1,141 feet—almost as high as the Empire State Building—the Stratosphere towered above Las Vegas, offering breadth-taking views of the surrounding metropolitan area from its observation decks. During construction Stupak even proposed making the Stratosphere higher than the CN Tower in Toronto, then the tallest structure in the world (the Stratosphere is not considered a building because it lacks floors for most of its height), but the FAA and McCarran Airport officials objected, and his plan had to be scrapped.[28]

Stupak's success in securing an unrestricted gaming license for his casino resort near the north end of the Strip reflected the City of Las Vegas's increased willingness to bend its traditional red-line policy to accommodate the growing demand for suburban casinos. Clearly, Vegas World was not within the city's red-line area. Like the earlier Moulin Rouge in West Las Vegas and the Showboat on Boulder Highway, the city wanted to promote commercial activity in a peripheral area—in Stupak's case, to lure some north Strip tourists into Las Vegas. So, the city council granted Stupak a zoning variance, just as it had for the earlier resorts. When these three resorts got unrestricted gaming licenses, each became, in effect, a new self-contained red-line district. But after more than a decade of discussion since George Franklin first raised the issue of abolishing the red-line ordinance, the city council on February 8, 1989, finally voted to end Las Vegas's red line, which dated back to the early 1930s.[29]

The municipality's sweeping new ordinance allowed more unrestricted gaming licenses while restricting smaller operations. Specifically, the law banned all *new* small gaming operations anywhere in the city. It also cut the number of existing slot machines that taverns could have and imposed similar restrictions on laundries and other businesses with limited gaming. The major reform, of course, involved those wanting to open new gaming establishments in town. In an approach similar to Reno's 1971 ordinance, Las Vegas tied new casinos to hotels. The city would issue an unrestricted gaming license only to casino operations that provided two hundred guest rooms. While city council members told reporters how they became concerned about revising the old ordinance when they received a laundry operator's request to install fifteen slot machines in his business, their reform policy was really tied to a much larger context. First, councilmen regarded the establishment making the request not as a laundry with a few slot machines, but rather as a slot arcade with a few washing machines. They were determined to stop the spread of these kinds of places.[30]

Much of their incentive, however, came from the concerns expressed by land developers, who were on the verge of extending the city's built-up zone dramatically westward. Support for the restriction of slot arcades and the requirement of a two-hundred-room hotel for unrestricted gaming came directly from the Howard Hughes Corporation, whose executives no doubt lobbied for some reform to close loopholes in the city's gaming ordinance even before the council brought up the matter for consideration. Even though most of the city's tavern owners, laundry operators, and other affected retail stores opposed the new measures, John Goolsby, president of the Howard Hughes Corporation, publicly supported the new ordinance. As he told reporters, it was his company's view that it was "not necessary to a proper quality of life for our citizens nor to the success of economic development programs to have gaming intrude into every sector of the daily lives of our citizens." That was it. With Del Webb's Sun City Summerlin opening that very month, February 1989, and the Hughes Corporation's even larger housing projects geared for all ages preparing to start selling homes in 1991, Las Vegas leaders were not about to antagonize the developers of the giant new affluent tax base being created on their city's western edge. Unlimited gaming would no longer be limited to the red-line zone downtown and to a few grandfathered-in resorts. Gaming would be allowed to spread outward as the city's suburbs spread outward, but only under strict zoning controls.[31]

This soon became the standard policy in both Clark and Washoe Counties. Later in the 1989 legislative session the State of Nevada officially recognized the right of governments "in a county whose population is 700,000 or more" to create "enterprise zones" to restrict gaming.[32] The goal was to protect residential areas from unwanted casinos. The evolving process mandated that the city planning commission propose such zones and hold hearings to gather public input before making a recommendation to the city council. This was the process that later governed the location of new resorts near or in Summerlin, Las Vegas, Henderson, North Las Vegas, and Clark County. Reno and Sparks also adopted the two-hundred-room hotel requirement in their jurisdictions to keep casino gambling out of residentially zoned areas.

This liberalization of Las Vegas's red-line policy promoted development, especially in more affluent suburbs. When it debuted in 1999, the Resort at Summerlin (later the J. W. Marriott Las Vegas Resort & Spa) brought an additional touch of class to that burgeoning community. Virtually encircled by golf courses and set on fifty-four acres, the resort, with its elaborately landscaped grounds, myriad waterfalls, and babbling brooks, offered the perfect getaway for vacationers anxious to enjoy the Las Vegas atmosphere without having to brave the hectic atmosphere on the Strip or downtown. Farther east, the Santa Fe Station opened in 1991 on thirty-six acres off Rancho Drive. With only two hundred rooms, the hotel was not large by most standards, but it met the city's current room requirement for an unrestricted gaming license.[33]

The continued growth of casino resorts and the suburbs surrounding them resulted in a more diverse population than in earlier decades. Beginning in the 1980s the local Hispanic population began to soar, as the growing number of jobs diverted them from their normal migratory paths through California and Arizona. In 1970 Latinos constituted only 3.6 percent of the Las Vegas SMSA's population. That figure rose to 7.2 percent in 1980, 11.2 percent in 1990, and 21.9 percent in 2000. By 2010 29.1 percent of Clark County's population was Hispanic, compared to roughly 10 percent for African Americans. Following passage of Nevada's open-housing law in 1971, Latino settlement patterns spread out across the valley, although the cities of Las Vegas and North Las Vegas were the most popular areas for businesses catering to Hispanic needs.[34]

The same was not true of the growing Asian–Pacific Islander population, which by 2012 constituted 8.7 percent of the county's population, up from 2 percent in 1980. While some Asians lived in Las Vegas and North Las Vegas, many resided in the more affluent southern and western suburbs. Over time an Asian commercial district began to emerge. In 1999 Nevada

TABLE 4.1
Latinos, Las Vegas Area
Percentage of MSA Population

Year	Percentage
1970	3.6
1980	7.2
1990	11.2
2000	21.9
2010	29.1

TABLE 4.2
Resident Minorities, Las Vegas Area
Percentage of Population

Year	African Americans		Latinos		Asian–Pacific Islanders	
	Las Vegas	Paradise Township	Las Vegas	Paradise Township	Las Vegas	Paradise Township
1970	11.2	.07	No data	No data	No data	No data
1980	12.8	3.3	7.8	6.5	2.0	2.6
1990	11.4	4.9	12.5	10.5	3.6	4.0

governor Kenny Guinn officially designated the place as "Chinatown." It developed, however, not in the old central city where Chinatowns usually appear but in the Strip city on county lands bordering Spring Mountain Road, approximately two miles west of the Venetian hotel. The process began in 1995 when Taiwanese American developer James Chih-Cheng opened his Chinatown Plaza, a strip mall featuring Asian restaurants and other businesses. More commercial developments followed, and by 2010 the district ran for several miles down Spring Mountain Road.[35]

However, if one breaks down the figures a bit to distinguish between just the city of Las Vegas and Paradise Township (which covered most of the Strip and its eastern, southern, and western suburbs), it becomes obvious that the emerging Strip city, at least before 1990, was mostly white and Anglo. In 1970 African Americans composed 11.2 percent of Las Vegas's population, compared to .07 percent of Paradise. In 1980 the figures were 12.8 percent and 3.3 percent, and in 1990 (almost twenty years after Nevada's open-housing law took effect) they had changed little, at 11.4 and 4.9 percent, respectively.[36]

The pattern for Hispanics and Asian–Pacific Islanders varied. Hispanics at first settled mainly in Las Vegas and North Las Vegas, but by the 1990s they began heading for the Strip city, too. In contrast, Asian–Pacific Islanders preferred the Strip city's suburbs, but these populations were still not high enough to change the fact that Las Vegas, like Reno, remained largely white and Anglo into the next century.

In 2000 and 2010 the minority share of the population rose in both metro areas and in their suburbs. As blacks, Hispanics, and especially Asians began securing better-paying jobs, modern housing, and better access to credit to allow financing of their businesses, more were able to move out to the suburbs. Many minority lower-income workers also moved farther out to be near their jobs in suburban resorts and other service businesses. However, in both the Reno and the Las Vegas metropolitan areas, Anglos continued to dominate the outer suburbs and the overall population at the same time that Hispanic and Asian numbers rose.[37]

All of these trends continued into the new century—as did the boom. While the terrorist attacks of September 2001 slowed tourism for a while, by 2004 Las Vegas had rebounded to post its highest numbers ever. In that year 37.4 million people visited the valley, thanks to "a strong convention industry, low-cost and abundant air service . . . and a popular advertising campaign." The room occupancy rate was 88.6 percent, despite 1,000 new rooms coming on line. And the weekend figure was 95 percent, far more than New York City (81.1 percent), Honolulu (79.7 percent), and other rivals. Figures for Las Vegas were expected to rise further in 2005 with the April opening of the Wynn Las Vegas resort, and they did. By 2006 Las Vegas claimed a record 38.9 million visitors staying at its 132,605 hotel rooms with an annual occupancy rate of 89.7 percent.[38]

In the early to mid-2000s Las Vegas investors and developers responded by preparing to build even more sumptuous resorts and residences. The big project, of course, was MGM Mirage's City Center. In September 2005 MGM Mirage announced plans to build the multiuse project on sixty-six acres of land between the Bellagio and the Monte Carlo (which it got in the deals with Wynn and Mandalay Bay Resorts) hotels. Plans called for a sixty-story, 4,000-room hotel (Aria) and two boutique hotels (the Mandarin Oriental and Vdara) as well as condominium towers, restaurants, and retail and entertainment venues. The company reserved more than 2,000 of its planned 7,200-unit complex for condominiums. The so-called city-within-a-city project promised to transform the Strip once again while increasing the number of visitors and residents to the area. In June 2006 MGM Mirage broke ground for Project City Center, which experts predicted would employ more than 7,000 workers when construction peaked in 2008. Once finished, the company estimated that more than 12,000 employees would work at the complex.[39]

Donald Trump also set aside many units for residential living in his proposed tower. In 2004 Trump planned to build a sixty-four-story condo hotel on the Strip, just north of the newly expanded Fashion Show Mall. In the end, the Great Recession forced him to postpone construction of a second tower, but he still succeeded in selling out his apartment units.

By the spring of 2005 there were no fewer than sixteen projects on the drawing board just for Harmon Avenue near the Strip. Some were new towers (the Hard Rock Hotel), some were expensive renovations of older hotels (Alexis Park), some were new hotels (the Cosmopolitan), some were multibillion-dollar projects (City Center), and some (including a few luxury condo towers) never happened because of the recession that began casting a shadow over investor optimism.[40]

The early to mid-2000s witnessed other trends before the recession hit. Hilton resorts led the way in the construction of time-share housing on the Strip. The company popularized the trend with its Grand Vacations Club (200 units) behind the Flamingo Hilton pool in 1993. It added another 230-unit tower near the Las Vegas Hilton a few years later and in 2004 opened its twenty-eight-story, 283-room high-rise on the Strip near Circus Circus. The corporation then drew up plans to erect several more high-rises on its ten-acre site there, but the recession delayed those projects. Unlike Reno, where Hilton's hotels were located in the city, none of its resorts or vacation homes were located in the city of Las Vegas. The company built its time-shares exclusively in the Strip city, where wealthy tourists could enjoy extended vacations in the sumptuous atmosphere of the great resorts.

While new buildings went up, some venerable old ones came down. In June 2006 Kansas real estate mogul Phil Ruffin announced that he would close his aging New Frontier (on the site of the old Frontier Hotel) and replace it with a new 2,750-room $2 billion palace, the Montreux. But he never built it. Ever the shrewd businessman, Ruffin, unwilling to pay the soaring interest rates that lenders demanded for construction loans, sold the New Frontier to Israeli developers and used the money to buy Treasure Island from MGM Mirage. Later that fall the Boyd Group closed the Stardust Hotel to make room for Echelon Place, the upscale resort it planned to open by 2010. The Boyd Group had purchased the Stardust, for years a Mob domain, in 1985 and spent millions upgrading it with new restaurants, a tower, and other improvements. Twenty years later the new Wynn Resort, plans for Encore, plans for the Fontainebleau, and the dramatic expansion of the nearby Fashion Show Mall obligated Boyd to replace the aging Stardust with a worthy successor. In March 2007 crews imploded the resort's thirty-two-story tower to make way for Echelon Place. Boyd planned to build five boutique hotels with a combined 5,000 rooms along with a 140,000-square-foot casino, 300,000 square feet of retail space, and up to thirty restaurants. Plans also called for three-quarters of a million square feet for meetings and conventions in a complex spread over eighty-seven acres that included twenty-four Boyd got from Harrah's Entertainment in a land swap.[41]

Small motels along the Strip also faced the prospect of demolition to create sites large enough for more major hotels. In July 2004, after forty-five years on the Strip, the family-owned Tam O'Shanter closed to make way for the Palazzo, as another relic of the midcentury Strip yielded to its modern successor in the seemingly endless process of the Strip reinventing itself. A few years later the Algiers Hotel, a Strip mainstay since 1965, closed its doors to make way for the projected Fontainebleau Hotel.[42]

By the early 2000s the preferred site for new megaresorts had clearly shifted from the south to the center Strip. In March 2004 Las Vegas Sands executives announced they would soon begin phase 2 of the Venetian expansion, construction of a new resort just north of the Venetian. Originally planned to stand forty-two stories high, the Palazzo was redesigned to a height of fifty-three floors so it would rise above Steve Wynn's fifty-story tower across the street.

Despite their occasional feuds, it was Wynn and Adelson who together helped establish the central Strip as the new site for megaresorts in the 2000s. Flush with more than $500 million he received from MGM Grand for the Mirage, Treasure Island, Bellagio, Monte Carlo, and the Golden Nugget, Wynn purchased the Desert Inn Hotel and its 215-acre site in 2000 for $270 million. In November 2003 Wynn told the press that he wanted to exploit planned expansions at the nearby Las Vegas Convention Center and Adelson's Sands Expo Center. He hoped to build a luxury hotel to convince the chief executives and other officers of many American corporations to hold their annual board dinners and banquets at his 50,000-square-foot ballroom area.[43]

When Wynn Las Vegas opened on its 25-acre site on April 28, 2005, the resort reinforced its proprietor's well-deserved reputation for transforming the Strip's landscape. The Wynn's fifty-story curved tower, with its pine-covered mountain in front boasting waterfalls near the Esplanade entrance and the big curtain waterfall "inside," along with Tom Fazio's redesign of the historic Desert Inn golf course, set a new standard for excellence on the Strip and encouraged more resort construction on the north Strip up to the Sahara Hotel. As Mandalay Bay Resort Group chief executive officer (CEO) Glenn Schaeffer noted, "Steve has the talent each and every time to raise the profile and price in the market. [Wynn Las Vegas is] a positive in terms of bringing more visitors. Steve never lets anybody down."[44]

Although some pundits predicted the Wynn's opening would spawn a rapid development of the north Strip, others argued that it would have little effect. Still others insisted that the north Strip would have developed anyway even without Wynn, because that is where space was most available. Former Mirage executive Alan Feldman offered perhaps the most insightful comment: "When The Mirage opened in 1989, there was little competition. It's important to remember that the cost of building The Mirage [$611 million] was greater than the combined cost to build all the hotels in Las Vegas that came before it. Now the level of investment has exploded to billions of dollars."[45] In other words, all the new hotels on the Strip since Treasure Island (1993) had limited the effect of any single property on the market.

As the Strip city slowly began to emerge at midcentury, each new resort on the highway and each new expansion of an existing property exerted a multiplier effect on the lands beyond, raising their value and transforming them into sites for residential subdivisions, apartment complexes, office parks, commercial centers, and suburban resorts. The once empty desert now became a canvas where entrepreneurial developers could work their magic. It has been said that into the 1980s, "the right twenty-five people in a room could accomplish anything in the Las Vegas Valley." That was probably no longer true by the 1990s because of the area's larger population and more diverse elites, but in the earlier decades of the Strip city's development the wide-open real estate frontier on county land presented unlimited opportunities for influential capitalists. The Strip exemplified this trend—even more than the developments around it—even into the 1990s. The Venetian, Paris, New York–New York, and Bellagio epitomized the innovative approach to resort construction that made the Strip another Parthenon, another Taj Mahal, another spectacle to be visited for its own merits. In the last half of the twentieth century, Las Vegas, thanks to the ingenuity of Strip executives, became more than the false-fronted western town of the 1940s. It evolved an idiosyncratic nature all its own, and, in the process, the larger Strip city reinvigorated and sustained the metropolitan area around it, a process that did not occur to the south of Reno.

But as the approaching Great Recession ominously slowed resort and gaming profits, the march of development up the north Strip came to a virtual halt. As 2007 drew to a close, Las Vegas promoters took solace in the fact that Steve Wynn's Encore was on track to open in late 2008. Wynn's newest resort, with 2,034 rooms and a convenient free shuttle through the property to the Las Vegas Convention Center, was designed to be more intimate than its older sister next door. As reporter Liz Benston noted, Encore would "feature a chambered casino floor divided by draperies and columns—a nod to the more intimate gaming rooms in Macau and a departure from Las Vegas' cavernous casino floors." Wynn explained that he got some of his ideas for Encore and its pool and use of natural light from resorts he visited in St. Tropez. Wynn was able to open Encore in the midst of a major recession because he had a sound business plan for his company and secured the credit to finance his building before construction began.[46]

Encore itself was a tribute to Wynn's attention to detail and genius for design. Its five restaurants, luxury spa, and what soon became the world's most profitable nightclub quickly swelled the company's profits and its ability to bankroll more construction in Asia. Wynn hardly rested on his laurels. Within a year he was already planning to demolish Encore's attractive Strip entrance and replace it with a posh beach club, providing "dayclub" services for Encore guests as well as those in other hotels. The hotel featured much of Wynn's signature style expressed through the creative genius of designer Roger Thomas: the artwork at Botero, the crystal dragon at Wazuzu, the retracting wall and ceiling decor at Switch, the goddess Daphne chandelier gracing the lobby bar, the green-eyed serpent sizing up bar patrons at Surrender, the rock-crystal parrots at the front desk, and Frank Sinatra's stately Oscar greeting diners at his namesake restaurant. These new venues supplemented Encore's instantly successful XS nightclub that Wynn opened with Victor Drai in 2008.[47]

Despite a worsening economy, Sheldon Adelson still managed to open his Palazzo next door to the Wynn in late 2007. The resort proved to be a magnificent extension of the Venetian. By connecting the Palazzo with the Venetian at a strategic point, the latter's Grand Canal Shoppes, the Las Vegas Sands Corporation created a seamless entry into the Palazzo's inviting retail mall. And, by shrewdly linking his two hotels, Adelson saved himself $40–$60 million in other back-of-the-house operating costs. The Palazzo was the first new Strip resort to open during the Great Recession and the first since the Wynn Las Vegas debuted in April 2005. The opening of the $1.8 billion Palazzo next to the expanded Venetian gave Adelson more than 7,000 hotel rooms for convention delegates using his newly enlarged Sands Expo Center. The two hotels and the center together offered conventions more than 2.25 million square feet of meeting space—more than all of the convention space in San Francisco. Adelson, who made much of his early fortune in the 1980s and '90s running the huge Comdex convention, was one of the first resort leaders to realize that in the "New Las Vegas," conventions were no longer a "filler" for Strip hotels during the week, but were quickly becoming a central "pillar" of the Strip's resort economy.[48]

Together, Adelson and Wynn further solidified the Strip city's control of the big conventions and the high-level events and meetings surrounding them. By providing all-suite, high-end accommodations and dining facilities in close proximity to the main convention center just down the street from Wynn's hotels and practically at the doorstep of Adelson's cavernous Las Vegas Sands Convention Center, both men kept the lion's share of business on the center Strip. At the same time, Caesars Entertainment (Harrah's) and the MGM Resorts International, the oligopolistic group down Las Vegas Boulevard, captured a lot of the remaining delegates for the south Strip. As a result, the city of Las Vegas's Cashman Center, built in 1983, attracted much smaller trade shows and meetings than the Strip city's facility.

But Wynn and Adelson were not the only ones investing heavily in the Strip city's future. New resorts, expansion of existing ones, and other innovative projects filled the drawing boards of architects and engineers in the early to mid-2000s. In September 2005, for example, new Aladdin owners Starwood Hotels International and its partner announced plans to spend millions to revamp that resort completely by ending its decades-long Middle East theme. Their dream was to rebuild the front entrance and casino to create the spectacular new Planet Hollywood resort to maximize profits at their strategic location across from the soon-to-open City Center.[49]

Expensive new hotels also appeared on the metropolitan periphery. In April 2006 Station Casinos opened its $925 million Red Rock Resort on West Charleston Boulevard and the 215 Beltway to cater to upscale tourists and suburbanites in the Summerlin area. Veteran gamer Frank Fertitta Jr. had opened the Bingo Palace in 1976 and soon after expanded it into the Palace Station. With profits made there he later bought the Boulder Highway site for the Boulder Station. Fertitta retired from the company in 1993, turning control over to his sons, Frank and Lorenzo, who went on to build Sunset Station, Red Rock Station, and Aliante Station. In addition to the Santa Fe (1991), the Suncoast (2000), Castaways (2000), and other new resorts on the edges of the city of Las Vegas, new resorts also appeared in the suburbs of other cities, including the Sunset Station (1997), the Reserve (1998), and the M Resort (2009) in Henderson as well as the Texas Station (1995), the Cannery (2003), and the Aliante Station (2008) in North Las Vegas. This trend resembled one in Reno during the 1990s and early 2000s. While the Silver Legacy and a few other places were new additions to the downtown landscape, several large resorts appeared in the suburbs after smaller existing places were dramatically enlarged. These included the Atlantis and Peppermill, among others.[50]

In the Las Vegas area there were also significant expansion efforts on or near the Strip at the Hard Rock Hotel, at Caesars Palace, and elsewhere. In March 2007 the Hard Rock's new owners, the Morgans Hotel Group and DLJ Merchant bank, announced plans for a $750 million expansion and renovation for the twelve-year-old resort that included a new fifteen-story, 550-room tower with a separate 400-suite VIP tower. New visitor attractions were also on the agenda of many Strip resorts. There were several proposals to build a wheel similar to the London Eye, but only one resort group actually did it. The plans for upgrading the area south of Harrah's were in the works a few years later. Finally, in 2012, Caesars (formerly Harrah's) Entertainment knocked down O'Sheas Casino between the Flamingo and Imperial Palace (later the Quad) to begin work on the Linq. This $550 million entertainment complex, featuring new restaurants, bars, and shopping leading to the 550-foot "High Roller," the largest observation wheel in the world, opened in 2014.[51]

Then there were also grandiose projects that were envisioned but never built. In April 2008 Station Casinos announced plans to construct a multibillion-dollar, mixed-use, mega-size project on 110 acres west of Interstate 15 at Tropicana Avenue that would be even larger than MGM's City Center. To be built in phases, the Viva Project would eventually feature three hotels with more than 5,200 rooms and a large casino. While one Deutsche Bank consultant predicted that Station would have little trouble raising the capital for the development, the firm was already overextended with its $675 million Aliante project in North Las Vegas and other new facilities such as the Red Rock resort that had not yet paid for themselves. Little did anyone realize at the time that these and other drags combined with the world economic slowdown of 2008 would send the once profitable company spiraling into bankruptcy by 2009.[52]

Virtually everyone misjudged the changing economic climate. Nothing but optimism led the Elad Group of New York and Israel to buy the New Frontier in 2006 from Phil Ruffin. Plans called for imploding the old resort, which Elad did in 2007, and replacing it with a $5.8 billion Strip version of Manhattan's famous Plaza Hotel. Elad was looking to develop the Plaza brand and its worldwide reputation for luxury and excellence, not only in Las Vegas but in other major US cities too, just as Donald Trump and Steve Wynn had begun to do with their names. At the time there was no thought of suspending the project. But the global recession changed everything, and in 2008 progress stopped just as it had next door at Echelon Place and the Fontainebleau. All of the heady predictions about the north Strip's rapid development following the opening of Wynn Las Vegas disappeared almost overnight.[53]

In addition to resorts the prerecession boom had also fueled an enthusiasm for building more combined-use projects in the suburbs. Developers planned the Curve, a high-rise condominium project surrounded by a suburban village of cobbled streets, on forty-seven acres off the 215 Beltway where it curves north to Las Vegas after Durango Drive. The forty-acre village at Centennial Springs promised to enhance land values in the northwest valley, and the second stage of the District at Green Valley Ranch in Henderson on a twenty-acre tract promised to boost its predecessor across the street with a Whole Foods, a Cheesecake Factory restaurant, and fifty thousand square feet of office space and stores. And there were similar, and even bigger, developments on the drawing board, including Tivoli Village on Rampart Boulevard. The advantage of these projects was, as one executive put it: "You're able to live, work and play in one environment." But the recession halted most of this work. Although the second phase of the District opened in time, the place went bankrupt in 2010. And most of the mixed-use projects on the drawing boards got caught in the recession's backwash.[54]

Still, before the full force of the recession hit, Las Vegas continued to grow at a rapid pace. The boom of the 1990s and early 2000s had only encouraged major hotel operators such as Harrah's, MGM, Wynn Resorts, and Las Vegas Sands Corporation to emphasize high-end megaresorts, and LVCVA advertising was shaped to package that approach. In 2006 the

LVCVA spent $82 million on advertising, more than the combined amount for Hawaii, Florida, and New York. Slowly, the Strip, with its high-priced shows, gourmet restaurants, retail shopping, and suites, began to distance itself from the longtime marketing strategy of offering deluxe accommodations and entertainment at low prices. Wynn, the Venetian, and other Strip properties built during and after the late 1990s appealed to high-end visitors. As one observer noted, casino investors and executives assumed that "for every tourist priced out of the Strip, one or more new, higher-end visitors [would] come to replace them."[55]

The continued boom on the Strip only reinforced the growth of suburbs in all directions. Into the early 2000s Summerlin continued to be America's new home-sales leader, with other developments in the valley selling nicely as well. As noted earlier, having witnessed the transformation of Las Vegas's once desolate western suburbs with Summerlin and Henderson's escape from its unwanted factory-town status with Green Valley, North Las Vegas, with help from the Southern Nevada Public Lands Management Act, had been able to help developers assemble a large tract for its own upscale community far from the city's crime-ridden center. These lands attracted the interest of builders as the century drew to a close and infrastructural work began in earnest at Aliante in 1999–2000. In 2002 Del Webb began selling homes in Sun City Aliante, its third age-restricted community in the metropolitan area. Six years later it reached full build-out, with all of its homes sold. In 2003 Aliante, North Las Vegas's 1,905-acre master-planned community north of the 215 beltway, opened and immediately began selling homes built by D. R. Horton, Pulte, Pardee Homes, and KB Home. In 2004 the Aliante Golf Club and Nature Discovery Park opened, and the city announced plans to begin construction soon on two more. The debut of the Aliante Station resort in 2008 also boosted sales—until the recession dramatically slowed them. Nevertheless, city officials and builders expected that once recovery came, more than seventy-five hundred homes would ultimately fill Aliante by 2020, if not earlier.[56]

In the new century the metropolitan area's rapid development posed a major challenge for local governments. Unprecedented growth pushed the once little railroad town out to the valley's borders and beyond. As Las Vegas celebrated its centennial in 2005, economic analysts continued to see a bright future for its namesake metropolitan area. With a monthly average of 4,000 people moving to southern Nevada, planners were preparing for a metropolitan area that would eventually sprawl southward along both sides of Interstate 15 down to California and across the Colorado River into Arizona, thanks to the new 2010 Mike O'Callaghan–Pat Tillman Memorial Bridge. They also expected growth to extend westward over the mountains to Pahrump and northeastward along I-15 toward Mesquite, "as more local workers showed a willingness to drive farther to work so they can live in outlying areas where single-family homes are more affordable"—just as in Greater Los Angeles. By the fall of 2007 Clark County's population officially surpassed 2 million people. On July 1 the city of Las Vegas counted 603,093, Henderson 265,790, North Las Vegas 215,026, Mesquite 19,194, and Boulder City 16,206. The rest of the county's rural hamlets had slightly more than 10,000. But the largest place of all was the Strip city. Indeed, the unincorporated portions of the Las Vegas valley, which encompassed much of the Strip city, boasted more than 840,000 residents. These numbers, however, would drop by 2010, once the Great Recession forced thousands of construction and resort workers to leave the valley in search of jobs elsewhere.[57]

Of course, in 2007 the boom was still on, but the Las Vegas area's dramatic growth had its drawbacks. With all these people, building projects, and the appreciation of land values as well as property taxes, the cost of living continued to rise in a place where the low cost of living had always been a draw. In 2004 the Las Vegas area led the nation in housing-price increases with a jump of 32.4 percent over the previous year. With land prices soaring, new home front and backyards shrank to sizes that one would expect to see in Brooklyn and older urban areas that tended to build duplexes. Gone were the generous distances between homes. Soon, privacy took a backseat to the developer's need to conserve space and build vertically, as two- and even three-story homes replaced the single-story structures that once dominated the valley. In 2004 the cost of living in Las Vegas surpassed Reno, Phoenix, Salt Lake, and Denver, prompting conservative state senator Bob Beers to lament that the cost of living was "going up, and up, and up. If the government isn't doing something to drive it up, the economy is." But this was another consequence of frantic growth, and some business leaders worried that it might throttle the boom.[58]

As the growth process continued, opportunistic governments, such as Henderson's, acted to widen their tax base east of Interstate 15. In 2006 the BLM approved the city's proposal to annex thirty-five hundred acres from

St. Rose Highway southward to near Sloan—much to the chagrin of Clark County commissioners, who wanted the revenue that development would bring for their own treasury. Henderson officials salivated, because the BLM's action now positioned their town to become the gateway for Southern California motorists entering the valley on Interstate 15 as well as for airline passengers deplaning from the then projected new airport at Ivanpah. Henderson expected to complete the annexation process later in 2006, but had no schedule for asking the BLM to auction off the land for sale to developers. Analysts predicted the city would zone the area for master-planned communities and for resorts along Las Vegas Boulevard South. Because Henderson officials planned to extend sewers and other public works into the corridor from the municipality's main grid farther north, they expected to have little trouble convincing existing private landowners to join the city. While the BLM awarded Clark County an eight-hundred-foot-wide corridor (mostly from Las Vegas Boulevard to Interstate 15) to extend utilities down to the planned airport at Ivanpah, it was obvious that Henderson could easily realign Las Vegas Boulevard to host more gaming resorts and condo towers. The BLM's decision surprised Clark County commissioners, given the county's long track record of successfully developing Strip resort and suburban communities on former BLM lands. But Henderson leaders were delighted.

The city had battled the county commissioners before, back in the 1960s, when the latter tried to use its Clark County Sanitation District to lay large-diameter sewer mains down Sunset Road in an effort to outflank Henderson. In the 1970s and '80s this trunk line could have been used to connect with homes and businesses on Pecos and Warm Springs Roads, Green Valley Parkway, and other main drags, servicing the future Green Valley and keeping these communities along with their middle-class tax base safely in the county. But Henderson built its sewer mains quickly and fended off the Strip city. Thirty-five years later, in 2012, this time on lands east of Interstate 15, Henderson once again prevailed over the county commissioners. City councilwoman Amanda Cyphers described the BLM's action as "a way to continue to assure Henderson's future." She and her colleagues were "excited about making sure that if Henderson needs to grow in the future, that opportunity will be afforded to us." Blocked by the county to the north, Lake Mead on the east, and Boulder City in the southeast, Henderson finally secured a corridor through which it could continue to extend the city's tax base southward.[59]

Of course, not every municipality joined the expansion movement. Little Boulder City, with its longtime commitment to slow growth (approving about thirty new houses per year), acted to counter Henderson's imperialistic expansion southeastward. In December 2003 Boulder City's mayor and councilmen directed their staff to draw up a plan to annex eight square miles just west of the city before "developer-friendly" Henderson took it. As Boulder City mayor Bob Ferraro told reporters, "I think we have to be very, very concerned with the growth that is going on in the Las Vegas Valley. We need to do everything we can posthaste to take control" of Eldorado Canyon. In this case Boulder City succeeded in capturing its western flank, but developers were already drawing up plans for prospective communities that leapfrogged Boulder City and Hoover Dam onto the Arizona side of the Colorado River.[60]

In 2006 Clark County commissioners, faced with the prospects of developers planning to build large communities in the exurbs, forty to fifty miles away from Las Vegas, began to consider the formation of a "super regional task force" to guide the planning of infrastructure projects. This group would also try to guide developers regarding locations for their new communities. By 2006 the twin forces driving the appeal of exurban communities for home buyers were larger lots and lower prices than they could get in the Strip city and its suburbs. State legislators even suggested that the state help guide the task force. As Nevada Assembly majority leader Barbara Buckley noted, "I always thought it makes sense to coordinate before we find ourselves with huge communities that don't have roads to get into and water to service it." For these needs and for the services offered by doctors, dentists, teachers, and other needed professionals, "the satellite communities are going to be relying on metropolitan areas."[61]

Even new developments closer in sometimes began with just a narrow access road branching out from the metropolitan area. This was the case at Mountain's Edge, an ambitious master-planned project slated to host 14,500 homes at full build-out. When the development opened in 2004, Blue Diamond Road was mostly a two-lane highway with no paved connections to Rainbow Boulevard or other north-south thoroughfares in the western Las Vegas valley. Clark County commissioners had to work overtime to widen and light Blue Diamond from Mountain's Edge eastward all the way to Interstate 15 to accommodate the horde of new residents and commuters who invaded that new community after 2004. In this case the

Great Recession proved to be helpful, slowing the arrival of new home buyers dramatically after 2007 and giving county and state highway officials time to finish road improvements.[62]

Clearly, the 1980s and '90s marked a crucial turning point in the metropolitan area's development. Las Vegas met the challenge posed by Atlantic City and the national recession head-on by broadening its appeal, shedding its midcentury Sin City image, and becoming a true global destination. With the southward trend of new Strip megaresorts largely complete by 1999, Steve Wynn, Sheldon Adelson, and others planned ambitious new projects that seemed destined to shift the center of activity toward the center and north Strip. Even more important, the population surge and resort boom helped give Clark County a leading role in guiding the metropolitan area's overall development. The 215 Beltway, McCarran 2000, and other key projects enthroned the Strip city as the dynamic entity connecting all three cities in the valley and as the driving force behind metropolitan expansion.

The years between 1975 and 2007 represented an unprecedented period of growth. In all parts of the valley, subdivisions and master-planned communities filled the desert. While Las Vegas benefited greatly from the increased population and revenue generated by Summerlin, and Henderson expanded its borders farther west to accommodate Green Valley, Anthem, and other developments, and North Las Vegas looked confidently to Aliante for thousands of new affluent residents, the Strip city spread out even farther to the southern and western hills. The Mirage Revolution on the south Strip promised to inspire still more rounds of growth to its north. In 2006 only a few farsighted people saw the storm coming. It took about two years for it to fully hit, but the worst recession in Las Vegas's history would eventually take a toll on the Fontainebleau, the Las Vegas Plaza, the Sahara, Echelon Place, and a lot of other big projects and their companies. The boom of the 1990s and early 2000s set the valley, the state, and even the nation up for the inevitable fall when fortunes and dreams vanished almost overnight.

Truckee River flooding in downtown Reno looking east toward the Mapes Hotel, 1950. (Courtesy of Special Collections, University of Nevada–Reno Library)

Elegant Mapes Hotel on Virginia Street, ca. 1965. (Courtesy of Special Collections, University of Nevada–Reno Library)

Aerial view of downtown Reno looking northwest, 2003. The dome is part of the Silver Legacy Hotel and Casino. The building in the foreground, with a graduated roof line, is the National Bowling Museum. (Courtesy of University Archives, University of Nevada–Reno)

Aerial view of the former MGM Grand Hotel, Reno, at dusk, ca. 1980. Now the Grand Sierra Resort. (Courtesy of Special Collections, University of Nevada–Reno Library)

Aerial view of downtown Las Vegas in 1968 looking northwest toward the future site of Summerlin, with the northern end of the Union Pacific railroad yards just beyond the casinos. (Courtesy Special Collections, University Libraries, University of Nevada, Las Vegas)

Aria Resort and Casino at city center with monorail running in front, 2013. (Courtesy of the author)

Wynn Las Vegas, 2013. (Courtesy of the author)

The Palazzo, 2013. (Courtesy of the author)

The Fontainebleau and its half-built marquee, 2013. Construction was halted by the Great Recession. (Courtesy of the author)

Chapter Five

RENO AREA

Transition and Depression, 1990–2014

RENO WAS NOT IMMUNE from the crash either, but its slowdown had begun much earlier. The Reno-Sparks area entered the 1990s on a vastly different course than Las Vegas. Although tourism was still relatively strong, Reno was not riding the wave of prosperity that the Las Vegas valley enjoyed. The sense of optimism that buoyed city leaders and gaming executives in the 1960s, 1970s, and even the 1980s slowly gave way to concern. Indications that California might soon legalize Native American gaming, along with the continued presence of a managed-growth sentiment in the city, did little to raise gaming-industry hopes for the future.

Reno's increased reliance on the bus crowd from the Bay Area and the shift of high-end customers to places such as Las Vegas also worried promoters. An RSCVA visitor-profile study in 1985 found that gambling was still the "main reason" visitors came to Reno. In particular, bus travelers credited Reno for being less expensive than other destinations; 90 percent of them were repeat visitors and averaged five trips per year to the city. All of these figures were far less for air travelers, but the latter obviously were more affluent. Almost half of the bus travelers were retirees; many car drivers had managerial white-collar positions, and air travelers ranged up to the managerial and professional ranks. Yet the number of visitors to Reno arriving by jet did not markedly increase in the 1990s, and American Airlines' 1999 acquisition and shutdown (just seven months later) of Reno Air, a popular new carrier in the city, only worsened the situation.[1] While the buses continued to do a brisk business, Reno needed more affluent visitors and conventioneers. But ominously, in the late 1980s when the Reagan tax cuts were finally benefiting most American travel destinations, Reno's convention business was beginning to flatten out. In 1987 the area hosted 288 meetings, which drew 180,000 delegates, just 3,000 more than the previous year.²

While Las Vegas boomed in the 1990s, Reno struggled to increase gaming profits and its visitor count. In 1979 tourist-industry leaders and many gaming executives had been concerned about Reno voters' support for Barbara Bennett, the first mayor in recent memory with whom the big casino operators had little influence. Her opposition to most new hotel-casino projects and the expansion of existing ones did little to please tourist-industry boosters such as former chamber of commerce head Jud Allen. In 1983 Allen decided to run for mayor against Pete Sferrazza, who had pledged to continue Bennett's slow-growth policies. Allen steadfastly opposed this position and argued that a managed-growth agenda would discourage investors and limit Reno's access to capital. But, according to historian William Rowley, plans to build a large new resort near the convention center, a place that might spawn even more resorts, greatly hurt Allen's candidacy. In 1983 voters elected Sferrazza—then reelected him twice more. As a result, slow-growth advocates continued to influence Reno's development until Sferrazza left in 1995. This differed greatly from the trend in the Las Vegas area, where, as late as 1997, state senator Dina Titus's Portland-like effort to limit mushrooming growth by putting a so-called ring around the valley failed to win much support locally or in the state legislature. In the end, the measure died.³

Of course, Reno had its bright moments in the 1990s and early 2000s, as a number of important new properties opened. These included the Siena in 2011, the Ramada Reno Hotel Casino near the Reno Livestock Center, and smaller places near the airport and around town. One of the brightest moments was the opening of the Silver Legacy, the brainchild of Circus Circus CEO Clyde Turner and Reno attorney Don Carano, who owned the land upon which it was built. Plans for the project evolved somewhat in the early 1990s, but in the end the owners decided on a Victorian-themed resort that paid tribute to Nevada's mining days. To this end, developers built a 127-foot mining rig over the casino, topped by a twenty-one-story dome. The outside architecture resembled the resorts on the Strip. Instead of a long entryless wall such as the one at Circus Circus that did little to help the shops across Virginia Street, the Silver Legacy featured false-fronted shops and Gilded Age lampposts all along its frontage in an effort to replicate somewhat the streetscape and sidewalk scene of nineteenth-century Reno. Inside, the mining rig was in constant motion, much to the delight of visitors, and the hotel conveniently linked them directly with the Eldorado and Circus Circus via skywalks on either side. This awarded guests easy access to more than twenty dining spots and allowed them to stay inside, especially during the cold-weather months. Although the Silver Legacy proved to be a good job and revenue provider for the city, it did little to promote downtown revitalization. Not only was the complex north of the railroad tracks and far from the river, but, even more than for most casinos, its effect was to contain people inside and not encourage them to stroll around downtown.[4]

In contrast, the Atlantis grew up several miles from downtown. The resort evolved out of the old Golden Road Motor Inn and was developed gradually by the Farahi family, which over time constructed twelve- and eighteen-story hotel towers, among other improvements. The place changed names several times, becoming the Atlantis in 1996, after which the owners added a twenty-seven-story hotel tower and a grand-lobby atrium complete with glass elevators. The resort's glass-covered indoor pool, fountain-lined entrance, signature restaurants, and luxury spa only reinforced the Atlantis's growing reputation for excellence. But like the Peppermill, John Ascuaga's Nugget, and the Reno Hilton, it was isolated from the casino core downtown. As a result, it catered heavily to conventioneers.[5]

Taken together, the Silver Legacy, Atlantis, and the greatly expanded Peppermill (also near the convention center) strengthened Reno's position as a tourist city, but the overall trend was not good, thanks to growing competition in Las Vegas and other states. In the 1990s Reno's resort industry faced twin challenges: a slow but steady decline in the city's appeal to visitors and widespread slow-growth sentiment among residents, who did not want Reno to become another Las Vegas. Declining tourism, epitomized by downtown's growing number of vacant gaming properties, was the major problem promoters and resort executives faced. In an alarming chain of events, between 1995 and early 2001 eleven downtown gaming properties closed. This list included the Colonial Inn, the Holiday, the Comstock, Harolds Club, Horseshoe, Nevada Club, Riverboat, Speakeasy, the Virginian, and the Pioneer. Some underwent renovations; the Colonial Inn Hotel and Casino became an attractive timeshare; the Club Cal Neva reopened the Virginian for a while and renovated the Riverboat into a convention facility. However, the Cal Neva later bought the Nevadan/Onslow and remodeled its rooms to compete more favorably with Harrah's down the street before closing the Virginian for good. But other former clubs and hotels remained empty in the early 2000s, victims of Reno's cracked crystal ball.[6]

Even worse, some of Reno's biggest hotels eventually closed or were shaken to their foundations. Nothing more graphically illustrated the decline of Reno's once bright gaming-tourist industry than the fate of Hilton's properties in the city. In 1985 Kirk Kerkorian's Tracinda Corporation sold its MGM Grand hotels in Reno and Las Vegas to Chicago-based Bally Technologies, a manufacturer of gaming machines. In 1992 Hilton outbid Harveys to buy the Reno resort from Bally's; Hilton later purchased the Bally's resort in Las Vegas, too. In 1995–96 the company spent millions upgrading what became the Reno Hilton. At century's end Hilton spun off its gaming division into Park Place Entertainment, and in 2001 this company purchased Caesars Entertainment, Inc., which merged with Harrah's Entertainment in 2010 to become Caesars Entertainment Corporation. While the many gaming properties now controlled by the new corporation generally performed well, this was not the case in Reno. In many ways the Reno Hilton exemplified the city's and the company's growing problem. The resort had decent earnings until century's end. But revenue dropped precipitously, from $153 million in 2000–2001 to $142 million in the next fiscal year. The same was true of resorts across town. Circus Circus profits fell from $26 million in 2001 to $17.8 million the following year—far below the company's take from its Las Vegas resorts. Even the Eldorado Hotel, one of the "best-appointed" resorts downtown, had steadily lost customers after the airlines cut flights to Reno in half.[7]

What was the major cause for this cut in service? In 1998 California voters legalized Native American gaming. By 2002 tribal casinos began to make serious inroads on Reno's customer base, as many former Bay Area and Central Valley visitors stayed in California to gamble. The winter months were particularly bad for tourism, because Northern California motorists preferred traveling to the new 2003 Thunder Valley Casino Resort just east of Sacramento rather than taking the long drive on Interstate 80 across the snowy Sierra and down the treacherous Donner Summit to Reno—much less the trip back. By 2003 more than fifty Native American casinos operated in the Golden State; a decade later the number had risen to sixty-eight. By 2013 forty-eight more operated in the Pacific Northwest, and all of these steadily ate away at Reno's traditional market.[8]

Western tribal casinos' siphoning of visitors who formerly came to Reno by car and plane did little to help the Reno Hilton. Finally, in 2006, with Reno-area tourist spending in decline, Hilton decided to sell the hotel to the Minnesota-based Grand Sierra Resort Corporation, which bought it for $150 million—just a few million dollars more than it cost MGM to build the place. The property was renamed the Grand Sierra Resort, but its new corporate owner lacked the capital to make all of the expensive upgrades needed. The later recession not only made capital scarce but forced tourist revenues to drop too, and the Grand Sierra closed for a while. Eventually, the lender, J. P. Morgan Chase, took back the property from Grand Sierra Resorts and sold it in 2011 to the Meruelo Group for $42 million. The new owner reopened the place and pledged to make $25 million worth of renovations to restore some of the hotel's former grandeur.[9]

A similar fate befell Hilton's other big property in town, the Flamingo. The Del Webb Corporation had opened this property as the Sahara Reno in 1978, four years after Webb's death. As company executives gradually began to shift their firm's course away from resorts, they sold the property in 1981 to Hilton, which spent millions renovating what eventually became the Flamingo Hilton Hotel. In 2001 Hilton ceased licensing the Flamingo name, and the place simply became the Flamingo Reno. But Reno's sagging tourism and declining profits as well as the company's merger with Caesars World all hastened the Hilton's closure on October 23, 2001, an event that shocked residents and boosters alike. In 2003 new owners reopened the resort as the Golden Phoenix, but the hotel tower and big casino on North Sierra Street closed permanently in 2005, the victim of Native American gaming in California and downtown's declining tourist economy. The little casino (the onetime Primadonna) that had given the Flamingo an entrance on Virginia Street, next to Fitzgeralds and across from Harrah's, limped along until October 2006, when it also closed. Then in a dramatic turnaround, a developer came in, bought the hotel, stripped it down to its steel and concrete bones, and transformed it into the Montage condominiums. This represented a major step forward in the effort to shift downtown back to the residential-commercial center it once was and away from gaming and tourism. The Montage condos opened in April 2009. But all signs of the former Sahara/Flamingo, one of Reno's flagship hotels for more than a quarter century, were gone.[10]

The key to Reno gaming's problems lies in the statistics. A 1998 visitor-profile study found that the typical visitor to Reno was older and gambled also in Native American casinos, but would return to the city for more visits. The survey also found that 30 percent of this group also gambled in Las Vegas. In the 1990s, however, motels got a declining percentage of the tourists coming to Reno. By 1997 motels attracted only 3 percent of that figure, down from 9 percent in 1990. The main finding was that perhaps 50 percent of all Reno visitors came from California—clearly a prime market for the state's Native American casinos. The San Francisco Bay Area accounted for 20 percent of all visitors to Reno, and California's Central Valley represented 14 percent. But ominously in 1998, 70,000 fewer visitors came to Reno from the Bay Area than in the previous year. In addition, 170,000 fewer visitors traveled to Reno from the Pacific Northwest in 1998 than in 1997. Even the Bay Area's weekly "Fun Train" to Reno, a winter staple since 1963, seemed near its end by 2014. The two major reasons for this were competition from Las Vegas and the emergence of Native American casinos.[11]

The decline of Reno's gaming industry, especially since 2000, has been remarkable. If one adjusts for inflation, in the 1990s real gross income actually went up slightly, but from 2000 to 2010 it plummeted, thanks to the proliferation of Native American casinos. Casino employment is another index demonstrating northern Nevada's stagnant gaming economy. In 1990 the casinos had approximately 25,000 employees. By 1996, at the height of the dot-com boom, that figure reached almost 30,000. But in 2003 it fell to about 22,000. The Great Recession then dealt a mortal blow to Reno-area casino workers. In 2010 there were only 14,586 workers in the Reno-Sparks hotel-casino industry, a 50 percent drop from 1996. Room occupancy also reflected the downward trend. The Reno area's occupancy rate fell from 87.2 percent in 1990 to 79.8 percent in 2000 and to 69.6 percent in 2010.[12]

Neighboring Lake Tahoe also struggled. By 2010 real gaming revenue declined by almost 38 percent from its 1990 level and hotel-casino employment by almost 68 percent. These figures reflect an important fact for Renoites who think the Sierra and Truckee River can be used to attract tens of thousands of tourists to town. Natural beauty alone is not enough to bring the crowds that Tahoe casinos need to be highly profitable. True, there is more visitation in summer largely from Californians and others looking to escape the heat and daily grind of city living, but the number of vacationers is hardly overwhelming. The four or five large hotels and the line of motels and cabin courts rimming the south shore have been handling roughly the same number of tourists since the 1970s. The debut of the Red Hawk Native American casino at Shingle Springs near Placerville in late 2008 was largely responsible for the recent decline in Tahoe's gaming revenues. While the basin has a distinct winter advantage over Shingle Springs in the ski season, the skiers have never gambled enough for the casinos to even approach summer profits. Lacking a significant locals market, Lake Tahoe runs the risk, according to one study, of someday becoming a one-casino market. In contrast, the Reno area in the 1990s developed a strong locals market, which partially helped offset the declining tourist trade. Since 1990 the percentage of gaming revenues from locals increased from about 10 percent to 40 percent in 2010. But the Great Recession, especially the loss of casino and construction jobs, has cut into this market, too.[13]

Although Las Vegas has siphoned off potential Reno visitors since at least the 1960s, into 2012 the Reno area continued to battle twin tsunamis: the recession and the growth of Native American gaming in Northern California and the Pacific Northwest, traditionally northern Nevada's two strongest markets. Part of the problem has been the failure to attract more distant visitors. Through the years Reno has tended to be a "drive-to" market. Despite "adequate" jet service, the RSCVA's various marketing efforts have not been able to substantially increase demand from distant points in the past few decades. So the town continues to rely heavily on car and bus traffic. Though certainly welcome, bus visitors are not big spenders and tend to reinforce Reno's unwanted reputation as a "budget market" and not a "glamorous" destination like Las Vegas.[14]

Like Tahoe, Reno's tourism also tends to be seasonal. Although visitors certainly appreciate the town's natural beauty, the promotional events—Hot August Nights, the Reno Rodeo, the Reno Air Races, and major tournaments at the National Bowling Stadium—are what really fill the hotel rooms and casinos. In winter the Sierra may just as well be the Himalayas for Reno casinos looking to draw California gamblers on Interstate 80. With gambling spreading to virtually every state—even into Brooklyn and Queens, much less into the heart of the Bible Belt—distance has become a mortal enemy for casinos in Reno, Tahoe, Laughlin, and other points in the state. But even in the midst of recession Las Vegas continued to be a draw, thanks to the Strip city, whose lower but still substantial revenues helped get Las Vegas and the rest of the metropolitan area through the recession. Almost forty million people visited in 2011. Why? Because the Las Vegas area offers more attractions: shows, high-end retail, fine dining, more deluxe accommodations, and better year-round weather.

Despite their frustration with tribal gaming competition, Reno hotel executives have largely failed to develop popular attractions at their own resorts to divert potential visitors from their home states' tribal casinos—and have also failed to divert the homeless from the streets of Reno's tourist center. As one 2007 visitor to Reno in the summertime observed, "Lake Tahoe has a lot of glitz, some glamour, dining, exciting live music, great outdoor activities and a ton of gambling. Reno has ... well ... gambling." In contrast, "Dining options in Reno are relatively standard, ... night clubs are mostly non-existent and the physical vibes of the downtown area away from the Eldorado/Silver Legacy/Circus Circus corridor is quite seedy and a bit dangerous." He appreciated the revitalizing downtown area, but voiced a familiar refrain: "The riffraff is still there. If they want tourists, they gotta clean up the streets"—something Las Vegas and Clark County did years ago with strict enforcement of vagrancy and teen curfew ordinances. Local businessmen felt the same way. Indeed, Julian Mandelstam, manager of the Lerner's store downtown, complained to reporters that "something has to be done to stop the erosion of downtown. We need a plan." The chronic homeless problem in parts of downtown prompted UNR students in 2012 to produce a video highlighting the issue and the ongoing efforts of groups to provide relief to help solve the problem. On the other hand, there were people, including writers such as Tom Chiarella, who saw Reno as a real city and portrayed it as such in their publications.[15]

Sands Hotel owner Pete Cladianos was outspoken about Reno's failure to eliminate the homeless problem downtown. He traced its origins to the early 1970s, when the Gold Dust Hotel's owners donated some downtown land to the Catholic Church, which put a St. Vincent's Kitchen on the property. According to Cladianos, once the homeless population learned about the free meals it served, they funneled into the area. Panhandlers continue to accost tourists downtown to this day. Casino managers recognized the problem but could do little to end it. As Cladianos recalled, "We've done everything under the sun, and so have the Hilton and the Eldorado and Harrah's, the Cal Neva, and other places. All of us have tried in every way we could to get the [city] council to solve the problem, and the council has simply failed." Why? Because "they haven't had the guts." Because no part of Reno wanted a homeless shelter and because local voters would have punished any politician who tried to relocate one near their neighborhood, no city council action was ever taken. By default, the homeless remained in the city's casino core for decades, where they did little to help the city's struggling tourist economy. As Cladianos concluded, "It is a problem that has really hurt downtown Reno, and it is probably one of the reasons why the Peppermill and the Atlantis and maybe the Nugget [in Sparks] have done so well in locations away from downtown."[16]

Aside from his reference to the homeless problem, the California visitor's overall point was simple: "Rather than blame industrious tribal casinos who are offering great casino resort product, Reno's casinos should reassess their own offerings and provide a better product that northern Californians wouldn't think twice about passing up." This, however, became more difficult to do as the twenty-first century progressed, because, as gaming analyst Ken Evans explained, Reno's declining gaming profits have tended to dry up capital for existing and new resort projects. Investors, Evans explained, "are going to put [their capital] into the area where they would get the best return on investment." In a nation where casino construction is exploding, there are many cities today that would trump Reno's chances of getting the money. In short, it is going to be hard for any future Bill Harrahs to get the funds to build a major new resort or an Auto World–type theme park in Reno's metropolitan area—until the situation changes.[17]

All of these problems hurt the local economy in the 1990s and early 2000s. It also affected government revenues, because gaming and sales tax revenues accounted for nearly 70 percent of Reno's revenues and almost that much for Washoe County. Not only were there tax delinquencies and bankrupted businesses paying no revenues, but some of the largest resorts in the metropolitan area wanted their tax rates lowered. In 2003 auditors estimated that Washoe County would lose $1.5 million in property tax revenues, because the county assessor had to slash the value of ten operating casino hotels by a total of $117.8 million. The Reno area's economic downturn had begun in 2001 following the terrorist attacks of September 11. Whereas Las Vegas eventually won back its tourists and thrived for several more years thanks to a construction boom and bullish real estate market, Reno never fully recovered before the Great Recession started in 2007–8. The end of the so-called dot-com boom of the 1990s also damaged the city, because tourism fell off there and at Lake Tahoe, since Silicon Valley residents had less discretionary income to spend in northern Nevada casinos. These events affected everyone's balance sheet. So, it was hardly surprising when Reno's casino owners in 2002 complained that the Washoe County assessor, Robert McGowan, had not cut their property taxes enough. Circus Circus executives wanted him to trim another $12 million off their resort's assessed value, which he refused to do. But as Reno's economic slump continued to worsen, pressure on the assessor mounted. Even before hearings began for the 2003 tax year, McGowan had to reduce the Reno Hilton's assessed valuation by $55 million. He also had to lower the valuation of the Club Cal Neva, John Ascuaga's Nugget, the Sands Regency, the Sundowner, and other properties, which gave the county less money to spend on urban services. Reno's short-term prospects were not bright. Indeed, casino executives warned the assessor that the growth of Native American gaming in California would allow only a slight recovery in 2003. As the Eldorado Hotel's financial director glumly observed, "It's tougher than anyone who is not close to it can believe." And he was right.[18]

The demise of Reno Air, the sale of the Hilton properties, and the death of so many other hotels and casinos downtown only reinforced the Reno area's decline as a tourist destination. Even Harrah's, long a mainstay of downtown's casino core, faced problems. For example, when Harrah's purchased Harolds Club in 1999, it promised to build an exciting new attraction on the hallowed ground where Reno's most famous club once stood. But Reno's economic downturn in the new century delayed those plans. In 1999 Harrah's replaced Harolds Club with a nondescript plaza. Today, the former hub of Reno gaming sits meekly across the street from a group of shuttered casinos.

All of this carnage led many in the 1990s to wonder anew about what it would take to rejuvenate Reno as a vibrant tourist destination. There were no lack of suggestions. Some argued that Reno should follow Boise's example and reinvigorate downtown with a sports arena. Reno developer Larry Leasure, who helped construct the CenturyLinkArenaBoise, was impressed by its stimulus effect upon downtown business. Reno ultimately built a modern ballpark downtown for its minor league team, but this was largely a summer facility. Others argued that a downtown convention center was the answer. But, as John Stearns reported, many felt that two convention centers in a city the size of Reno was one too many. "The project," Stearns wrote, "was either a silver bullet or a potential wooden stake through the heart of public purse strings and community unity." Although residents were hardly pleased to see so many gaming properties close, many still opposed the expansion of downtown gaming. Even with more than twelve downtown casinos gone, Renoites were still divided about the future role of gaming and tourism—industries that had propelled their city upward in the twentieth century.[19]

Some in the Reno media wondered if the area's foundering tourist industry resulted from poor leadership. They were hardly encouraged by Steve Wynn's crack that "you need Bill Harrah to come back." John Stearns, a longtime reporter and observer of the tourist scene, complained that even though the Reno-Sparks Convention and Visitors Authority in 1998 hired Phil Keene, an experienced leader, to direct the organization, as yet there had been no major breakthroughs. This was the problem. As Stearns himself conceded, "Unfortunately, downtown's struggles have divided the town ... [and] division, parochialism and finger-pointing still prevail." What Reno needed, he felt, was the bold, innovative, aggressive leadership and the kind of public support that Las Vegans bestowed upon their resort sector. As one former casino executive told Stearns, "Everyone is still locked into their own narrow self interest." The different Reno groups were less strident in 1999 than they had been in the 1970s and '80s, but tensions could quickly rise again "at the first disruption" of the status quo. Almost everyone agreed the city could be a "base camp" for tourists visiting the majestic natural beauty nearby. But, as Stearns pointed out, the other half of Reno's lure would have to be "more conventions, bolstered with a better convention center," but this would only create more hotel-casinos and require some expensive bond issues, both of which many residents opposed. Stearns ended by insisting that Keene needed to hire a talented marketing director with a "firmly articulated plan to gain converts among the resident population."[20]

Keene, however, took control just as Native American gaming was moving toward approval in the California Legislature and the dot-com boom of the mid-1990s was ending. He certainly recognized, as Jud Allen had earlier, that Reno had been underperforming in its tourist and convention business for years. In 1999 Keene declared that Reno had "abdicated its rightful position as a legitimate western destination for too long," but, at the same time, he conceded that the RSCVA was "cash strapped." While Keene and others spoke about devising some western attraction to bring visitors in,

Reno largely ignored the 150th anniversary of the California Gold Rush in 1999 as well as the 150th anniversary of the Comstock Lode in 2009. However, municipal leaders and the Historic Reno Preservation Society in 2012 formally observed the 150th anniversary of the death of the city's namesake, Major General Jesse Lee Reno (née Reneau), at his statue in Powning Park. But the western history appeal was largely over. In the twentieth century building cowboy towns, scheduling trips to tribal villages, and staging scripted cattle drives had been tried in other western towns and were hardly the key to drawing millions of visitors in the new millennium.[21]

Keene and his marketing staff, like Stearns, recognized the lure of Reno's scenic setting. In 2003 the RSCVA regularly marketed the area by emphasizing its natural beauty and affordability. "Nestled at the base of the Sierra Nevada Mountains, Reno-Tahoe," the brochures proclaimed, "is a four-season destination." It was where "world class golf courses and magnificent alpine and Nordic ski resorts combine with an extra ordinary mix of history and culture, 24-hour gaming and entertainment." At the same time, it offered "world class accommodations and facilities at average costs 30 percent less than competing destinations."[22]

Keene did what he could to attract more visitors but whined about the obstacles in his way. The RSCVA needed to spend $105 million to add two hundred thousand square feet to the convention center, and downtown really needed a convention center but lacked the space for a building site. There was no economical way to cover the lanes of the National Bowling Stadium to create more exhibit space, so Keene had to rely on the Silver Legacy's new forty-thousand-square-foot exhibit hall, slated to open later in 1999, to fill the need. This was hardly the case in Las Vegas, where growth and good management had given the LVCVA enough funds to build the second-largest convention facility in the nation and a budget to promote it worldwide.[23]

At the very least, Keene felt that Reno needed to construct a dedicated transit system of buses to connect the airport, the Reno-Sparks Convention Center and adjacent hotels, the Reno Hilton, and Victorian Square in Sparks with Reno's casino core. Reno opened a downtown transportation center for buses in the 1990s, and the Regional Transportation Commission replaced it in 2010 with the new $13 million Fourth Street Station, just a few blocks from the baseball stadium the city was building off Evans Avenue for the Reno Aces Triple A team. The new RTC Centennial Plaza

Transit Center opened in Sparks in 2009. And although this made it easier for especially lower-income residents to travel around the metropolitan area (something that could have reduced car use and air pollution in the 1970s), it did nothing to attract tourists. Keene, however, was not really the answer to Reno's marketing problems, and he left after only two years on the job.[24]

Keene, much like other local promoters in the 1990s, sought a panacea to put the city back on track. Clearly, Reno needed special attractions, like most of the Las Vegas Strip resorts were creating, to draw customers. As UNR gaming analyst William Eadington noted, casinos no longer need be the main draw for many people to want to come to Reno. There could now be other attractions beyond gambling. Indeed, he observed that gambling in Reno and Tahoe was slowly losing its power to draw. Innovative planners proposed a variety of ideas for transforming the situation, including construction of a special events center, a sports arena, and an aquarium and even enclosing several blocks downtown to create a Disney-like family entertainment center with Hollywood special effects. But in the end, nothing of such a major scale was undertaken; no one came forward with the financing or the willingness to implement any of these ideas, and Reno was none the better for it.[25]

In his newspaper columns John Stearns kept emphasizing Reno's need to reinvigorate its marketing approach and strengthen its tourist market in the face of growing Native American competition. In a later column he paraphrased Jud Allen, who, after thirty years in Reno marketing and business leadership and several years on the city council, fervently argued, "We have to bring the area together.... It's all about broadening the kinds of visitors Reno should seek rather than fighting over the same video poker players." This represented a subtle shift from his position in the 1970s and 1980s. As Allen told Stearns, "The East is far more interested in the West than it is in the Eldorado Hotel." But, at the same time, he cautioned, "Selling the area means packaging attractions so potential visitors can visualize what they'll do, ... and how much fun they'll have." In still another column Stearns noted that the Venetian in Las Vegas, set to open in 1999, was devoting sixty-five thousand square feet to a high-end health spa with hydrotherapy and other amenities, much like the famed spa in Baden-Baden, West Germany. Stearns wondered aloud why Las Vegas's gaming community expected the spa to be a "big draw," while, at the same time, resort executives in Reno showed little interest in the idea. He implied that Reno suffered from a lack of leadership in the private sector. Stearns complained that Reno, with its alpine setting, possessed all the prerequisites to be a health mecca. "We have everything it takes right here: thermal mineral springs, mountains, forests, rivers, Lake Tahoe, favorable climate and so much more." But no innovative entrepreneur stepped up to exploit the opportunity, although the Atlantis in 2003 followed a growing trend in the resort business and constructed a luxury spa. In later years several other places also built spas of different sizes.[26]

As Stearns noted, strong leadership, innovative ideas, and investment were what the city and the resort sector needed in the 1990s. At this time Clark County commissioners were spending millions to dig up the Strip for the installation of large sewer lines in anticipation of the megaresorts then on the drawing boards. The City of Las Vegas also drafted ambitious plans for a stadium and other venues to draw tourists, using bond issues and redevelopment funds. In short, Las Vegas and the Strip city were acting, while officials and promoters in northern Nevada continued to debate the future of Reno's tourist sector and how best to enhance its future development.

Joining Stearns in this discussion was former chamber of commerce head Jud Allen, a city councilman by 1987, who insisted that Renoites, even if they preferred slow growth, should follow California's model and support tourism as the best way to boost the area's economy. He explained that places like Reno and San Francisco employed different ways of luring tourists and emphasized that with beautification of the Truckee River, downtown could do the same. Allen pointed out that while the contrast between Los Angeles and San Francisco is enormous, "each offers its own unique appeal." He insisted that Reno "should strive to capitalize on our differences [with] Las Vegas instead of being identified as a poor man's Las Vegas. Our goal should be to follow the goal of California." He stressed that the only factor standing in Reno's way was "us" and urged residents to overcome that obstacle "by each of us putting the community first." Underlying this statement was Allen's assumption that "downtown Reno is not only the heart of our economy, it also is the heart of Reno's future."[27] Unlike many American central cities where manufacturing or some other key industry that had originally spurred the central city's expansion left for the newer suburbs, unrestricted gaming in Reno had largely remained downtown.

There were a few casino resorts near the airport and the convention center and in Sparks, but most of these places were still in the city of Reno.

Although the importance of the river to downtown had been championed by numerous redevelopment groups and consultants in earlier decades, Allen's argument in 1990 was particularly forceful, because he was a city councilman as well as a longtime gaming promoter who was now embracing the river as part of the equation for downtown redevelopment *and* tourism. Allen emphasized the symbiotic relationship he saw between the river and downtown gaming and not between the river and Reno residents—as many growth critics did. He contended that "numerous studies over the years have identified it [the river] as Reno's greatest asset. Other communities with river development projects have discovered that water is a magical tourism tool." Although he did not specifically mention St. Louis and the Mississippi or San Antonio and the Riverwalk, Seattle and Puget Sound, Chicago and its lake, or San Francisco and its bay, they were surely on his mind, as were Miami Beach, Honolulu, Acapulco, Rio de Janeiro, and other resort cities with their seaside settings. Allen was a well-traveled promoter who understood tourism's profit potential, and these places definitely influenced his thinking. For him, beautification of the Truckee was the key to attracting more tourists to his city. With river beautification and more nearby walkways, shops, and restaurants, he predicted that downtown "Reno will be offering family fun and nighttime adult entertainment all within walking distance. Reno will, at last, have a permanent identity that is different from Las Vegas. And it [Reno] doesn't have to pursue runaway growth in order to enjoy economic vitality."

This had been the thinking underlying downtown redevelopment since the late 1960s, when Project RENOvation was proposed.[28] Barbara Bennett, the mayor who first pushed for legislation to create the Reno Redevelopment Agency, had been an advocate of river beautification and renovation of the neighborhood around the Truckee in the 1970s and '80s. Under her successor, Pete Sferrazza, the approach was more multifaceted but still oriented toward renewing the urban core. Whereas some of the agency's initiatives were centered in the neighborhoods like the University Gateway Project around UNR, most of the focus has been downtown. The 1991 Raymond I. Smith Truckee Riverwalk, the 1992 Wingfield Park Amphitheater, the 1995 National Bowling Stadium, the 1999 Century Riverside Theatre, the 2005 Reno Events Center, and the eighty-one-million-dollar Aces Ballpark in 2009 were just some of the initiatives undertaken. These projects, combined with more private ones such as the 2000 Riverside Artist Lofts (in the former Riverside Hotel), began the process of transforming downtown.[29]

Supplementing these facilities were a variety of other projects, reflecting the millions of dollars that the public and private sectors invested to create a downtown environment of apartments, nongaming businesses, and attractions serving the community rather than just tourists. The Nevada Discovery Museum, the Truckee River Whitewater Park, along with Wild Island in Sparks, that city's white-water park for kayaking and other water sports, attracted residents and guests. In addition to its other roles, the Truckee River's Wingfield Park area served as a community crossroads where residents and tourists could swim, inner-tube, and raft down the water in the summer months. The river and its park also hosted parts of the Artown Festival each year.

But Reno did even more to revitalize downtown. The city also helped fund the West Street Plaza, a market-area gathering place for food, shopping, and entertainment, along with an expanded Riverwalk for bicyclists and pedestrians, as well as other improvements to induce restaurants, shops, residences, and other businesses to move back to downtown. Future plans to convert the old 1934 post office into a historic mixed-use center for offices, bistros, and stores as well as new midsize hotels in various stages of development will only further benefit downtown. In 2004, after buying and renovating the building, Reno moved its city hall into the impressive sixteen-story high-rise on the corner of Virginia and First that served for years as the upstate regional headquarters of Wells Fargo and First Interstate Bank. So, even in the midst of recession, the city of Reno, like its counterpart in southern Nevada, continued to revitalize its core area to create an appealing street scene for visitors, residents, artists, bicyclists, students, and others.

The key to this process has been the city's ability to move away from expensive and controversial bond issues that require voter approval, which, in the 1970s, became a very unreliable source of support. Once the state legislature legalized tax-increment financing in the 1980s, most of the increase in property and sales taxes in the district resulting from the agency's improvements went to the city and then to the agency to help pay for the work. Only the additional money needed for an improvement project came from bonds and Reno's Community Development Department, which also applied for federal funding. So, in the 1980s, Reno, like Las Vegas, which also raised millions for redevelopment through the tax-increment mechanism, finally had a dependable source of income it could tap for downtown projects.

Reno, like Las Vegas, needed strong leadership at city hall to direct its redevelopment effort. Mayor Pete Sferrazza and his successor, Jeff Griffin, were capable leaders who helped push the effort. Then in 2002 Reno voters elected Bob Cashell, a longtime gaming executive and respected political leader, as mayor to guide the city into the new century. Cashell, who had previously served as a university regent and as lieutenant governor, faced many challenges, not the least of which was the long-festering issue of what to do about the railroad tracks downtown. This was perhaps the biggest challenge proponents of downtown revitalization faced. By the twenty-first century Reno was about the only city in America not to have either diverted or depressed its old railroad tracks downtown. This was just another obstacle to Reno improving its CBD and its image as a modern, progressive city.[30]

As the new century approached, Reno's political and business leaders realized they had to take action. In 1995 the Southern Pacific Railroad began the process of merging with the Union Pacific. Because the merger was expected to double or triple the number of freight trains moving through Reno in future years, the railroad, the federal government, Mayor Griffin, and the city council finally entered into serious negotiations to lower the tracks below street grade for approximately two miles through the downtown area. To accomplish this, the Reno Transportation Rail Access Corridor (ReTRAC) was established to facilitate the largest public works project in the city's history. Paying for it was another obstacle the city eventually overcame. Twenty years earlier voters had rejected bonds for the project, but in the end the city enacted a hotel/motel room tax to fund much of its portion.

Residents had an opportunity to block the project by electing anti-ReTRAC candidates to the mayoralty and city council seats in the 2002 municipal election. But voters chose Cashell and the two pro-ReTRAC city council candidates, and so the project proceeded. Construction immediately began in 2002 on the 54-foot-wide, 2.25-mile-long railroad trench 33 feet below street grade. By late 2005, with some work still ongoing, trains began moving through the trench. Though controversial, the project benefited downtown. Not only did the trench, once covered, create 120 new acres of land for development downtown, but it also substantially reduced traffic congestion and air pollution at numerous intersections. Still, the cost was high and burdensome for a city whose main industry has been suffering a recent decline. By the spring of 2012 the cost appeared to be even greater than originally thought at $282 million, plus untold millions more in interest still to be paid—a point not lost on ReTRAC's conservative opponents. They argued that bypassing downtown would have been cheaper, but complained that, once again, the municipality gave in to major hotel executives who wanted to give potential visitors AMTRAK access to their properties. In April 2012 the city sued Goldman Sachs, its bond underwriter, for misleading officials about the risk involved. The bank had advised Reno officials to issue auction-rate bonds whose interest rates soared when the Great Recession hit, forcing the city to refinance and pay millions in extra fees and interest payments. Despite all of the problems, Reno's ReTRAC project was an absolute necessity, although it probably should have been undertaken years earlier.[31]

While the centerpiece of downtown revitalization, ReTRAC was just part of the larger redevelopment process whose roots lie in the 1960s–'70s growth period. Historians of Reno note that despite widespread public support for implementing the key recommendations contained in the ten blue-ribbon panels' reports, many contemporaries believed these improvements would never happen because the big hotel-casino operators preferred the city's lackluster approach to downtown development, which saved them money.[32] For more than a decade few proposed improvements were actually undertaken. In 1975, a year after the reports appeared, ten members of the American Institute of Architects' Regional Urban Design Assistance Team had visited Reno and urged the city to begin planning immediately for future growth, citing the problems outlined by the blue-ribbon panels. The group met with local officials and recommended that Reno build a cultural arts complex and more housing for low-income as well as elderly residents and engage in more neighborhood preservation. The team also advocated "improving the street life of the central business district." Members heard from some Reno critics that the Project RENOvation Master Plan had been fully drawn up at great expense by 1969 but, as of 1975, was not yet implemented. As Alicia Barber has pointed out, Reno had a notorious reputation for funding all kinds of studies, plans, and proposals that never saw the light of day. So, this was yet another chapter in what proved to be a long story that stretched into the 1990s.[33]

One critic observed that downtown Reno presented "unique obstacles to redevelopment" that continued into the new century. These included "the enormous cost of downtown building and the fragmented ownership of many parcels of land, which makes it extremely difficult to put together a major development." In the mid-1970s Mayor Bogart had sought to convert Virginia Street into a mall, a tree-lined, pedestrian-oriented boulevard with perhaps a single lane of traffic, but despaired that he would ever get the money and support from enough voters and property owners to do it.[34] Into the twenty-first century Virginia Street, unlike Fremont Street in Las Vegas, was still a busy thoroughfare that tourists and vehicles had to navigate. Instead, many Renoites looked to the Raymond I. Smith Riverwalk to be downtown's pedestrian mall—*away from most of the casino traffic*. As one editorial noted, preserving and restoring "the mountain stream beauty" of the Truckee River were crucial to transforming downtown into "a place that local residents can enjoy." Here was the major conflict that would play out over the next four decades. Should Renoites continue the process of ceding downtown to gamblers and tourists and permitting resort executives to dominate city policy making? Or should residents take back downtown by using their redevelopment agency, as they had since 1983 and especially after 1990, to build a river walk and a white-water park and encourage art galleries, shops, and more nongaming businesses like river cities in other states?

One of the larger questions surrounding downtown revitalization and its antigaming dimension, as well as the slow-growth/managed-growth movement, is whether Renoites even agree about their city's identity. UNR cultural geographer Paul Starrs observed that downtown Reno, much like the Fremont Street area, is what urban studies specialists call an "epitome district," an area that epitomizes what the city is really all about—its historic identity. Just as the French Quarter in New Orleans and the Fisherman's Wharf and Embarcadero area of San Francisco epitomize their respective Mississippi fur-trading port and Gold Rush seaport identities, so too the casinos and railroads as well as the old jewelry and pawn shops, bars, and apartments of downtown Reno and Las Vegas epitomize the cultural landscape of those cities and should be preserved in any revitalization movement. In Reno, however, Starrs found that even as recently as 2002, numerous constituencies within the city still insisted on their own version of what downtown should look like and who should pay for it.[35] As noted earlier, in the late 1970s, '80s, and '90s, voters regularly elected slow-growth mayors citywide but at the ward level regularly chose city councilmen who often supported growth projects—much to the frustration of Barbara Bennett. Minds could be changed and there was a wide range of opinion regarding each new building project, but the progrowth coalition usually won out.

The same range of opinion also affected, and sometimes confused, the downtown revitalization process. As Starrs explained, "The whole tension ... is between these constituencies, each of which wants something slightly different and none of which has the least inkling of how to talk to the others." He noted that city councilmen and county commissioners are willing to fund revitalization projects that will please their constituents, but their constituents are a fragmented group. According to Starrs, the elected officials' view is: "We'll do this for our people," but the question is: "Who ... are *these* people?" For Starrs, this was the political dilemma that has slowed downtown revitalization for years. Today's riverfront area has been beautified, but even after millions of dollars in spending, many gaps remain in Reno's vernacular landscape. On the streets downtown, boarded-up buildings, empty parking lots, and blight juxtapose continuously with artist lofts, condos, casinos, and outdoor cafés to produce a "Renoscape" exhibiting a dizzying array of images that symbolize the city's built past as well as its present.[36]

At the same time all of these events and public debates were occurring, another old foe once again appeared and demanded a response. Floods have victimized Reno throughout its history. Major flooding downtown in 1950, 1952, and 1955 had forced the Army Corps of Engineers to construct three dams to protect the city, which seemed to be enough. Reno's situation differed from Las Vegas's, where the Colorado River was roughly twenty miles east of the city and several thousand feet below it in altitude. For Las Vegas, the danger was not the Colorado River but the mountains west of town, especially when it rained in the summer. Winter posed little threat because moisture fell as snow, and most of it stayed conveniently on Mount Charleston. It was the thunderous downpours of summer that forced residents to take action, as urbanization and suburbanization spread rapidly across the valley and its myriad washes in the later twentieth century. For a while, after the Army Corps built the three diversion dams, it seemed that Reno might be safe. But massive floods (on New Year's Day when the town was packed) in 1997 and again in 2005 did little to help tourism rebound and only exposed downtown's continued vulnerability. In January 1997 Truckee River waters closed Harrah's, the neighboring Hampton Inn, and other hotels and casinos as well as the airport. Incredibly, plans for a comprehensive flood-control system to protect the city were still in process in 2013, slowed by the usual divisions and by conflicts with the federal government over costs. Reno's flood problem is similar to neighboring Boise's, where 1997 storms almost filled that city's three reservoirs to the brim. By 2010 the City of Reno and the Army Corps were busily reviewing plans for building additional storage capacity upriver.[37]

While Renoites spent the better part of several decades deciding how to protect as well as transform downtown, an unplanned transformation occurred on the urban periphery. Over the past four decades, Reno's housing market has ebbed and flowed with the fortunes of its gaming and tourist industries. In the 1970s and early '80s, as more casino resorts opened and more workers and their families moved in, the local housing market began to boom, much like Las Vegas's. The Reno-Sparks built-up zone expanded steadily outward, and a small metropolitan area began taking shape. Although there were no densely master-planned communities yet, there were planned subdivisions. On the southern edge of town in the 1970s and '80s, construction of middle-income homes proceeded apace, especially in the Donner Springs area. More affordable housing, including new single- and multioccupancy dwellings, concentrated in south-central, east, and northeast Reno and Sparks.[38]

Into the 1990s before Native American casinos arrived in the Sacramento area, Reno-area gaming and tourism continued to grow, if no longer at the pace of earlier years. As a result, the suburbs continued their march inexorably outward even into the new century, thanks to the area's natural beauty, outdoor sports, and gaming. Suburban sprawl began to engulf southwest Reno all the way to the Carson Range. This was also true of southeast Reno, where the construction of the US 395 freeway shortened the commute to downtown, resulting in the subdivision of ranches and open country. In southeast Reno the development of Hidden Valley with homes and retail centers quickly transformed former scrubland around the Hidden Valley Regional Park into valuable real estate. In southwest Reno the appearance of the South Meadows development, containing Double Diamond and other popular communities, began to fill in that part of the Truckee

Meadows with homes and businesses. By 2000 southeast and southwest Reno claimed the highest median incomes in the metropolitan area along with northwest Reno, to which home builders flocked in the 1990s and 2000s to exploit its proximity to the Sierra and Interstate 80's easy access to downtown.[39]

In the 2000s Summerlin-style, densely master-planned communities also appeared on the scene. Damonte Ranch in southeast Reno near South Meadows was especially popular. Backed up against the Virginia Range, the 2,000-acre development featured 174 acres of wetlands and several miles of walking trails with scenic views of the mountains from virtually every vantage point. Although there was only one retail center in the community, residents knew there was plenty more shopping at neighboring South Meadows. Double Diamond Ranch, also on the southern edge of the metropolitan area, had four parks, two schools, and twenty-six miles of walking trails for its three-thousand-plus residents. Similarly, Cyan in South Meadows was another master-planned community with a 14-acre park trail system and community garden landscaping using native plants to reinforce the high-desert quality of life the developers promoted. Somersett in west Reno was a sprawling golf course community featuring homes by Legacy, Toll Brothers, Pulte, and other builders bordering tree-lined fairways and winding trails with full country club privileges and other amenities, as well as local shopping.[40]

In Sparks one longtime ranching family decided to subdivide 800 acres of its property and develop the "smart" community of Kiley Ranch. The project was in Sparks, where front and backyards tended to be smaller than in south or west Reno. The idea was to follow Portland's example, reduce downtown sprawl, and save $75 million in utility-line installations and other infrastructure costs. By 2007 550 home lots were laid out, and designers planned to have eleven million square feet of professional, retail, and living space once full build-out was reached a decade later. As one company promotion noted, the Kiley Ranch master plan called for "country lanes, walking trails, pocket parks and a wetlands preserve to counterbalance a strategic blend of big-name commercial venues and neighborly cafes and boutiques." Although some apartments were built and rented, Kiley Ranch soon became another casualty of the Great Recession.[41]

When local gaming began to tank in response to the arrival of California casinos and the national housing bubble began to burst at roughly the same time, Reno real estate followed suit. Construction virtually halted at all major developments, including prestigious Damonte Ranch. Pulte, which tried to construct a Del Webb–type Sun City community for retirees at Somersett in west Reno, eventually conceded defeat and opened the home sales to all ages. Then, in 2009, the developers of Kiley Ranch declared bankruptcy, and in 2010 their entire development, which contained little more than half-finished infrastructure and foundations, was sold at auction for $9.8 million to investors who were obviously prepared to wait for the next housing bubble. By 2010 foreclosures and short sales filled the metropolitan periphery where, just a few years earlier, prosperity and optimism had reigned supreme.[42]

The recession hit Reno especially hard. By July 2009 housing and real estate indicated the depth of the problem. Of four thousand actual listings of homes and sales, 59 percent were distressed properties. In commercial real estate, Reno's vacancy rate was 15 percent, and office space was even higher, at 22 percent. But the news was not all bad; the area became one of the more affordable housing markets in the nation, and its overall cost of living, a perennial advantage, remained low. So, with interest rates still low and the national economy improving, Reno looked forward to some recovery in 2012 and thereafter. But the Silver Legacy's declaration of bankruptcy in May 2012 (even though the resort remained open) hardly boosted hopes for a quick recovery.[43]

To combat the national recession and its own economic problems, Reno worked hard on two fronts: to improve its ability to accommodate larger conventions and to recruit new industries to its area. By the 1990s, as conventions became a larger part of the economies of Las Vegas, San Francisco, and other large cities, leaders in Reno's meeting industry realized they had to expand the amount of convention space in the metropolitan area and especially downtown if they were to remain competitive. Although the RSCVA's marketing effort accurately described Reno as a "second-tier destination" in terms of capacity, by 2009 Reno's hotel-casinos and the convention authority had spent millions to attract more and larger meetings. Many building projects were on the drawing board before the economic downturn, and falling labor costs after 2007 made it worthwhile to start construction then. In November 2008 the RSCVA completed the Atlantis Sky Bridge, connecting that resort with the newly enlarged Reno-Sparks Convention Center and its 565,000 square feet of meeting and exhibition space, its fifty-three meeting rooms, and its 35,000-square-foot ballroom. The Atlantis itself finished $70 million worth of expansion projects, while the nearby Peppermill spent $400 million building an all-suite tower, new restaurants, and other amenities.[44]

By the mid-2000s Reno's downtown convention space finally had enough capacity to attract large meetings. The Silver Legacy had the most, with 90,000 square feet, but Harrah's, Circus Circus, the Sands, the Eldorado, and the Siena together contributed another 168,500 square feet. At the same time, the Reno Livestock Center, besides its two outdoor arenas, provided another 20,000 square feet of exhibit space in addition to the Reno Event Center's 118,000 square feet, the Reno Ballroom's 32,000 square feet, and the National Bowling Stadium's 65,000 square feet, which could be modified to seat twenty-nine hundred. The Grand Sierra Resort and John Ascuaga's Nugget in Sparks added another 310,000 square feet to this total. So, by 2009, forty-five years after the Centennial Coliseum opened, downtown finally possessed the requisite amount of space needed for hosting larger conventions.[45]

But attracting larger conventions was just part of the solution. By the twenty-first century it was obvious that Reno, as well as Las Vegas, had to pursue economic diversification more aggressively. In casino cities such as Las Vegas, Reno, and Atlantic City, casino gambling had always tended to discourage other industries. True, Las Vegas had a chemical industry in Henderson, a vestige of its World War II–era magnesium plant. The city also claimed a few other prominent businesses such as Ocean Spray Cranberries, Ethel M (Mars) Chocolates, and Bally's Manufacturing. Reno had its wood products industry with a number of large and small companies as well as other relatively small industries. Both metro areas also had an abundance of warehousing, thanks to Nevada's 1949 Freeport Law and the presence of interstate highways, major railroad lines, and substantial airports. As noted earlier, in 1979 J. C. Penney's built a massive facility in Reno just to serve Northern California stores, and similar structures went up over time in the Las Vegas valley. But both metro areas needed more nongaming enterprises.

Clearly, Atlantic City helped legitimize gaming, which encouraged the construction of casinos across the country in the 1980s and afterward. This in turn eliminated a decades-old concern in corporate boardrooms about locating nongaming businesses in Las Vegas and Reno, where twenty-four-hour card games and liquor sales threatened employee attendance. Recruiting companies would be easier after 2000, but there was another problem. The two cities and the state, content for years with expanding revenues from casino gambling and gold mining, had never adequately funded business recruitment. As both Jud Allen and Reno mayor Bob Cashell have noted, casino companies had never been eager to fund development authorities to pursue the acquisition of other industries in northern Nevada. The serious effort to lure industry to Reno dates from the 1970s, when local business leaders helped create the Northern Nevada Development Authority. Later, the Economic Development Authority of Western Nevada joined with the Nevada Commission on Economic Development and the Cities of Reno, Sparks, and Fernley as well as UNR, along with seven western counties, to recruit jobs and companies to the region. This effort has become even more important in the twenty-first century with the decline of gaming tourism in the Reno area worsened by the Great Recession.[46] In Las Vegas and Reno the growing recognition that new companies and jobs broaden the tax base and enlarge revenues has won even wider acceptance among people who for years expected that gaming would always support the state and its cities. But by 2008 the long period of boom was finally over in Las Vegas, as the pundits began to realize that the Strip's effort to globalize its product and reach out to all classes and not just to growing lists of high rollers made the place more vulnerable to economic downturns in America and the world. Both Reno and Las Vegas built their major economies around American discretionary income and now faced the consequences stemming from reduced consumer demand for their product during the Great Recession.

The statewide debate over whether low taxes alone could draw more business to Nevada continued, as it has since the late 1930s when Governor Richard Kirman first championed the "One Sound State" approach that emphasized low taxes and reliance on divorce, tourism, and gaming as the keys to Nevada's prosperity. In 2011 new Nevada governor Brian Sandoval predictably cut funding for education and announced confidently that Nevada's tax-friendly business environment would draw more companies, but although there were some gains, no stampede from more heavily taxed California, Oregon, and Washington occurred. Moreover, budget cuts at UNR and UNLV threatened to make a bad situation only worse—as both campus presidents warned, along with such respected figures as longtime Reno Republican state senator Bill Raggio.

Both UNR and UNLV had substantially upgraded their research faculty since 1990, but state budget cuts (including salary and benefit reductions) at both schools over time exerted a depressing effect on talented young faculty who were mobile and able to move elsewhere, which a significant number ultimately did. Only time will tell if low taxes alone will attract industry or whether more funding for education is needed and how much. Still, there is hope for cities like Reno and Las Vegas that host numerous conventions, which expose thousands of businesspeople from other states to their cities. As America West Airlines vice president of public affairs C. A. Howlett explained about the company's experience in Arizona, "Historically, particularly when Phoenix was an emerging giant of a city, market studies showed [that] a significant percentage of people who located their businesses in the Phoenix area were first exposed [while] either being a conventioneer or a tourist," rather than through a local or state development agency.[47] Of course, Phoenix was a more attractive alternative than Reno for many businesses because of its milder climate, accessibility to markets, and lack of gaming.

Regarding the recruitment of new industry, the best model for Reno to emulate was not so much sprawling Phoenix but Boise to the north. Both Reno and Boise were smaller Intermountain West cities, whose early prosperity relied on the railroad, mining, and nearby agriculture. Like Reno, Boise lost jobs to the Great Recession, but, unlike Reno, Boise's prerecession economy was strong, diversified, and likely to recover more quickly from the downturn's effects. Prior to the recession Boise exemplified the kind of urban transformation Renoites dreamed about. In the 1970s, as MGM, Del Webb, Circus Circus, and other resort companies came to Reno, Hewlett-Packard and Micron were entering Boise, which for decades had been little more than a rail center for potatoes, fruit, and wood. But computers gave the city a new horizon. As one observer of the computer industry noted, "Reminiscent of a high-tech biblical lineage, HP began companies like Computrol, which begat Synpet, which begat Design Concepts International and so on." Some of these companies later boosted their profits by establishing joint research ventures with major companies such as Intel. There was no stopping the momentum. Graduates of Boise State and other nearby institutions often majored in computer science and formed their own companies. All the while, the city's critical mass of high-tech workers continued to grow in the 1970s, '80s, and '90s, which generated more companies, more products, and more profits. Over time, the "City of Trees'" reputation as a high-tech center spread. By the 1980s Boise had grown far beyond its traditional role as a potato- and fruit-shipping town. By 2008 Idaho hosted more than a thousand computer firms—not just manufacturing but research companies—and many of them were in the Boise area.[48]

Like Reno, Boise's natural beauty and access to rims and ridges, white-water rafting, and hiking trails was a major draw. But rather than using these attractions to lure millions of tourists and casino-resort employees, the city's proximity to nature drew thousands of highly educated, skilled, and well-paid workers who contributed substantially to the local tax base. As one former Texas-based executive, Faisal Shah, told a reporter, "I started technology companies [in Boise] because we had initially looked at Silicon Valley, but felt we had a large pool of developers and engineers that we could access here." Neither Reno nor Las Vegas appealed to him, because they lacked highly educated and skilled workforces. It was not low taxes or a low cost of living that attracted him. As Shah concluded, "What made the company successful was the talented pool of people we had access to. It's remarkable the number [of] engineers and computer scientists there are in Boise." And he added, "We have talented individuals coming into the market from Boise State all the time."[49]

MGM went to Reno in the mid-1970s because of the low cost of labor and the pool of qualified casino workers there. If Reno or Las Vegas had been able to diversify their economies and if Nevada had invested more in its two urban universities and in its K–12 school systems, maybe the history would have been different. But the Strip city, like Reno and Las Vegas, was built on casino gambling, an industry that eagerly hired high school graduates for many positions and required a substantial education only for its corporate managers. This was not the case in Austin, Silicon Valley, Seattle, and other high-tech centers like Boise. And while Boise, like Reno and Las Vegas, also suffered during the Great Recession with unemployment and thousands of home owners underwater with their mortgages, the city's growth was impressive up to that point. By 2008 1,335 high-tech firms employed more than thirty-four thousand skilled workers. Two years later, even in the midst of the recession, the Boise-Nampa metropolitan population topped six hundred thousand. Boise State University, whose 175-acre campus sits just a mile from downtown, kept pace with the city's economic development by substantially upgrading its science and engineering programs with new faculty, laboratories, equipment, and programs to attract major funding. All of this provided the school's undergraduates with experience and training that have empowered many of them to enter the area's high-tech workforce and contribute as productive employees and even founders of innovative new companies.[50]

In her oral history Mayor Bennett wondered aloud why Reno could not attract industries that would benefit from UNR's pool of talented research faculty. "Here we have a university town, and we really don't have any industry that could or was interested in taking advantage of it." In 1989 she also noted prophetically that if California ever adopted gaming, Sparks would suffer less than Reno, because Sparks "had some pretty good planning measures." And with all the warehousing "out at the end of the community," Sparks "was in a position that if no more hotel-casinos were built, their economy was pretty safe." At the same time, although Bennett saw Reno's gaming industry as essential to the continued employment of many residents, she also felt casino gaming hurt the city's economic diversification effort, but not for the usual reason: employers feared that the twenty-four-hour party environment that gaming created was a threat to worker discipline. No, it wasn't just that. She recalled that while she was mayor, UNR conducted a survey of firms asking them why they decided not to relocate to Reno. When asked why they would not move their business to the city, "one of the most persistent answers that we got was the power of the gaming community. Many people didn't feel that their businesses would be very important in a community like ours." Given the actions of past mayors and city councils since midcentury, their concern was well placed.[51]

But there was progress on the diversification front during the last years of Mayor Sferrazza's administration and especially in Jeff Griffin's. As the *Christian Science Monitor* reported in 2001, Mayor Griffin, recognizing that rents in Reno were one-tenth the cost of those in Silicon Valley, actively recruited business from the San Jose–Cupertino areas. By 2001 iGO and Sorb-Tech had already relocated to Reno, while Cisco Systems, Intuit, Lucent, Microsoft, and others had established some warehousing, assembly, and support operations in town. But Reno's computer industry had not taken off like Boise's in the 1970s and '80s.[52]

In 2012, however, a potential game-changing event occurred that might give Reno's nascent computer industry the momentum it needs. In that year Apple, Inc., proposed spending $1 billion in the area over the next decade. The outcome resulted from months of negotiations with officials at Apple, Unique Infrastructure Group, and government authorities. Apple announced it would build a data center in UIG's technology park east of Sparks to house its cloud computing service and also create a business and purchasing center in downtown Reno. For several years Apple maintained a small office in Reno to collect and invest the company's profits as a way of dodging California's 8.84 percent corporate income tax as well as taxes in about twenty other states. This Apple subsidiary operation had netted the Silver State relatively little in revenue. But analysts estimated that the new facilities would give the area 241 permanent jobs as well as 580 construction jobs and that the overall monetary infusion for the area would top $343 million. Of course, the pact included $89 million in city, county, and state tax abatements, which reduced Apple's net taxes by 79 percent, not a bad deal for the company. According to the plan, the company would still pay plenty of property and other taxes. Although storage data centers do not buy and sell goods and services like traditional businesses, they do purchase a lot of computer equipment because servers have a relatively short life span. Analysts estimated that the Apple facility would buy about $1 billion in computer equipment (which is taxable under the agreement) over the next decade. Aside from taxes, a major reason Apple went to Reno was because of its proximity to the firm's headquarters in Cupertino.[53] Whether other Silicon Valley companies will follow suit remains to be seen. But the area may be able to parlay Apple's move into something bigger, just as Hewlett-Packard's and Micron's move to Boise helped jump-start that city's computer industry. But only time will tell.

Still, Apple's expanding presence in Reno may lead America's "Biggest Little City" into a new era of development. As of 2013 the Reno area had established a good foundation for a computer industry, but it still lacked the volume of business and revenue that would significantly benefit it and the state. However, the Apple deal may finally provide the critical mass needed to make the industry a major contributor to the economy, as it has in Boise and other cities. The arrival of Native American casinos in Northern California may be the proverbial "blessing in disguise" for Reno, forcing local and state officials to undertake the effort necessary to secure new industries to invigorate the city's struggling economy. While the closing of so many hotels and old-time clubs was a body blow felt by all residents who love their city, the diminished role of gaming may now induce more mainstream companies like Apple to consider the Reno-Sparks area as a suitable location for their operations.

Further promoting this option may be Reno's success in reinventing itself and in converting its downtown, as much as possible, back to a typical American downtown with which most people can identify. This parallels the effort in downtown Las Vegas, not to marginalize gaming, but to use former railroad lands to utilize hundreds of new acres west of Fremont Street for specialized medical institutes, performing arts centers, and other businesses that may or may not complement the city's main industry. So, after more than a half century, both Reno and Las Vegas recognize they can no longer rely so heavily on gaming and tourism. For years they had trouble attracting other industries because of gambling's shady reputation and all-night cocktail atmosphere, but the nationalization of gaming in recent decades has largely eliminated that traditional concern. Today, the future is bright for Reno and Las Vegas *if* they can recruit the industries they seek to their metropolitan areas.

Chapter Six

LAS VEGAS

Depression and Some Recovery, 2007–2014

THE POPULAR VIEW had always been that Las Vegas was immune to recessions, and, to some extent, that was true in earlier decades when the town relied more on high rollers and upper- and middle-class vacationers and conventioneers. But the so-called Eisenhower Recession of the late 1950s, along with some overbuilding, helped close the Dunes Hotel and other properties. The town also slowed down in the early 1960s, the mid- to late 1970s, the early 1980s, parts of the 1990s, and for a while after the 9/11 terrorist attack. However, the Great Recession had the greatest impact of all, because the Las Vegas market had grown so large and no longer relied primarily on high rollers. By the early 2000s, the area had substantially widened its appeal to foreign tourists, low-income travelers (thanks to family-friendly Circus Circus and the Excalibur), and younger American adults. So, the slump in US and world discretionary income after 2006 hit the tourist business in Las Vegas, as it did in Reno, especially hard.

The so-called Great Recession's first local impacts were felt in 2006–7 and then gained momentum in 2008 and seriously affected business valley-wide. The number of visitors to southern Nevada dropped gradually in 2007 and continued to wane into the autumn of 2008 as the recession deepened. In October visitor volume plunged by 10.2 percent over the previous October, the worst nose-dive since the 14.1 percent number in September 2001. Gaming revenue also fell throughout the state compared to the previous October. Statewide revenues languished; October 2007's figure of $1.165 billion was only $909.9 million a year later. The Strip's gross take dipped from $639.8 million to $475 million, a decline of 25.7 percent. Downtown Las Vegas's figures went from $60.1 million in October 2007 to $48.3 million a year later. By comparison, Washoe County's revenues skidded only 9 percent, from $85.5 million to $78.1 million, but, because of Native American casino competition and other factors, its revenues were already low in 2007.[1]

Thanks to decreased visitor spending, corporate profits began to shrink along the Strip and downtown, which affected stock prices and the companies' ability to borrow and finance construction projects. In February 2009 gaming stocks plunged to levels not seen since the months following 9/11. Just between January and February 2009, MGM Mirage stock plummeted by 53.1 percent based on fears that City Center would not be finished, Las Vegas Sands stock declined by 48.2 percent, and even rock-solid Wynn Resorts, Ltd., saw a 34.5 percent drop.

Some of the Strip city's older hotels were in trouble, including the Las Vegas Hilton. Opened by Kirk Kerkorian as the International in 1969 and sold to Hilton in 1971, it was the company's first casino venture in Nevada. But its off-Strip location and age slowly reduced its visitor appeal and value. In 2004 the company sold the Las Vegas Hilton for $280 million to Colony Resorts, a private-equity firm that earlier had purchased Harveys Resorts and other hotels. In the deal Colony was allowed to retain the Hilton brand. But the recession of 2008 seriously destabilized the gaming industry and especially companies such as Colony that were carrying a lot of debt. In 2011 Hilton Worldwide informed Colony that it would pull its brand by early 2012, which it did, due to declining service and quality that fell below Hilton's standards for excellence. The hotel became the LVH in early 2012, but business continued to drop, as the loss of the Hilton brand, the aging resort's need of renovation, and competition from newer Strip resorts took their toll. In October 2012 the hotel was sold to Goldman Sachs and Gramercy Capital. Given the amount of capital it would take to restore the off-Strip resort to its former grandeur, its future remains uncertain.[2]

At the north end of the Strip, the venerable Sahara Hotel actually closed. No one expected any problems at the Sahara after Bill Bennett's widow, Lynn, died in 2006 and the place was sold. The resort was a prime candidate for remodeling and a general upgrade. In 2007 its new owners, SBE Entertainment and its San Francisco–based partner, had already invested $2 million to spruce up the property for customers. SBE also envisioned a major renovation of the historic Moroccan-themed resort. To that end, the company hired Marnell-Corrao, builders of Wynn, Bellagio, and other Strip resorts, as well as Bergman, Wall, and Associates, architects for the Mirage,

Paris, and other Strip icons, to begin planning a dynamic redesign. In February 2008 Clark County commissioners approved SBE's plans to build a new 520-foot tower with 1,000 rooms, as well as the renovation of two existing towers and the removal of the resort's original 200-room tower. Driving these plans were the $2.9 billion Fontainebleau down the street and plans by Crown, Ltd., of Australia and partners to build a $5 billion resort on the old site of Wet 'n Wild next door to the Sahara. But SBE based these actions on the assumption that the north Strip would continue to boom with Encore, the Fontainebleau, and all the other new resorts in the pipeline—until the recession suddenly cut off the flow of credit and much of the planned nearby construction. In late 2010 SBE canceled its plans for the Sahara's renovation and in May 2011 closed the resort, to the shock of residents and guests. In 2012, however, with the Strip in the midst of a recovery, SBE and a private-equity group announced plans to spend $300 million to downsize the old resort and replace it in 2014 with a luxurious boutique hotel, the SLS Las Vegas.[3]

Clearly, many business-savvy analysts and Strip CEOs were caught off guard by the recession's effects. In evaluating the problem Las Vegas faced at this time, former Harrah's CEO Phil Satre remarked that resort executives never appreciated "how much the town's appeal was based on discretionary income that people had developed through 401(k)s, appreciated home values, and easy access to financing." Former Boyd Group president Don Snyder also agreed that the continued growth of US discretionary income had been the key factor sustaining Las Vegas–area growth into the 2000s. As he explained, "Before the recession, each new building cycle in Las Vegas would create more demand." But the assumption in 2007 that "we can create a new demand and fill all the rooms no matter what happens" proved to be an illusion. Once declining real estate values and a slumping stock market began to influence the process, a lot of business decisions by even the shrewdest executives suddenly proved to be ill-conceived.[4]

Las Vegas's largest gaming companies struggled just to stay afloat during the storm. Leading the pack was MGM Mirage with its City Center project. Despite the guidance of experienced executives, Project City Center—although a great idea—almost blew up in the company's face. A greatly relieved Murren, even with Dubai money, had come perilously close to a Chapter 11 filing in late 2008 when credit markets dried up. Murren was the Wall Street financial genius who joined MGM in 1998 as its chief financial officer. A world traveler, Murren had visited Kuala Lumpur, Abu Dhabi, and many other places featuring striking modern architecture. Murren had longed to build an "urban gathering place" of stunning beauty—something more than another large hotel. By 2004, when he completed the process of raising the billions necessary to acquire the Mandalay Bay Resort Group, he already had the germ of his City Center idea: a mixed-use campus of buildings where people could live, work, and play. It took more time to convince the full MGM board about the plan's feasibility and chances for success. By 2006 construction began, but no one—not even the astute Murren—expected the world's economy to implode, sharply cut discretionary income, and imperil not only the project but the company too.[5]

By March 2009 MGM Mirage had used up its $4.5 billion line of credit trying to build City Center and was desperately seeking new investors—and finding few qualified takers. Eventually, the company secured funds from Dubai World. But by year's end even large Middle East concerns such as Dubai World were shaky due to oil's falling price on world markets. Adding to the problems of MGM Mirage CEO Jim Murren were the steadily rising costs for City Center's construction as well as news later that Perini Construction had allegedly bungled the steel buttress work on the Harmon Hotel—a charge that eventually sparked an orgy of litigation. By April 2009 MGM Mirage had cut the troubled hotel's height in half by slicing off two hundred condo units, but there were many other unresolved issues with the center's other buildings. For its part, Perini Construction officials countered that MGM was not paying all of its bills and sued the company for the money to reimburse contractors.[6]

Fortunately for MGM, this massive undertaking, like Encore, Palazzo, and Cosmopolitan, was far enough along and able to attract enough financing to be finished. The Las Vegas area badly needed these projects to demonstrate some continued momentum. Even in the midst of a severe recession, the Strip city remained the most vibrant part of the metropolitan area and a beacon of hope for the valley's economic recovery. New resorts always attract visitors. So, it was a highly significant event when, in December 2009, MGM Mirage opened the Aria, Vdara, and Mandarin Oriental hotels as well as the Crystals retail mall in City Center. It should be noted that former MGM CEO Terence Lanni, who had overseen MGM's acquisition of Mirage Resorts and later Mandalay Bay Resorts, before leaving the company in 2008, provided crucial support for the City Center complex that his successor, Jim Murren, helped conceive and finish.[7]

The recession plagued not only Strip resorts, but also properties on the metropolitan periphery. As thousands of suburban construction workers lost their well-paying jobs, they gambled less in neighborhood properties run by Coast Resorts, Station Casinos, and other firms. But even resorts that catered to the usually reliable golfer clientele struggled. In the go-go 1990s the next great resort spot in the Las Vegas area seemed to be Lake Las Vegas, on Henderson's extreme eastern edge. The Mediterranean-like community on the shores of a new artificial 320-acre lake, with three signature golf courses, palm tree–lined streets, and expensive homes set in beautiful desert foothills, seemed a sure thing.

Reinforcing Lake Las Vegas's appeal were two hotels. In 1999 the Hyatt Regency Lake Las Vegas opened, complete with three pools, a spacious beachfront on the lake, a casino, and upscale rooms in the Grand Hyatt tradition. Then in 2003 the Ritz Carlton, another elegant Mediterranean-themed resort, opened next to MonteLago Village and its casino. The development resembled a mini–Palm Springs community. With Celine Dion buying a $1.2 million villa at Lake Las Vegas in 2002, it seemed that nothing could stop the momentum. But Lake Las Vegas went into foreclosure in the fall of 2007 when developers defaulted on a major loan. The trouble was that the development was highly vulnerable to recession and the place was way out—nearly twenty miles from the airport and Strip hotels. Many of its home owners were second- and third-home buyers, who, once the Great recession hit, could not afford their home-owner-association fees and mortgage payments. Hotel guests and the golf crowd also cut back on their recreational spending and travel as the stock market and real estate investments collapsed.[8]

Lack of visitors and the decline of Las Vegas's meeting industry eventually closed the Hyatt Regency (which, in 2006, became the Lowes Lake Las Vegas) and put the Ritz Carlton out of business in 2009. The golf courses went bankrupt also, and by the fall of October 2011 the MonteLago Village was barely hanging on, although in 2011 the Ritz Carlton reopened as the Ravella, which helped breathe some new life into the place. A year later, in 2012, as the recession began to wane, Westin Hotels bought the old Hyatt from Lowes and reopened it. This acquisition by a national chain with a substantial reservation system increased room occupancy. Then in 2012 Kam Sang, a California company, bought the Ravella and in June 2012 rebranded it the Hilton Lake Las Vegas & Spa. Besides this, starting in

2012 Wall Street billionaire John Paulson through his firm began purchasing almost a thousand acres of Lake Las Vegas land. He then undertook various aesthetic improvements, including turning on the resort area's big mountain waterfall again. His apparent goal was to raise the area's land values again before selling his holdings to home builders. Despite these signs of recovery, however, two of Lake Las Vegas's three golf courses, including Jack Nicklaus's Reflection Bay course, remained closed into 2013. However, the decision in June 2013 to extend Sunset Road directly to Lake Las Vegas should greatly improve its accessibility and shorten visitors' commuting time from the airport. This improvement, along with the fall 2013 announcement that developers would use the so-called Green Grass Project to "restore the Reflection Bay and The Falls golf courses to their original lush appearance," can only stimulate business and land sales in the area.[9] Of course, the long-term viability of this plan will depend on the western drought not dropping the waters of Lake Mead below Basic Magnesium's 1940s supply line from which Lake Las Vegas draws its water.

New resorts on the town's periphery struggled to survive even as formerly "can't miss" projects on the Strip failed to open (the Fontainebleau) or even break ground (the Las Vegas Plaza). In the midst of Las Vegas's worst downturn since the 1930s, Anthony Marnell opened his $1 billion 390-room M Resort Spa Casino in March 2009 on the western outskirts of Henderson near Interstate 15. With its rooftop Veloce restaurant and the ground floor's appealing "in-laid wood and cantilevered glass" design, the M was an instant hit with locals in Henderson and the southern valley as well as with motorists approaching Las Vegas on Interstate 15. But the recession slackened demand and devoured Marnell's profits, forcing him out as principal owner in 2010. A year later, with Penn Gaming now in charge, the M chugged along, but Veloce closed its doors, a victim of the continuing recession.[10]

Henderson was particularly hard hit by the economic downturn. The area around the M illustrates the point. In early 2006 work began to prepare a site for Inspirada, west of the Henderson Executive Airport. This master-planned community epitomized the "New Urbanism" approach to home building that was becoming increasingly popular at the time. The community of 11,500 residences (at full build-out) on two thousand acres promised "dense, pedestrian-friendly neighborhoods interconnected with narrow streets, village squares, parks, and open space." But the project fell victim to the recession, and much of it was never built. In 2013 the nearby M Resort still sat in a sea of empty desert where the rest of Inspirada should have been.[11]

During the real estate boom in 2006 Gary Goett was developing many residential projects in the county west of Interstate 15 in Southern Highlands, his 7,000-home master-planned community south of the 215 beltway in the largely vacant southwest portion of the valley. Goett, along with an affiliate, Olympia Gaming, announced plans to build a 3,200-room resort hotel near the M, but the recession put a halt to Goett's dream, as his development, with its high-priced homes, soon became a major foreclosure zone.[12]

The carnage hit hotel workers as well as owners. As in the Reno area, the economic downturn of 2008–9 took a substantial toll on Culinary Union members. By December 2008 MGM Mirage had cut its full-time workers from 54,700 a year earlier to 46,000, while its part-time force rose from 12,700 to 15,000. Union workers also lost their full-time benefits at Harrah's Entertainment and at other companies, but MGM Mirage led the field. Pay cuts and layoffs, which occurred at virtually almost every casino property in the Las Vegas area, exerted a depressing effect upon workers and their families and upon the local economy that was already struggling with high vacancy rates and declining retail sales.[13]

Workers not only lost their jobs, benefits, and savings, but also saw their homes depreciate in value. Many in the tourist industry who bought new and larger homes in the flush times now struggled to make their mortgage payments, as property values plummeted. Since the 1990s the median price of new homes had always increased, which had only made real estate more alluring. In 1994 the median new home price in the Las Vegas valley was $129,000. By 2004 it ballooned to $232,270, a jump of 22.8 percent over the previous year. Analysts worried that rising interest rates could slow the market. Gone were the days when Las Vegas home prices sat well below the national average. Still, in 2004 analysts were not worried about sales tapering off in the face of high interest rates. Why? Because, except for Phoenix, none of America's housing markets had Las Vegas's job and business growth, wealth, or entertainment. Out-of-state buyers continued to represent more than 28 percent of new home buyers in the metro area. The thinking was that as long as Las Vegas's cost of living and taxes remained below California's, Golden State residents would continue to fuel southern Nevada's housing market.[14]

By 2007, however, the local media began to report an emerging foreclosure crisis. Analysts and local boosters initially blamed out-of-state speculators looking to flip their properties quickly rather than on local home buyers, since unemployment was still relatively low in the valley and median household income continued to rise. But by July 2007 the Las Vegas real estate market was in the doldrums — even before Wall Street's financial collapse began. Already, median home prices in Las Vegas had plunged by more than 20 percent from the previous year, and 26 percent of available inventory was listed as short sales. Stalled projects abounded all over town, including several large hotels and commercial developments such as the half-built Great Mall of Las Vegas near the Red Rock Resort, Vantage Lofts, Sullivan Square, Verge, Inspirada, and many other developments.[15] Worse still, soaring oil and gas prices raised jet fares to the point where they began to cut visitor volume and spending, whose ripple effect began to slow local business. By the summer of 2008 the office vacancy rate in the valley reached 16.1 percent, up from 11 percent a year earlier. The unemployment rate hit 13 percent in 2010, as Las Vegas led the nation in joblessness and foreclosures.[16]

The slowdown also halted the "condo craze" in the Strip vicinity. With Metropolis on Desert Inn Road near Paradise, the Panorama Towers on Dean Martin Drive south of Harmon Avenue, and the fourth and final Turnberry Tower behind the Riviera hotel all nearing completion and seventy other towers breaking ground soon or on the drawing boards, it appeared that the Manhattanization of the Strip area would continue unabated. But there were ominous signs it would not. By December 2005 several residential projects had been canceled for lack of demand, including Aqua Blue, Krystal Sands, and Ivana Las Vegas, the 923-foot luxury tower with interiors designed by Ivana Trump, slated for the northeast corner of Sahara Avenue and the Strip. Prior to the recession, rising land values in the Las Vegas valley had contributed to the soaring cost of new homes and, along with the growing cost of living, threatened to short-circuit the boom and reduce Las Vegas's century-old advantage of being more affordable than California or Arizona. By the spring of 2009, however, land values valley-wide had crashed, falling by 74 percent from their all-time high just a few years earlier. Specifically, the value of all land in the metropolitan area averaged $391,877 an acre at the end of 2008 compared to $1.5 million an acre just a year earlier — and this included higher-priced Strip property. Not surprisingly, the building industry took a major hit during the recession; only 39,000 construction workers remained in the spring of 2011 compared to

46,800 in January 2010—a 17 percent decline in just one year. Resort and gaming employees also left town by the thousands in search of work, and the recession even slowed the in-migration of retirees who lost millions in their 401(k) plans and other investments.[17]

As a result, population growth in Clark County dramatically slowed. From 2001 to 2007 the county's average annual growth rate was 3.9 percent, compared to just 2 percent in 2008. Las Vegas and Henderson also saw their growth rates fall in 2008 to just 1.5 percent for Henderson and .4 percent for the city of Las Vegas. North Las Vegas saw the most significant decline. From 2000 to 2007 the city gained 93,108 residents, an increase of 78.9 percent and an average yearly increase of 8.6 percent. In 2008 that figure sank to 2.9 percent—even with the opening of Aliante. But all was not bright for North Las Vegas; from the summer of 2011 into 2012 it teetered on the brink of bankruptcy, a victim of the recession and excessive municipal spending. Despite its expanded tax base, Henderson had to pull in. Aside from building a greatly expanded new city hall in the early 2000s when times were flush, Henderson had to postpone most of its plans for downtown revitalization.[18]

Even the Clark County School District saw the first prolonged downturn in its history. In 2009–10 CCSD enrollment dipped by 1,700 students. Since the school district's birth in 1956, with the exception of 1983–84, there had never been a drop in enrollment. In fact, during most of the mid- to late twentieth century the school district could barely build enough schools to meet demand. But the recession's impact on resorts and construction finally reversed the long growth trend. In 2011, partly because of falling enrollment and severe budget cuts, the district ended its year-round schools and eliminated many administrative and teaching positions.[19]

All of these events transpired because Las Vegas's core business, gaming-tourism, declined. Local resorts responded by lowering prices. By August 2009 Las Vegas was "on sale" and attracting thousands of middle- and lower-income visitors, who exploited the tough times by reserving rooms on the cheap at some of the Strip's most luxurious resorts. Steve Wynn, faced with only a 72 percent occupancy rate at Wynn and Encore, slashed room prices in 2009, as did Caesars, the Venetian, Bellagio, and other high-end hotels. As a result, tourism rebounded—if not profits. At least for a while Las Vegas resumed its old role as the place for a bargain vacation. Hotel owners had no choice because they needed the cash, having borrowed too much to build or expand their gaming properties in town and around the world—just as the economy was crashing. *Time* reported how the price cutting extended even to Las Vegas's condo market. As one column noted, condos at Newport Lofts that went for $600,000 in 2007 now sold for $179,000, as values declined everywhere. In just two years, Sheldon Adelson, one of the richest men in the world, lost more than $36 billion of his estimated $45 billion worth, although he made much of it back by 2012, largely thanks to his lucrative gaming palaces in Macau.[20]

Several projects begun before the economic downturn opened during the recession in an effort to make back the money spent on construction. Deutsche Bank, for instance, opened the Cosmopolitan of Las Vegas in December 2010 after pumping almost $3.9 billion into the resort it had acquired at a foreclosure sale. In a rare practice the bank actually built the place from the ground up—and did a good job. To be sure, the Cosmopolitan was a tribute to innovative design. The Vesper Bar and the Chandelier shopping mall and bar, with its curving staircase and outdoor Strip-view terrace of the Comme Ça French restaurant, wowed visitors and players alike. The hotel was certainly large enough and met the standard of elegance established by the Bellagio and City Center for the neighborhood. But the Cosmopolitan opened at the height of the recession and lacked the built-in customer base that MGM Mirage, Steve Wynn, and other operators possessed when they unveiled their new resorts. Not surprisingly, the "Cosmo" struggled in its first year, with management leaving an entire tower closed for lack of demand.[21]

City Center was more successful, but it too struggled. After a year of operation, CEO Jim Murren reviewed City Center's ups and downs for the local media. The good news was that the facility generated thousands of new customers and did not siphon off an inordinate number of gamblers from the company's other resorts. In addition, none of City Center's stores closed, despite the ongoing recession. Although Aria's 63 percent occupancy rate in the first quarter disappointed Murren, the hotel's 82 percent rate in the third quarter demonstrated the giant hotel's growing popularity. As for the bottom line, after $383 million in losses during the first two quarters, City Center's third-quarter profit of $413 million was gratifying. Still, there were problems. The Harmon's disastrous fate along with the filing of nearly $500 million in mechanic's liens against MGM Mirage by City Center's contractors and the ongoing litigation between Perini Construction and MGM were the leading issues. But the closing of Eva Longoria's nightclub and later her restaurant in Crystals, reduced hours and profits at various restaurants, and a substantial vacancy rate in City Center's condominiums were also disappointing. Nevertheless, City Center benefited from two notable trends. Despite the recession, in 2009 the Las Vegas area still attracted more than 36 million tourists who spent more than $20 billion. And while room rates did fall valley-wide, they stabilized more quickly at high-end resorts such as City Center than at the mid- to low-end properties.[22]

The year 2010 showed some improvement in the Las Vegas area's gaming economy, with revenues up 1 percent over 2009. And while filling hotel rooms in the slow midweek period was still a challenge for many properties, analysts believed Las Vegas's recovery was under way—albeit very slowly. After companies slashed costs and paid down debt, most were ready to roll up some badly needed, if relatively small, profits. But Southern California's double-digit unemployment rate in 2010–11 did little to help Las Vegas's plight. By 2010 only 36 percent of Las Vegas visitors lived in the Golden State (down from the 70 percent or more at midcentury); of this number, only half were from Southern California. But even as late as the fall of 2010, these visitors *spent and gambled* much less than in 2007, when 39.1 million people visited Las Vegas compared to 39.6 million six years later.[23]

Still, there were bright spots. Even in the midst of the recession, some building projects continued or were begun, because many believed that the downturn would end once discretionary income increased. When that happened, the town had to be ready. Most of these projects, public and private, were located in the Strip city. The Clark County commissioners once again led the way with a major project designed to prepare the metropolitan area for the next boom. Bob Broadbent's protégé and successor, Randall Walker, oversaw the latest phase of airport expansion. To accommodate the growing number of flights and visitors, the airport had undertaken its twenty-year plan, dubbed "McCarran 2000," in the late 1970s to create more gates, parking, and a greatly expanded Terminal 1. Then in 2006 Walker and the county commissioners hired the Bechtel Corporation to build the largest project in McCarran's history, the massive 2,300-foot Terminal 3. Despite misgivings expressed by Southwest and other airlines serving Las Vegas, Clark County commissioners moved ahead with plans to finish the D Gates and build a modern Terminal 3 to replace the aging Terminal 2, which had served foreign flights since 1991.[24]

After pointing out that construction costs usually fall during depressed times when unemployment grows and materials are cheap, Walker insisted that the airport had to keep pace with Las Vegas's recent and projected growth. He observed that since the airport last expanded in 2008, the metropolitan area had added 11,500 rooms and planned to build more. He emphasized that as the Las Vegas Convention and Visitors Authority and the Strip's high-end properties attracted more foreign visitors, it was necessary to build a new terminal complete with modern customs facilities to serve these international flights more quickly. In June 2002 foreign airlines flew more than 1.1 million passengers to Las Vegas, and by 2009 that figure had doubled. With the Asian market for gambling growing by the month, Walker argued that McCarran had to prepare for the day when more transpacific flights would be landing. Domestic flights had surged in number during the 1990s and early 2000s, thanks especially to America West, Southwest, and a growing number of new airlines serving smaller cities. By mid-2005 McCarran was the fifth-leading airport in the nation for departures to US destinations. To handle the growing traffic, McCarran in 2005 opened the northeast wing of its D Gates less than two weeks before the debut of the Wynn Las Vegas resort. All that remained was to finish the ten-gate northwest wing of the D Gates and construct the $2.4 billion Terminal 3 (which opened two years late in June 2012) to reach 120 gates and full build-out. With 42 percent of all visitors arriving by plane in 2012, there were also plans to build a second passenger airport near Ivanpah, near the California line, but the recession put them on hold. In the end, county planners decided that, whenever built, the Ivanpah facility would be better suited for cargo flights.[25]

The county's actions resembled the same kind of approach to expanding the Las Vegas Convention Center east of the Strip. It was the county commissioners, working with Las Vegas city officials on the Convention and Visitors Authority in the 1950s, that made sure the location of the Strip city's main convention facility was built on land near the great resorts and not on lots near Fremont Street. They also made sure the site was large enough to accommodate substantial expansions, a process that has continued unabated from the 1970s up to the present. In later years the LVCVA board membership changed, but county commissioners and Strip executives still enjoyed a major presence. In 2012 the Las Vegas Convention Center, with 3.2 million square feet, was the second largest in the United States after McCormick Place in Chicago. And the LVCVA has begun laying plans for even more expansion to maintain southern Nevada's major position in the nation's convention industry.

Building enough gates for the airlines and enlarging the convention center to handle more trade shows and delegates were just part of the problem the valley's government leaders faced. Expanding the water supply to accommodate the projected needs of future residents and visitors was an even bigger task. As the metropolitan population continued to soar, surpassing two million briefly in 2007, area leaders once again faced the challenge of securing more water. Worsening matters was the prolonged drought of the early 2000s, which reduced Lake Mead from 91 percent of capacity in 2000 to 54 percent by 2004. This prompted Southern Nevada Water Authority (SNWA) general manager Pat Mulroy to begin negotiations with the federal government and the other six states in the Colorado River Basin to get Las Vegas more water. The authority, created in 1991 by leaders in Boulder City, North Las Vegas, Henderson, and the Las Vegas Valley Water District (which included Clark County and the City of Las Vegas) to coordinate the distribution, acquisition, and conservation of water in the metropolitan area, had to be vigilant and active to ensure the continued growth of the metropolitan area. With agriculture taking most of the 7.5 million acre-feet of water compared to Las Vegas's meager 300,000 acre-feet, it was clear that there had to be more for the metropolis. As Mulroy correctly pointed out, if Las Vegas ever filed suit for more water in an emergency, the issue would fall to the courts to decide, and, she added, "A judge will not shut off a city, . . . [Indeed,] never has a judge or the federal government shut off a city."[26]

While Mulroy never specifically said it, she knew that no judge would shut off what Las Vegas had really become: a metropolis of nearly two million people, powered by the Strip city that showed every sign of continued growth once the recession subsided. It was the substantial growth of the Strip and the emerging city around it that got Las Vegas the Great Society funding it needed to build the Southern Nevada Water Project in the 1970s and '80s. Forty years later it was the Strip city's potential for future growth that cleared the way for another Mulroy initiative: the pipeline into eastern Nevada. By the twenty-first century the state greatly depended on a healthy and growing Strip to supply its revenue needs. The billions in revenue that the Strip resorts and the city around them contributed in the 1980s and

'90s had powered the state through this period of unprecedented growth, allowing it to fund K–12, its universities, and many services at levels it could never afford before. Despite a sentimental nod toward ranching and recognition of its value to any western state, no governor or state engineer was about to block Mulroy's project. She began the effort to get Carson City's approval for the controversial three-hundred-mile pipeline into eastern Nevada to tap groundwater supplies at the same time that her successful water conservation and rebate program was saving the authority millions of gallons in local consumption. But the pipeline approval process was bumpier than she and many business and political leaders expected. Despite her assurances that, because of legal and environmental constraints, "another Owens Valley" could never happen in this century, farmers and ranchers in eastern Nevada, as well as environmentalists, remained unconvinced and organized to block her effort.[27]

There was little the water authority could do but remain patient and determined. Its 1990s initiative to pay customers to switch from grass lawns to desert landscaping had greatly cut water use and served as a model for other metropolitan water districts, but Las Vegas's continued growth forced Mulroy to build the controversial pipeline. Short of Clark County adopting a controlled-growth policy, there was no other choice, since residents of Las Vegas, North Las Vegas, Henderson, and the county expressed little support for controlled growth. True, a 2004 survey found that 75 percent of Clark County residents who were polled felt that halting new construction would ease the metro area's water crisis. But no moratorium on building seemed likely. Why? As Las Vegas city councilman Michael Mack noted, residents would not want to deal with the economic fallout. Mack, who represented the booming northwest part of the city, told one reporter, "I grew up in Reno where they did have an anti-growth policy, and it stymied Reno." He went on to warn, "We can stymie growth here, and we can send the price of a home off the charts, and it won't be affordable to live here anymore."[28] Support for controlled growth in southern Nevada was mostly confined to Boulder City.

So, Mulroy pressed forward with construction plans even as the boom gave way to recession. In April 2007 Nevada state engineer Tracy Taylor approved a plan to let the SNWA pump forty thousand acre-feet of water per year from eastern Nevada rather than the ninety-one thousand acre-feet it had requested. He did allow some leeway—perhaps another twenty thousand acre-feet annually *if* there was no threat to local aquifers. Soon after, the SNWA began construction on its $2 billion three-hundred-mile pipeline with completion slated for 2015, but a judicial decision temporarily blocked the project, while BLM opposition and rising costs threatened to delay the work indefinitely. Of course, eastern Nevada farmers and ranchers continued their protests and lawsuits to stop the project, but Las Vegas leaders were determined. The conservative *Review-Journal* viewed the pipeline as crucial to the metropolitan area's continued expansion. In a strongly worded editorial, the newspaper supported the SNWA's efforts to safeguard Las Vegas's water supply by seeking water in the state's eastern counties, because securing enough water for Las Vegas was crucial to all of Nevada's economic recovery. After numerous delays, in early 2012 the state engineer and the courts finally cleared the way for construction, although future litigation could again halt work for a while.[29]

At the same time, the water authority also had to authorize construction of a new pipeline under Lake Mead to meet the potential threat posed by the lake's water levels dropping below those of the intake pipes. In 2011 the water authority, using a massive tunnel-boring machine, began excavating a twenty-three-foot-diameter tunnel three miles under Lake Mead to draw water from the lake. But the contractor hit a fault, and water flooded the tunnel just months into the project, forcing drillers to take a new route under the lake. Work on the new tunnel was also time-consuming and dangerous—there were fatalities—but the authority remained committed to completing this new, more reliable "straw." In all of these initiatives Mulroy retained the backing of the local business community, powerful gaming executives, and residents who recognized the value of a water supply large enough to serve current needs and future growth—once the recession ended.[30]

This same optimism pervaded segments of the nongaming business community. Despite the February 2010 auction sale of the District, Green Valley's signature tribute to the New Urbanism, the developers of Tivoli Village in Summerlin pressed boldly forward with their mixed-use project on Rampart Boulevard, across from the Suncoast resort. The first 225,000 square feet of commercial and restaurant space opened in 2011, with another phase, consisting of 300,000 square feet, scheduled to debut in 2012. The key was that the consortium of developers each had the cash in hand to fund construction—unlike their counterparts at the still unfinished Summerlin Centre, whose effort faltered once credit markets dried up. Located near the high-end Queensridge Place condominium towers and the elegant J. W. Marriott Las Vegas resort and surrounded by affluent new home communities and golf course, Tivoli Village seemed destined for a successful future. The Boca Park shopping center just south of Tivoli, with Fry's Electronics coming and other "big box" retailers already there, only reinforced the strategic importance of the Rampart Boulevard location so close to the US 95 freeway. Tivoli's developers were convinced their project would prosper once fully built out.[31]

This optimism was duplicated in the Strip city by a number of developments that may or may not pan out. "Trop 42," on forty-two acres just east of the MGM Grand, will have six high-rise condo towers encircling a resort, with a condo hotel, shops, and restaurants. "McCarran Village," a similar project on Tropicana Avenue with a lot of "residence over retail," high-rise condos and a thirty-story hotel amid plenty of restaurants, are among the mixed-use projects either in progress or on the drawing board in the Strip city. All of this, of course, depends upon a healthy rebound from the Great Recession.[32]

The same is true of residential real estate across the metro area. By 2012–13 there was some improvement in residential real estate. Although the Las Vegas valley remained the nation's foreclosure capital until 2012, new home sales picked up in the midst of the recession. This was especially true in master-planned communities, which still proved to be a most popular site for home sales. In 2010 Mountain's Edge, the thirty-five-hundred-acre development in the southwest valley, ranked fifth in the nation, and Providence, a twelve-hundred-acre community in the northwest valley, ranked seventh, with the Villages in central Florida being first.[33]

In the midst of the recession, work also continued on downtown revitalization, just as it did in Reno. As noted earlier this work had begun in 1986 and proceeded with notable successes and failures through the administrations of Ron Lurie and Jan Jones. Beginning in the spring of 1999, incoming mayor Oscar Goodman took up the effort and eventually raised it to new heights. For all mayors one of the key obstacles to developing land along any major downtown street was the need to assemble enough lots to create a spacious-enough site. This had been a problem in Reno, but the challenge faced along Fremont Street was especially complicated. By early 2004 a major obstacle to the redevelopment of property abutting this thoroughfare was the "parcelization" of land. Developers complained that the "leasehold tracts" rather than fee-simple landholding complicated the task of acquiring enough parcels to build new resorts. In 2004, for instance, the presence of so many owners with veto power over land use nearly held up the purchase of Benny Binion's Horseshoe casino by Harrah's and the MTR Gaming Group.[34]

But the real centerpiece of downtown redevelopment, the sixty-one acres of former train yards behind the Plaza Hotel, had only one owner, the railroad. In October 1988 the Union Pacific announced that it would move its yards out of the dense urban core, creating an opportunity for Las Vegas to develop the site. In October 2000 Goodman and the city council acquired the tract in a land swap with Lehman Brothers. A year later another stadium developer, Southwest Sports, pushed for a large events complex on the property financed with public revenues, but the city failed to reach an agreement with the company.

The municipality began to consider other options. In January 2003 it hired consultants to draft plans for an "urban village" of high-density residences above stores in a series of high-rises. Later that year the city council endorsed the plan and estimated it would take $23.1 million to clear the site and install infrastructure for streets and buildings. In April 2004 retired Boyd Gaming president Don Snyder volunteered to direct a multimillion-dollar capital campaign to raise funds for an elaborate performing arts center on part of the sixty-one-acre parcel. Several months later a consultant's report strengthened Snyder's appeal for donations by arguing that Las Vegas badly needed such a complex. In 2005, the same year that prominent architect Frank Gehry agreed to design the Cleveland Clinic's Lou Ruvo Alzheimer's Center nearby, Dan Van Epp, former president of Newland Communities, the city's master developer of what became Union (later Symphony) Park, consented to oversee the arts-center project. A year later architect David Schwarz agreed to design what became the Smith Center for the Performing Arts, a palatial, state-of-the-art venue that opened its doors to rave reviews in March 2012.[35]

The Smith Center joined a developing business neighborhood around Symphony Park. In the summer of 2005 Los Angeles businessmen Jack Kashani and Shawn Samson prepared to open the first phase of their World Market Center—a $2 billion furniture-expo facility on a fifty-seven-acre vacant tract bordering what soon became Symphony Park. Resort analysts expected that the city's first furniture show would bring the center eight hundred temporary and permanent exhibitors and seventy thousand attendees, who would account for at least four hundred thousand "room nights" at local hotels. The analysts were not disappointed. In July 2005 the first building of the World Market Center opened to a furniture show attracting fifty-three thousand buyers, a gathering that virtually filled the city and Strip's hotel rooms and restaurants, providing a real boost to the town's already booming economy. For a while it seemed that Las Vegas would replace San Francisco as the center of the West Coast's furniture-expo trade and even challenge High Point, North Carolina's longtime dominance of the national market. But the East Coast expo corporate rivals eventually united to end that threat—until May 2012, when Bain Capital with partners formed a large corporation that bought the World Market Center and most of the High Point facilities.[36]

Mayor Goodman's decision to use the city's redevelopment resources to locate a popular mall near Symphony Park was another master stroke that gave momentum to downtown revitalization efforts. At the August 2003 opening of the $95 million Las Vegas Premium Outlets, Goodman characterized the shopping mall's debut as "the spark that is going to reignite development in downtown Las Vegas." A month later Mark Fine, who helped develop both Green Valley and Summerlin, announced plans to build a mixed-use building near the new retail center. As he explained, "A lot of the migration out of downtown had to do with the fact that it was difficult to hire staff when they had options like being in planned office parks that had better options—like nearby restaurants and stores." But, as Fine concluded, "Now is the time to start looking back to the center of the community." The mall's developers had first proposed building their complex during Jan Jones's administration, but she reluctantly opposed their requests for city support. Why? Because, as she later recalled, "They were coming to us in the '90s for the outlet mall.... They wanted too much tax deferral. I wanted the money." But, as she later pointed out somewhat critically, "Oscar was willing to let it go."[37]

Goodman wanted development and did not let tax revenues stand in the way. By any standard, his record of promoting downtown revitalization was impressive. By late 2004 work on a range of important projects had begun. Phase 1 of the billion-dollar campus for the World Market Center was already under way, as was developer Irwin Molasky's $17 million

Internal Revenue Service building and the $75 million Molasky Corporate Center, housing the Southern Nevada Water Authority's headquarters. The mayor already envisioned a mixed-use, high-rise residential tower on the tract that the city had acquired from the Union Pacific Railroad. Several private developments supplemented these initiatives, including Sam Cherry's Soho Lofts and the Newport Lofts apartment buildings in the city's Arts District. The latter had begun to develop during the 1990s in an eighteen-block zone north of Charleston Boulevard. By 1998, when the city officially designated the Las Vegas Arts District, a growing number of galleries, artists' lofts, and off-beat restaurants, coffeehouses, and shops already catered to a sophisticated clientele. Beginning in 2002 they came by the hundreds each month for "First Friday" and faithfully attended other events as the district grew in popularity. In this regard, both Reno and Las Vegas moved in the same direction after 1990, trying to add a cultural dimension to their downtowns that casino cities had traditionally lacked.[38]

Mayor Goodman also encouraged developments in other parts of downtown. He regarded the twenty-one-story Streamline condo tower rising on the site of the old Golden Inn Motel on Las Vegas Boulevard as crucial to his goal of gentrifying parts of downtown to bring more suburbanites back to the city. Additionally, the L'Octaine Apartments on Gass Street, the Holsum Lofts for small businesses in the old bread factory on West Charleston, new county buildings on and near Grand Central Parkway, and other projects on the drawing board combined to spur much excitement about downtown's future in the years before the Great Recession slowed progress.

Just as Reno entered the new century determined to liberate downtown businesses and traffic from its street-grade train barrier by lowering its railroad tracks, so too Las Vegas had its own project. For more than a decade, the dream had been to remove the rail yards behind the Plaza Hotel and redevelop the property as part of a new downtown. After finally acquiring the land from Lehman Brothers, planning for the sixty-one-acre railroad site started in late 2002. Municipal officials spent seven months working out their blueprint behind closed doors. The city also took a while to identify a master developer before choosing Newlands Communities of San Diego. In 2006 Newlands announced it would seek four billion dollars from private lenders to help develop the project. The plan called for extending the Fremont Street Experience's electronic canopy around the north side of the Plaza Hotel to the site. Buildings would include residential towers as well as brownstone walk-ups in the classic style of Philadelphia and New York. A hotel and what became the Smith Center for the Performing Arts rounded out the blueprint. There were no plans for the so-called Oscardome football stadium that the mayor had been pursuing, because having such a venue, the developer warned, would probably lead to game-day gridlock on the nearby "Spaghetti Bowl." Four acres were reserved, however, for an arena to host an NHL or NBA team and other events. Dan Van Epp, president of Newland Communities, noted that his company's design targeted young adults who wanted "to be where the action is," as well as baby boomers seeking to leave the suburbs for a city lifestyle.[39]

Historic preservation and restoration of a few venerable old structures that constituted part of the public memory of longtime residents were also part of the city's downtown revitalization effort. In September 2008 the city reopened the newly renovated Fifth Street School as a cultural arts center. Built in the 1930s with New Deal money, the memorable landmark where so many Las Vegans attended school as youngsters now became the home for several nonprofit organizations, as well as UNLV's Fine Arts program and the city's Cultural Affairs Division. Even more noteworthy was the Neon Boneyard that began to look more like a museum, once enough donations poured in to transform Paul Williams's shell-shaped La Concha Motel Office on the Strip into a visitors' center downtown. The roots of the museum lay in the mid-1990s, when the first restored historic sign, the Hacienda Hotel's horse and rider, was lit at the old Neon Boneyard on the corner of Las Vegas Boulevard and Fremont Street. Over the years the hotels donated more of their iconic signs, and the nostalgic display, along with plans for "Fremont East," helped inspire the effort to create an Old Vegas atmosphere near the Fremont Street Experience. In 2012 the Neon Museum, with 450 pieces, comprising 150 signs that shined from the 1930s till century's end, finally opened just north of the casino core, across from the Reed Whipple Center in the city's "cultural corridor."[40]

The latter began to take shape as a planned artery in the 1990s, featuring the Mormon Fort, Museum of Natural History, Reed Whipple Center (serving also as home to Las Vegas's Shakespeare company), Lied Discovery Children's Museum (which moved next to the Smith Center in 2013), Las Vegas Library, and Neon Museum and other venues. This was in stark contrast to the Strip, which has imploded its built past with marked regularity. Whereas the city of Las Vegas has embraced its history, much like

Reno, the Strip city paid it little mind, except for an occasional reference to the Mob or deceased entertainers from a bygone era. But the Strip city's devotion to the present and to the next cutting-edge version of entertainment or pop culture or land development has proved to be a winning formula, too.

An additional example of the city embracing its past was the project spearheaded by Pat Mulroy and the Southern Nevada Water Authority she directed. In 2007 the SNWA opened the Las Vegas Springs Preserve on land where white explorers, including John C. Frémont on his 1844 mapping expedition, Native Americans, and travelers plying the Old Spanish, Arrowhead, and other trails camped in the nineteenth century. The complex, with its exhibits, natural habitats and wildlife, trails, desert botanical gardens, trackless train ride, archaeological and historical sites, and educational center, galleries, and amphitheater, drew thousands of schoolchildren each year as well as residents and visitors eager to learn more about Las Vegas's earliest years. Then in 2011 the opening of the new Nevada State Museum and Historical Society building on the grounds, with its archives and exhibits documenting Las Vegas's early and later history, only reinforced the Springs Preserve's importance as a cultural heritage center.[41]

But this was not the only salute to Las Vegas's past during the early 2000s. Some used the city's colorful past to fight urban blight. In February 2007 the Goodman administration broke ground on Fremont East, a retro district of four-story streetscapes designed to bridge the gap between the end of the Fremont Street Experience and the El Cortez Hotel. At the time the road between Fremont Street from Las Vegas Boulevard to Sixth Street was a dark thoroughfare filled mostly with boarded-up businesses. But city planners looked to create a bright center median adorned with colorfully lit icons depicting downtown in the midcentury era, with a showgirl, a tilted martini glass complete with swizzle stick, a glamorously lit high-heel shoe, and a glitzy Vegas sign—all of which offered beckoning images for camera-toting tourists. Local planners first looked at the Bourbon Street and Beale Street districts of New Orleans and Memphis before deciding to sink more than $1 million in redevelopment money into the $5.5 million project. Unfortunately, the recession took its toll. By 2009 the area boasted few of the original businesses. Even the farmer's market was down to only four vendors. But with Tony Hsieh and his company, Zappos.com, pushing the area's reinvigoration, by 2012 business was much improved at "Fremont East."[42]

Into 2012 work progressed in Symphony Park and on the so-called Mob Museum located on East Stewart, two blocks north of the Fremont Street Experience. The museum was the brainchild of Mayor Goodman. In 2000, after the federal government gave the old 1933 post office and courthouse building to the city for $1 on the condition that it be fully restored and used for cultural purposes, Goodman, a former Mob lawyer, soon realized the building could be converted into a museum depicting America's and Las Vegas's decades-old struggle between law enforcement and organized crime. After securing more than $50 million in private, federal, state, and local grants and with backing from the Federal Bureau of Investigation, the city opened the museum to large crowds in February 2012. But some of these venues, though popular, remained disconnected in a downtown whose revitalization process was only half completed. It was still quite a distance from the Smith Center to Glitter Gulch and even longer to Fremont East. Some of the streets were still relatively dark and even required strollers to pass through lonely underpasses.[43] The city took its time dealing with this issue, perhaps waiting for the brownstones to be built in Symphony Park.

While Symphony Park's performing arts center, the museums, and other downtown attractions, along with the Art District and condo complexes, all contributed to downtown revitalization, the infusion of new nongaming business was another crucial ingredient. For a while the prospects seemed bleak, as many business leaders continued to regard downtown Las Vegas as a place for court-related firms, some bank and insurance company headquarters, and gaming establishments. After all, the city for years had confined big hotel-casinos and clubs to the urban core with its red-line ordinance. And twenty-four-hour gaming palaces, with their honky-tonk atmosphere, did little to attract the companies, coffee shops, and watering holes that dotted most American downtowns. But Las Vegas's luck improved in 2010 when one key company began to consider moving downtown.

Both the City of Las Vegas and downtown businessmen lobbied Zappos .com CEO Tony Hsieh to move his firm's headquarters from Henderson to downtown Las Vegas. Hsieh had begun his online shoe store in San Francisco and moved to Henderson in 2004. The key person who convinced him to move downtown was Andrew Donner, CEO of the Resort Gaming Group. Donner raised the possibility of Las Vegas building a new city hall and allowing Zappos to locate its headquarters and one thousand employees in the old building. Over the course of several months Hsieh and the city came to an agreement. Donner's company would purchase the current city hall and its eighteen-acre site for $25 million, and Zappos would lease the property. The city agreed to vacate its facility by April 2012 and move into its new city hall, which it did. Over the next thirty years the deal called for Las Vegas to receive $97 million to offset much of the $147 million cost for constructing the new government center.[44]

Not only did Hsieh agree to move Zappos downtown, but he then tried to draw other out-of-state firms there, too. He developed a vehicle, the Las Vegas Downtown Project, for which he committed up to $350 million of his own capital in a concerted effort to transform downtown Las Vegas into something beyond a casino center. In 2013, for example, the project's Container Park for kids opened at Fremont and Seventh Streets. In early 2011 Hsieh told reporters that he was trying to convince some other San Francisco–based company leaders he knew to consider moving to a "high-tech incubator" that could be developed on acreage he was leasing. As Hsieh noted, "It's all about creating an environment [downtown] that appeals to the creative class and creating more serendipitous actions among employees and the community." It was therefore crucial to encourage Fremont East and places such as Vanguard, Griffin, the Beat coffee shop, and other nongaming venues where locals gathered. To this end, Hsieh and his little development company bought a 7-Eleven store plus other buildings in the area. Hsieh also established a $50 million fund to help small start-up companies if they agreed to locate their operations downtown. In 2012, for instance, Digital Royalty, a new marketing firm, moved downtown after the CEO and Hsieh met on Twitter to discuss the deal, and Hsieh concluded similar agreements with other companies in the months afterward.[45]

One of Hsieh's goals was to use the Downtown Project to help create a computer start-up-company environment east of the casino core that would attract creative people. One of the first to come was Michael Yoder, whose WinTech firm has developed ALICE, a virtual receptionist technology, which the company hopes to manufacture and ultimately market to businesses across the nation and the world. Nevertheless, in a 2013 Brookings study of tech-related jobs in America's one hundred largest metropolitan areas, Las Vegas ranked ninety-ninth, with only 12 percent of its workforce in that field. But there is much optimism about the metropolitan area's future because, as Tori Abajian, director of business services for IT Strategies, recently observed, Las Vegas's infrastructure "is excellent. We have data centers and connectivity to the Internet. We have good people in town that are very skilled." Abajian added, "We have the ability to fly in and out of nearly every place in the world. And there's no state income tax," as there is in California. Helping to push the momentum in downtown Las Vegas, out in the Strip city as well as in the Reno area are not just the local chambers of commerce and development authorities but also the Technology Business Alliance of Nevada, which recognizes that the best way to encourage tech-related businesses to move to the state is, as Hsieh has demonstrated with a number of small firms already, through concerted efforts by executives in Nevada's private sector rather than by an all-out government effort.[46]

Of course, the courting of software companies, the encouragement of Hsieh's development area, and building such attractions as the Mob Museum, Las Vegas Premium Outlets, and related projects all helped the city's revitalization effort, but Mayor Jones's idea for a stadium and major events center never really died. Mayors Jones and Goodman both knew what sporting events did, especially at night, for downtown business in St. Louis and Cleveland, and they wanted to bring these kinds of events to downtown Las Vegas to attract more visitors from the Strip as well as suburban residents. Although Goodman downsized Jones's stadium into a large arena, he never stopped pursuing the project. But he had competition. In the 2000s, even as Goodman courted NBA and NHL officials and owners in search of a franchise, Harrah's pursued its own plans to build a sports arena behind the former Imperial Palace on the Strip, but could not get its partial sales-tax funding plan approved by the 2011 state legislature.

Other arena projects also emerged. In 2011 Majestic Realty announced plans to partner with UNLV to build a sixty-thousand-seat stadium at the west end of the campus close to the Strip. The facility would host large convention-related events. But once the 2013 state legislative session began, MGM Resorts International, which was planning to build an arena of its own, announced its opposition to Majestic's plan. A few weeks later UNLV dropped Majestic as its development partner and began working more directly with the LVCVA and the Strip's large gaming companies to coordinate stadium construction with the meeting industry's needs.

The 2013 legislature authorized UNLV to establish a campus-improvement authority to begin the planning process. Such a mega-events center and stadium could potentially be a multimillion-dollar multiplier to the Las Vegas area's economy. It remains to be seen whether downtown Las Vegas will actually build its arena. Reno never did; both cities built baseball stadiums nearby for minor league teams, but neither appears to be on the verge of constructing a major league venue for any sport near its center.⁴⁷

Downtown revitalization certainly generated many good ideas that were eventually implemented—even during the recession. Nevertheless, the economic downturn took a toll on the city's urban renaissance effort, especially the residential side of it. By the early 2000s the construction of high-rise condominium projects had begun to change many residents' view of living in the urban core. No longer would they have to live in a cheap apartment or house built at midcentury. By 2007 Soho Lofts, the topped-off, Streamline tower, and the half-completed Juhl offered the kind of high-rise living one might expect in Manhattan or Miami. But the gentrification movement came to a screeching halt before it could threaten many of the lower-income, largely Latino residential districts nearby. The Streamline condo tower in the heart of downtown, which broke ground in 2004, had sold only 57 percent of its 256 units when it opened in May 2008. A weakening economy helped to hold down sales. Downtown resorts fared no better. In April 2008 one developer submitted plans for a sixty-one-story, 2,500-room Grand Central Hotel near Charleston Boulevard and Grand Central Parkway, but dried-up capital markets and declining demand for Las Vegas hotel rooms killed this project too.⁴⁸

As in Reno, the recession also hurt downtown gaming. But the decline of downtown gaming antedated the recession. From 1986 to 2006 the casino core added nearly 2,400 rooms, most of which were part of the Golden Nugget's 1986 expansion orchestrated by Steve Wynn. Although downtown casinos boasted a 5.7 percent increase in 1996 following the Fremont Street Experience's debut the previous December, every year thereafter gaming revenues either declined or remained flat. Still, there were some bright spots thanks to the Fremont Street Experience. In 2006 46 percent of the Las Vegas area's thirty-eight million visitors went downtown sometime during their stay.⁴⁹

Despite the allure of John Jerde's pulsating electronic canopy, gaming in downtown Las Vegas suffered a downturn in the early 2000s. In 1992 gross gaming revenue for casinos in and around Fremont Street was $703 million, 12 percent of total state revenues and 16.1 percent of Clark County gaming revenues. By 2009, however, the figures fell to $523.8 million (and 5 percent and 5.9 percent, respectively). The losses, tied to less visitor volume and growing Strip competition, contracted downtown's room inventory from 27,100 in 2004 to 23,700 by mid-2009. And while city officials talked about three new hotels opening downtown in the near future, stock analysts pointed to Moody's downgrading of Golden Nugget bonds to "extremely speculative" and predicted that investor capital would not be flowing into downtown properties as it had in earlier decades.[50]

To some extent, new ownership downtown fueled hopes that the casino core would once again thrive. In March 2004 the Barrick Gaming Group bought four of Jackie Gaughan's downtown properties—the Plaza Hotel, Las Vegas Club, Western Hotel, and Gold Spike—plus an option to buy his El Cortez. But Barrick never exercised that option. Despite promising to upgrade the four properties over time, the company soon sold them off. In June 2005, just fifteen months after purchasing Gaughan's four casinos for $82 million and proclaiming that it would re-create the old-time ambience of downtown, Barrick Gaming sold its interests to the Tamares Group, an international investment firm that was already serving as Barrick's silent partner at the properties. Barrick had planned to renovate the Plaza and add a 1,200-room tower for hotel guests and perhaps another tower for time-shares. It also announced plans to renovate the Las Vegas Club and retheme the Western Hotel for a Hispanic clientele. The good news was that Tamares closed the deal and then completely renovated the Plaza in 2010–11.[51]

As 2006 began a number of trends were evident. First, the Navegante Group, a company managed by veteran gaming executive Larry Woolf, prepared to take over Jackie Gaughan's former properties, because current owners Barrick Gaming and the Tamares Group remained locked in a legal struggle. Landry's Restaurants' 2005 takeover of the Golden Nugget and its $345 million in renovations helped boost downtown's gaming revenues in October 2005, which posted their first increase in seven months. At the same time, however, the announcement that the Lady Luck Hotel-Casino would close for a year or more for renovations was not welcomed news. But the arrival of Landry's at the Golden Nugget, the Siegel Group at the Gold Spike, the CIM Group at the Lady Luck, and other new-blood ownership gave downtown a spark of hope for the future. As Michael Crandall, the Siegel Group's director of business affairs noted, "It takes guys like us and some other guys downtown that really believe in it. Young, motivated guys that are going to roll up their sleeves and get in there and clean up not only our building but the neighborhood around our building."[52] Still, the boarded-up Lady Luck stood as a grim reminder of downtown gaming's decline amid the continuing drag exerted by the lingering national recession. However, reopening the completely renovated property as the Downtown Grand in the fall of 2013 restored hopes of seeing a gleaming new resort just across the street from the Mob Museum, finally connecting it with a bright path to the crowds on Fremont Street.

There were also other good news and other name changes. Following the death of Fitzgeralds' owner, Don Barden, the first African American to own a large Las Vegas casino, the owners of the historic Golden Gate Casino on Fremont Street bought the place. Derek Stevens, majority owner of the Golden Gate, announced that he would try to lay off none of the resort's employees. He also planned to renovate the casino floor and actually increase employment—yet another testimony to the business community's faith in the future of downtown gaming. Stevens not only kept his word, but in March 2012 announced that he would rename Fitzgeralds "the D Las Vegas," in honor of downtown's revitalization.[53]

Many hoped that Symphony Park and other Oscar Goodman–led projects opening soon would help downtown casinos escape the recession's worst effects. But downtown's gross gaming revenue fell by 33 percent in 2009 and 2010. Part of the reason was that when Strip-city resorts lowered their room rates, downtown was no longer the bargain it had been. Moreover, when the Golden Nugget opened a new five-hundred-room tower in November 2008, it drained customers out of other places. As a result, downtown gaming revenues in July 2009 were 19.2 percent below the figure posted for July 2008. Some optimists predicted that once the $100 million Lou Ruvo Center for Brain Health and $470 million Smith Center for the Performing Arts opened, they would help downtown. But that did not happen: the 2012 figure was still below prerecession gaming revenues. Critics complained that the Goodman administration was too focused on downtown and that the Mob Museum and city hall were a waste of taxpayer money. However, once these two facilities opened, along with the Smith Center, Goodman supporters pointed to the coup of luring Tony Hsieh downtown and cited his willingness to invest seed money to draw in more business. As Las Vegas mayor Carolyn Goodman correctly observed, you often "have to spend money to make money." Still, into 2013 critics wondered whether downtown land values would ever appreciate enough to help pay off some of the projects' deficits.[54]

Of course, downtown revitalization was just part of the equation in restoring the metropolitan area's economy. In the face of shrinking gaming profits and lost income, economic diversification once again became the subject of much debate, just as it had been periodically in the 1950s, '60s, and '70s when Phoenix, Tucson, Albuquerque, and many California cities were adding new industries to boost their economies. In 1957 Las Vegas banker E. Parry Thomas, Southwest Gas CEO William Laub, gaming executive Frank Scott, and others formed the Southern Nevada Industrial Foundation to promote the area as a low-tax, business-friendly option for companies looking to relocate or establish themselves. In the early 1970s the foundation morphed into the Nevada Development Authority, which, over the years, had attracted Ocean Spray Cranberries and a variety of other firms to the Las Vegas valley. However, with the exception of Citibank's credit-card processing center and a few other companies, most of these businesses were relatively small, and the tourist economy continued to be the mainstay of the metropolitan economy.

Still, the NDA had some success during the recession. In the late 2000s Las Vegas attracted a Foliot Furniture showroom and factory; the Hydro-o-Dynamic Corporation, which opened a plastic-molding injection facility in the county; and U.S. Micro Corporation, an Atlanta-based computer recycling firm that planned to build a two-story, 135,000-square-foot recycling plant, warehouse, and offices in the southwest valley. NDA president and CEO Somer Hollingsworth attributed these acquisitions to the proximity of McCarran Airport and southern Nevada's favorable "business climate," where taxes remained low. He explained that Las Vegas was still "in its infancy" in attracting manufacturers, as was the state. According to Hollingsworth, Nevada had a probusiness climate with relatively low property taxes, no income or corporate income taxes, and low unemployment insurance taxes.[55]

But not everyone agreed. One CNBC poll rated Nevada's business environment forty-fifth among the fifty states. It did not help that a "diverse mix of industry" was part of the criteria. CNBC also ranked Nevada forty-fourth in quality of life because of its crime rate and its lack of local attractions, health care, and other factors. Even worse, the network ranked the state last in education, a position that hardly improved with the budget cuts of 2007–12. As the network explained, "Not only do companies want to draw from an educated pool of workers, they want to offer their employees a great place to raise a family."[56]

Las Vegas may learn this lesson the hard way. Before its demise in 2001 Enron had constructed a huge fiber-optic network under the valley to connect with data carriers and major telecommunications networks. Switch, a new data-storage company, bought the network, and the firm's founder devised a unique cooling system to protect the firm's high-density servers from summer heat. By 2010 Switch and its three plants around the valley allowed major corporations to route data to any point in the United States and the world. Switch's system was unrivaled anywhere in the nation, and the company intended to stay, because Las Vegas was largely immune to tornadoes, hurricanes, volcanoes, major earthquakes, and other natural disasters that could disrupt the network. Already many major companies have opened offices in the metropolitan area to allow their technicians to be near Switch's data centers. Normally, Las Vegas would be in a great position to use Switch to entice these and other companies to move some of their larger operations to business-friendly southern Nevada. But one must wonder whether Nevada's notoriously weak and budget-cut school systems and casino gambling will discourage mass migrations of highly paid engineers and computer technicians to Las Vegas and whether Apple's data-storage center outside Reno will trigger the development of a dynamic new sector for information technology similar to Boise's.[57] Only time will tell. In the meantime, recognizing that Switch technology will promote the next generation of cloud computing and Internet development, UNLV soon negotiated an agreement with the firm to work together to create a cloud computing center that will train advanced graduate students in this area.

Education, however, was just one issue for those recruiting businesses to southern Nevada. As the Nevada Development Authority celebrated its fiftieth anniversary in 2007, Hollingsworth discussed the obstacles to attracting business to the Las Vegas valley in the twenty-first century. Some were already familiar. The higher price of land, housing, and the overall cost of living were issues that Las Vegas did not face in the previous century. Just from February 2006 to February 2007, land values rose 78.4 percent, raising the cost of an acre to $1.24 million—a far cry from the $10,000–$15,000 many such lands went for at midcentury. Land and high-priced homes, along with crowded freeways, soaring utility costs, and the presence of more than fifteen thousand other economic development agencies in the United States competing with the NDA for businesses greatly complicated Las Vegas's pursuit of economic diversification.[58]

To its credit, the NDA sought only those companies bringing in good-paying jobs that would contribute to the metropolitan area's overall wealth. By the 2000s, Hollingsworth noted, the NDA began to place more emphasis on high-tech companies, life science businesses, and alternative energy and green operations. With the skyrocketing cost of land, he explained that income taxes and other high levies in these and other states worked to Nevada's advantage, as did Las Vegas's proximity to California, where taxes and the cost of living and doing business were high. Nevertheless, like its counterparts in northern Nevada, the NDA suffered from the state's notoriously poor reputation for underfunding schools and its forty-ninth rank in per capita funding of higher education—a position weakened further by the dramatic spending cuts for the state's two research universities in 2011–12. As UNLV president Neal Smatresk consistently reminded business leaders, chamber of commerce officials, and community leaders, Nevada's universities were the key to conducting the research and workforce training needed by the modern industries Hollingsworth was pursuing.[59]

As the Las Vegas area continued to limp through the recession in 2011, critics questioned whether the Nevada Development Authority was pursuing the correct recruitment strategy. In 2010, when Hollingsworth outlined an advertising campaign to attract businesses from Southern California, Nevada Cancer Institute CEO John Ruckdeschel questioned whether the NDA's emphasis on low taxes would just draw businesses interested in paying low taxes and wages or whether it would lure significant companies that would truly enhance and diversify the metropolitan economy. In 2010 the NDA was a privately funded agency, operating with a meager budget of $2.2 million and a staff of eight, much like its counterpart in northern Nevada. Up to 2010 Nevada's Economic Development Commission, with a $6 million budget for the entire state, mostly offered companies tax credits to lure them in. In comparison, the LVCVA enjoyed a $90 million budget—plenty of money to market Las Vegas worldwide. Hollingsworth complained there was little money from Carson City to compete with states that offered cash incentives or to hire a resident promoter in California who could inform Golden State businesses of the advantages of Nevada's low-tax environment. To his credit, Governor Sandoval in 2011 supported legislation to create a new state economic development panel and give it $15 million to promote the state, but that money could be wasted if the recruitment effort is flawed. Luring companies to Nevada will not be easy. In the early twenty-first century the NDA enjoyed modest success in attracting business to the Las Vegas area. From 2000 to 2009 it played a role in helping to relocate or expand 526 mostly small companies, accounting for almost thirty-eight thousand new jobs. Many of these firms were in small manufacturing, warehouse distribution, and back-of the-office call centers, but no large companies moved a significant amount of their operations to the Las Vegas valley.[60]

Fortunately, the recession's destructive impact on Reno and Las Vegas brought some reform from Carson City and a glimmer of hope for promoters of a more diversified economy. State and local business leaders, including Governor Sandoval, who attended several conferences and spoke with other governors, began to consider what other states were doing. UNLV and some in the local media helped lead the way by raising questions and detailing some of the innovative ideas other states were implementing. As veteran Las Vegas reporter Dave Berns noted, Alabama, Georgia, and Tennessee spent millions of dollars at midcentury to pursue major companies in the Midwest and Northeast, offering grant money, low-interest loans, and forgiving property taxes. Ohio created a $150 million fund to invest in venture-capital firms that provided start-up funding for new companies settling in the Buckeye State. Finally recognizing that having the "friendliest low tax, limited business regulation climate in the nation" by itself might not be enough to compete with these states, Nevada lawmakers and the governor established a similar fund of $50 million in 2011 to be fully capitalized by 2016.[61]

Nevada had to take action because states farther west of Ohio and Tennessee posed a growing threat. Texas, another fiscally conservative state, also acted aggressively to recruit out-of-state businesses by awarding its counties the right to levy a quarter to half-cent sales tax to finance local economic development efforts. In Texas these local governments could also offer cash gifts and low-interest loans to attract businesses. At a meeting in 2012 Sandoval's Republican ally Governor Rick Perry helped drive home the seriousness of the Lone Star threat by telling his colleague that "he would like nothing better [than] for California firms to leap over Nevada and come to Texas." Perry further warned Sandoval, "If Nevada does nothing, Texas is going to kick your butt."[62]

Of course, in the twenty-first century one of the state's and Las Vegas's newer weapons in the diversification struggle was UNLV, which until the late 1980s had not been a real research university able to help its metropolitan economy much beyond training managers for the resort sector. This began to change with increased funding and support from Governors Richard Bryan, Bob Miller, and Kenny Guinn, but the recession's erosion of gaming and sales-tax revenues set a greatly improved UNLV and UNR back at least a decade. Republican governors James Gibbons and, early in his first term, Brian Sandoval both regarded higher education as an overbudgeted item in need of cuts. But reduced state support for UNR and UNLV did little to help the economic recovery of the state's two metropolitan areas.

UNLV's potential for helping Las Vegas's economic recovery became more apparent in August 2009 when Kirk Kerkorian's Lincy Foundation gave the school a $14 million gift to establish the Lincy Institute on campus to seek government grants and provide additional support for southern Nevada health care, social services, and education. This came after four months of negotiations between the foundation board and then-provost Smatresk and vice president for university advancement William Boldt, with help from Nevada's Lincy board member Lindy Schumacher. Two weeks later, thanks again to the efforts of Smatresk, Boldt, *Las Vegas Sun* publisher Brian Greenspun, and Harry Reid, the prestigious Brookings Institution announced its intention of partnering with UNLV through an "initiative" to create Brookings Mountain West and basing it at UNLV.[63]

This was a major acquisition for UNLV and Las Vegas, but it did not happen overnight. In the fall of 2008 UNLV held a series of meetings as part of its effort to promote urban sustainability. One of these conferences, the Brookings Institution Roundtable, brought many of the think tank's leaders to campus. Greenspun, a Brookings board of trustees member, helped make it happen. The conference allowed Smatresk and others to become acquainted with William Antholis, the managing director of Brookings and a senior fellow in governance studies. The conversations continued over ensuing months, and in September 2009 Brookings announced it would establish a western arm and base it at UNLV. Now-president Smatresk then secured Lincy funding to establish Brookings Institution's Mountain West Initiative on campus in September 2009.[64]

The goal was to provide a venue for leading scholars in growth, energy, and other subjects crucial to western development, where, in rotating residencies, they could teach, conduct research, and interact with UNLV faculty and others concerning issues vital to state, metropolitan, and regional growth. Both developments were intertwined, because in 2011 the Lincy Foundation became the Dream Fund (based at the University of California, Los Angeles), which helped support UNLV's Lincy Institute and partially support the Mountain West Initiative. Clearly, these were significant events that helped state and community leaders to appreciate the key role a research university could play in boosting the local and state economies.[65]

All of this came on the heels of a state legislative session during which lawmakers openly expressed concern about lost revenues resulting from the Great Recession and responded by approving major cuts in education. In response, President Smatresk warned state and local leaders about the consequences of such a policy, as did his UNR counterpart, Milton Glick. In January 2011, on the eve of a new legislative session almost certain to approve huge cuts in higher education, Smatresk wrote a column in the conservative *Las Vegas Review-Journal* citing the reasons for supporting higher education. After noting the all-to-familiar low ranking of Nevada in virtually every list relating to education and health care, he went on to argue that more cuts would only worsen the state's economy. Pointing out that Nevada already ranked forty-sixth among the states in college degrees per capita, Smatresk emphasized how the neighboring states of California, Utah, and Arizona far exceeded the Silver State in residents with degrees. He noted that in the Las Vegas metro area, only 20 percent of the adult population had earned a college degree. Smatresk also referred to statistics showing that cities with more educated workforces had more diversified economies than Las Vegas and were pulling out of the recession faster.[66]

To strengthen the link between local business groups and UNLV, Smatresk spoke to a meeting of the Las Vegas Metro Chamber of Commerce about the role a research university could play in diversifying and enhancing the metropolitan economy. He also became a member of the chamber's board of trustees as well as a member of the Nevada Development Authority's executive committee to better connect the university to the business community. Smatresk and UNLV took the lead following the unexpected death in April 2011 of President Glick, who saw his research university playing a vital role in diversifying the Reno area's economy.[67]

In early 2011 a few voices in the wilderness called for a change in Nevada's approach. Smatresk, Robert Lang (a noted urban sociologist and director of the Mountain West Initiative), and a few others in southern and northern Nevada pushed the idea that improving education and utilizing UNR's and UNLV's infrastructure and research faculty in a more dynamic way were key to diversifying the state's two foundering metropolitan economies. Smatresk emphasized that as the state with the highest unemployment rate in 2010, Nevada had to reconsider its traditional approach to education and invest more in its two research universities. He also pointed out that Colorado and Utah already had made strategic investments in theirs "to attract high-tech industries" and develop "strong public/private partnerships" to produce more advanced degrees, which helped both states lure new businesses and jobs to their cities. Smatresk observed that Utah's investments in higher education had already brought "R&D leadership and research teams" to Salt Lake City. In 2010 the University of Utah produced more patents than the Massachusetts Institute of Technology, and Salt Lake's "booming high-tech business base" generated more than ten billion dollars for the city's export economy. How did this happen? Smatresk explained that since 2006, Utah had invested eighty million dollars in the Utah Science and Technology Research Initiative, a five-year public-private partnership program to develop "technology-based start-ups," which resulted in many new patents, jobs, and an expanded economy.[68]

Other voices reinforced the idea that action needed to be taken to address Nevada's weaknesses. Mark Munro and Robert Lang from the Brookings Institution's Mountain West Initiative used their expertise to deliver an insightful "State of the City" address at UNLV. Not surprisingly, they emphasized the area's overreliance on gaming and construction and decried the lack of "research and development or innovative growth industries" in the valley compared to places such as San Jose and Salt Lake City. The reason for this was clear: Nevada's "mediocre schools, universities, health care and cultural facilities" drew few leaders and entrepreneurs from "knowledge industries." To help combat this trend, in September 2013 President Smatresk announced plans for a decadelong effort to transform UNLV's Carnegie Foundation designation to Tier One "Research University/ Very High," a ranking held by only 108 US universities in that year.[69] In 2014, following Smatresk's announcement that he would leave UNLV to become president of the University of North Texas, the Board of Regents appointed Donald Snyder, a major Las Vegas business executive and current executive dean for strategic development, as acting president. This was a clear message that the system recognized the vital role that Nevada's two universities could play in diversifying the state's metropolitan economies.

Brookings Mountain West and the Lincy Institute helped sponsor a variety of programs in 2009 and 2010 that clearly demonstrated the university's value to the economy and surrounding community. These events allowed UNLV to invite local business leaders to campus to participate in economic conferences, which provided Smatresk with information to use in his effort to discourage further budget cuts and push diversification. In a 2010 memorandum to UNLV's community, the president noted that the recent and idea-filled "National Clean Energy Conference 3.0" held on campus emphasized the school's key role "in creating a new workforce and as a partner with private industry in regional economic diversification centered on renewables."[70]

Liberal elements in the local media, friendly to funding higher education, summarized these ideas and transmitted them to the public at large. While the Salt Lake example clearly appealed to the valley's traditionally conservative Mormon business community, Phoenix's recent experience got almost everyone's attention, because Las Vegas's business community had traditionally viewed Arizona's capital as a rival whose postwar growth and promotion deserved emulation. Both the *Las Vegas Sun* and leaders of UNLV's Mountain West Initiative drove home the point that Las Vegas could learn a lot from Phoenix's strategic planning. As reporter Dave Berns explained, in the 1950s and '60s, with just mining, agriculture, and little else, Phoenix had worked to attract Cold War defense contractors and other businesses to town. But a lot of this sector slowed up with the Cold War's end. Then, in the 1990s and 2000s, the city again diversified its economy by capturing companies involved in semiconductor aerospace, electronics, renewable energy, and clean technologies. The normally conservative State of Arizona and Phoenix business and political leaders invested more than one billion dollars to seed a "bioscience and research economy," even raising taxes to do so. When Michael Crow, a scientist by training, left Columbia University to became Arizona State's president in 2002, he vowed to make ASU a "New Urban University—woven into the community," with the goal of enhancing the local economy by establishing public-private partnerships and undertaking innovative research. By 2011 ASU had already begun negotiations with the Mayo Clinic for a joint medical school. The university had also doubled its funding of research since 2005 and built almost a million square feet of new space for research. Crow also created the Global Institute for Sustainability and appointed the CEO of a former Seattle-based, and now Phoenix-based, firm that designs cancer diagnostic technology as director of the university's new Biodesign Institute.[71]

These events inspired ASU's perennial archrival, the University of Arizona, to construct a quarter-million-square-foot cancer center in downtown Phoenix. City and ASU leaders convinced the University of Arizona medical school to move part of its operations to Phoenix to help seed biomedical research. ASU also planned to move its law school downtown, and in 2008 a new light-rail system linking downtown Phoenix with the Tempe campus opened, reinforcing the growing symbiotic relationship between the city's economy and its university. As UNLV's Robert Lang explained, "They put the money in and built that capacity. But they had to [because] they don't have a gaming industry. And they knew their economy, much like Las Vegas', had to move away from retirees, master-planned communities and golf courses." Lang noted that, as a result of these and other growth-promoting actions, companies from other states, China, and other industrialized nations were moving to Phoenix. The city was becoming more recession proof, because it was building its economy around new innovative technologies, while Las Vegas, Reno, and the state were still relying on gaming, tourism, and mining. As Lang also pointed out, Texas may not be a great energy producer anymore, but its cities were still global headquarters for the energy industry, just as Silicon Valley, without many large manufacturing plants, was for global electronics, and just as Las Vegas was for the worldwide gaming and entertainment industries. The message was clear: Nevada had to adjust to a new century and begin emulating some of its western rivals by investing more in its universities.[72]

Aside from reigniting the periodic debate about the virtues of higher education and economic diversification, the Great Recession, more than any previous economic slowdown, affected every gaming property and building project in the Las Vegas metropolitan area. The halt to construction at the Fontainebleau—already sixty-three floors up in the sky—the multibillion-dollar Las Vegas Plaza, and even the resort projects of rock-solid gaming companies such as the Boyd Group was an unprecedented event in the Strip's history. Yet, in the midst of it all, construction continued on City Center, the Palazzo, and the Cosmopolitan. In the end, Station Casinos retained most of its suburban properties and climbed its way out of bankruptcy, despite the exodus of more than one hundred thousand workers and their families from Las Vegas and the sea of home foreclosures left in the wake of it all.

Downtown Las Vegas, like downtown Reno, experienced a major loss in gross gaming profits, but an infusion of new ownership and capital, including a dramatic expansion of the Golden Nugget, a total renovation of the Plaza and Lady Luck, and a change of identity for Fitzgeralds, helped invigorate Glitter Gulch. Supplementing this was the determination of Mayors Oscar Goodman and Carolyn Goodman to move forward with downtown revitalization, including the Smith Center, the "Mob Museum," the new city hall, and other projects—an undertaking that certainly matched Reno's effort as well as those in other American cities. Although the recession took its toll on condo projects in Las Vegas and on the Strip, forced the layoffs of many government workers, and almost plunged North Las Vegas into bankruptcy, southern Nevada still maintained its position as a leading tourist and convention destination for the nation and the world.

By 2012–13 the Las Vegas Strip also showed signs of once again expanding. In addition to the already mentioned SBS announcement that it would turn the closed Sahara into an upscale boutique hotel by 2014, the Malaysian-based Genting Group announced plans to spend two billion dollars constructing a thirty-five-hundred-room Chinese-themed resort, boasting a panda attraction and a replica of the Great Wall of China, on the former site of Echelon Place. In 2013 Genting bought that land from the Boyd Group to begin the first phase of a multiyear seven-billion-dollar complex that would eventually be called Resorts World Las Vegas. Within three weeks of that announcement, the value of nearby vacant lots on the Strip and Convention Center Drive had doubled.[73] In another move Caesars Entertainment also laid plans to supplement its Linq entertainment complex (featuring the 550-foot High Roller wheel) and its Quad Hotel (formerly the Imperial Palace) by transforming Bill's Gamblin' Hall on the busy corner of the Strip and Flamingo Road into the Cromwell, a classy boutique hotel. This would be a place with a rooftop pool, a Strip-view restaurant, and a posh nightclub fashioned by Victor Drai.[74]

In addition, MGM Resorts International announced in 2013 that it would not only construct a nineteen-thousand-seat arena between its New

York–New York and the Monte Carlo resorts, but also spend one hundred million dollars to build an outdoor plaza and mall, complete with retail stores and restaurants. Like the Linq Wheel and shops between Harrah's and the new Quad Resort and Casino, MGM sought to draw more visitors to its properties by liberating its guests from the traditional confines of its casinos.[75] As Bo Bernhard, a UNLV hotel administration professor, noted, this was another example of a new trend along the Strip. The resorts were abandoning their decades-old business model and no longer trying to hold customers captive inside their casinos, but were now emphasizing, in Bernhard's words, "open spaces and navigability."[76]

Clearly, by 2013 the Strip city's resort sector seemed headed for still more rounds of growth through the second decade of the twenty-first century. In addition, investors purchased thousands of foreclosed homes in the metropolitan area, which only promoted new construction. At the same time, UNLV, working with business leaders, the Nevada Development Authority (which became the Las Vegas Global Economic Alliance in 2013), Governor Sandoval, and state agencies, continued its efforts to promote diversification of the state and local economies.[77] Even though mortgage foreclosures remained high, new projects on the Strip combined with the state's increased effort to recruit and develop new industries sparked renewed optimism about Las Vegas's future.

Chapter Seven

THE RENO AND LAS VEGAS AREAS

A Comparative View

IN COMPARING the Las Vegas area with Reno-Sparks over the past half century, a number of subjects come to the fore. One of the most prominent differences between the two places has been the development of a Strip of resorts south of Las Vegas beyond its municipal limits. Of course, various Reno-area interests in the 1960s and '70s tried to create a "Strip" of gambling resorts, similar to the one in Las Vegas, a few miles south of their downtown core, but these efforts largely failed. For the most part, downtown Reno remained the city's tourist center. While John Ascuaga built a substantial resort, it was in Sparks and inspired little clustering around it. The Sparks Nugget resembled the individual Station and Coast casino resorts that sprang up to serve gamblers in the distant suburbs of the Las Vegas valley. The MGM Grand near Reno's airport also was relatively isolated. The same was true of other hotel-casinos such as the Holiday, Holiday Inn, Ramada, and the Sands, which sat several blocks or many blocks from Reno's casino core.

The most likely site for Reno to develop a "Strip" even remotely similar to Las Vegas's was several miles south of the downtown casino core at the Centennial Coliseum. But this area produced only the Peppermill and Atlantis—not a full-fledged Strip like Clark County's. South of Las Vegas, the Strip developed along US 91, the old highway that ran through downtown and Fremont Street on its way to Utah. At this time the railroad was still the main link delivering passengers from Southern California to downtown. By the late 1930s and early '40s, however, auto and bus travel became increasingly significant. A steady flow of cars and abundant cheap land, where one could buy a tract of many acres on either side of the highway approach to town, virtually invited entrepreneurs to give auto tourists a place to pull in before experiencing the traffic jams, parking problems, and crowds in and around Fremont Street's casinos. South of the city limits a line of major hotels began to form in the 1940s that soon began to compete with the city for gamblers and tourists. As more large resorts appeared during midcentury, the City of Las Vegas worked with county commissioners to acquire a jetport, an interstate highway, a convention center, and other amenities to help build up what became the Strip area that Las Vegas leaders fully expected to annex someday. It was not until the late 1970s that former mayor Oran Gragson and current mayor Bill Briare began to accept the fact that residents in the Strip's eastern, western, and southern suburbs had little interest in joining the city—because they now had an unofficial city of their own.

In Reno no similar Strip formed because there was no place where it could thrive. The MGM Grand remained isolated. Sparks provided no challenge, nor did the corridor along Interstate 80's approach from the west to downtown Reno. The area north of the freeway and the university stayed residential, just as the lands north of the railroad tracks had been for most of the twentieth century. Even lots south of the railroad tracks lured few hotels past the river. In fact, by 2000 the site for most of downtown's larger hotels, such as the Eldorado and Silver Legacy, had shifted north of the tracks, with Harrah's and the Club Cal Neva being notable exceptions. Even far down on South Virginia Street around the convention center near the new freeway to Carson City and Lake Tahoe's approach routes, only a few large resorts formed because the road to Lake Tahoe, though a popular tourist artery, led nowhere else for many miles.

Mayor Bennett recognized that "the reason for the hotel-casinos moving out there was cheaper land." Indeed, developers had acquired most of these tracts from farmers and ranchers. Despite Bennett's staunch opposition to building *more* casino resorts (a position that even many outlying residents supported), it still would have been easy to build a strip of resorts and big commercial developments in south Reno. Why? Because, in Bennett's own words, prior to 1981 "the [city] council almost automatically approved extensions to building projects which were sitting on the waiting list, because there had been a recession at the time. If they were not building, it wasn't because they didn't have approvals—they did." As she explained, "The fact was they didn't want to build because there was a recession during that time. Costs were too much to build, so they were coming in and getting approvals and leaving things sitting on the shelf until they were ready to go.... So we had a huge backlog of approved projects."[1] In the end, Reno's strip never materialized, due to lack of demand. The tourists and gamblers whom promoters had expected after 1980 were simply going elsewhere. Because of winter weather and other factors, Reno had its limits as a tourist destination; it could never be another Las Vegas.

Actually, a strip along Reno's southern edge would have been the most likely spot for a line of large casino resorts to form, since these places would have required a lot of space. From the beginning, the Strip along the old Los Angeles Highway attracted resort builders, because it contained larger tracts of land than the city could provide. In 1940 Thomas Hull was able to buy sixty-six acres for his El Rancho Vegas, space that he could never hope to get on the city's traditional grid of small blocks and lots. Even full-block sites were not easily available at midcentury on Fremont Street, because too many existing owners refused to sell or preferred to hold out for a higher price. Not only was it hard to assemble enough lots in downtown Reno and Las Vegas, but casino resorts also had to lie within the red line, the only area where the cities issued unrestricted gaming licenses. By 1931 there were enough houses inside the city limits along US 91's approach to town to prevent a developer from squeezing in an El Rancho Vegas-type resort. If they had, not only would home owners have protested at city hall, but municipal zoning ordinances would have posed a virtually impenetrable barrier to any resort plans. However, in the county lands beyond the municipal limits at San Francisco Street (today's Sahara Avenue), these problems abruptly ended.[2]

Although a downtown city environment may not have been the ideal place for modern casino resorts to sprout and prosper, Reno's geographic location was another disadvantage. By the late 1960s, traffic on US 50 hardly compared to US 91 in Las Vegas, which delivered thousands of visitors daily from the growing megalopolis in Southern California. US 91, replaced in 1971 by Interstate 15, crossed the southern Sierra at the relatively low Cajon Pass, which was usually free of snow or easily cleared for snow tires or chains in winter. By contrast, Bay Area visitors had to traverse the Sierra's full width to approach Reno by navigating either the treacherous Donner Summit or the avalanche-prone US 50 down the Carson Pass from the Lake Tahoe Basin. There was one obvious benefit: thanks to the smaller number of tourists, downtown Reno's gambling halls and casino hotels did not face the nearby competition their Fremont Street counterparts did from the Strip city's resorts. The only competition for Bill Harrah and the other downtown casino moguls lay completely within Reno's city limits at the airport with MGM and later with the Peppermill and Atlantis near the convention center. The downside, of course, was that the Reno area could generate no Strip of its own with which to attract millions of tourists. While Oran Gragson, Bill Briare, and other Las Vegas officials struggled to decide how to develop downtown to retain the small commercial businesses that every city needs *and* how to accommodate casinos spectacular enough to compete with the Strip's resorts, Reno's leaders struggled with a decade-long debate that split the metropolitan area and its business community. The overriding question was whether Reno should redevelop downtown to lure more tourists, gamblers, and resorts or manage growth, return downtown to locals, and keep taxes low by pursuing a more diversified economy.

But why didn't the question of growth-related concerns about higher taxes and bond issues arise in the Las Vegas area, as it did in Reno? The answer lies in the Strip city's development. It began as just two or three hotels that quickly blossomed into twelve. As it did, the future Strip city began to develop. In the 1950s and '60s small and scattered clusters of homes and apartments dotted lands behind the big resorts to allow employees an easy commute. From these nuclei, roads gradually spread eastward and a bit westward, as doctors, lawyers, dentists, and every type of professional and service business arrived to serve the new population where none had been before. Although Alicia Barber has correctly noted the negative response of many residents to the "commodification of Reno" by Harrah's, MGM, and the other casino hotels, no such reaction occurred in Las Vegas and especially not out in the Strip city.[3] Virtually all the people living in the area south of the Las Vegas city line (as well as many north of it) *owed their livelihood* to the Strip's continued success. No one, therefore, had an interest in blocking the nascent Strip city's expansion. Special service districts for water, sewers, schools, libraries, and other services quickly ensured that annexation to the city, with its extra taxes, zoning ordinances, and red-line mentality, would not be necessary. Unlike their counterparts in Reno, Strip-city voters approved bond issue after bond issue for new roads, schools, airports, and most public works, except for flood control, which was still not yet considered a priority—given the relative infrequency of floods. For the most part, Strip-city residents supported any reasonable measure that would promote the development of more gaming resorts along the old Los Angeles Highway. No one was, in the words of veteran newspaperman John Cahlan, "going to kill the goose that laid the golden egg."[4]

In Las Vegas even popular city commissioners such as Reed Whipple ran into voter opposition for backing such expensive and disruptive projects as the widening of Maryland Parkway. This was not the case south of town, where Clark County commissioners boldly supported many new streets as well as construction of an expensive new jetport in 1960—just twelve years after opening a new airport south of town. They also endorsed the building of a large convention center as well as interstate highway connections at the newly named Tropicana, Flamingo, and Sahara Avenues, in addition to a range of other public works and infrastructure improvements to support the eastward and eventually southward and westward thrust of building activity in the steadily expanding Strip city.

Every new generation of resorts brought more rounds of expansion outward into the largely empty desert, as a new and dynamic city took shape south of Las Vegas. The Strip hotels constantly raised the bar for Fremont Street, a challenge that men such as William Harrah and Charlie Mapes did not immediately face. In addition, the Strip rose up on a blazing desert floor surrounded by caliche and rolling sagebrush for miles on end. This was no Portland, Seattle, or Reno. According to the thinking of that day, expansion posed no serious or immediate threat to the environment. As a result, a different type of thinking governed the Strip city's development. Growth concerns were not part of the equation until the 1980s and '90s, and even then the level of concern hardly approached the levels present in Reno during the 1970s, '80s, and even earlier.

Las Vegas's advantage over Reno was not just its warmer weather, proximity to Southern California, and willingness to support a lot of public works bond issues. It also possessed more creative leaders in its resort industry, especially on the Strip, which provided a spacious, national stage for innovative thinking. Unlike their counterparts on Fremont Street and in Reno, Strip executives constantly searched the world for ideas to draw even more tourists to their properties. Indeed, the striking architecture and design ideas he picked up in his travels to Abu Dhabi, Kuala Lumpur, and other places inspired MGM CEO Jim Murren when he presented his ideas for City Center to board members. But Steve Wynn led the field in this regard when pioneering the "New Las Vegas" on the Strip. As his wife, Elaine, once explained, Steve got the idea for the Mirage in the 1960s while still living in Miami Beach and visiting the resorts along Collins Avenue and the Florida coast. In the mid-1990s Italy's Tuscan hill country and Lake Como inspired his Bellagio, as did the renowned art museums and palatial gardens of Europe.[5] A decade later his visits to the high-end resorts at St. Tropez and other exotic locales in the Caribbean prompted him to build the popular Encore Beach Club and even tear out the new resort's Strip entrance to make room for it.

Of course, the tradition of Strip executives attracting more business through the use of special attractions long antedated Wynn. In 1942 William J. Moore's "Last Frontier Village" on the grounds of the Hotel Last Frontier drew many more visitors and families to that resort than would have come without it. In the mid-1950s Warren and Judy Bayley offered multiple pools, an intimate showroom, and a kids' go-cart track to lure families to their Hacienda hotel-casino. In the 1950s and '60s the Stardust built rodeo grounds on its property, a Grand Prix race-car speedway west of the Strip, a golf course east of the Strip, and a state-of-the-art showroom—complete with hydraulic stage—for Donn Arden's Lido de Paris. In 1966 Jay Sarno contributed to the Strip's growing allure with Caesars Palace, his high-end tribute to the luxury and self-indulgence of ancient Rome. He did it again with Circus Circus (1968), a resort that, once modified by Bill Bennett and William Pennington, became a regional mecca for middle- and low-income families. With the exception of the Fremont Street Experience, the resort makers in the cities of Reno and Las Vegas never came close to matching the Strip's innovative performance.

Blessed with a larger valley than Reno's Truckee Meadows, the Las Vegas area had plenty of space south of the city limits for resorts capable of hosting Omnimax theaters (Caesars Palace, 1980), twin showrooms for headliners and production shows (the first MGM Grand, 1973; Kerkorian's International, 1969), Eiffel Towers (Paris, 1999), Dancing Waters (Bellagio, 1999), a Campanile Bell Tower (Venetian, 1999), and all manner of gourmet restaurants and high-end malls. Whereas Las Vegas, Reno, and the early Strip hotels were content to offer guests a coffee shop, a buffet, a steak house, and perhaps some seafood, Italian, or Chinese eateries, some Strip resorts gradually abandoned this tradition for a more ambitious approach. By the 1990s executives in the Strip city began to recruit celebrity chefs from leading American and European restaurants to serve their cuisine at Caesars Palace, Mandalay Bay, and other megaresorts—a trend that properties in the city of Las Vegas and Reno did not emulate (except for Charlie Palmer at the Grand Sierra) to any significant degree.

In the 1970s, with the Mob's presence fading, corporate gaming on the rise, and Atlantic City helping to open new sources of capital for casino resorts, the Strip's newly found access to billions of dollars in capital allowed Wynn, Adelson, and the other big resort builders to fund their innovative ideas, create a buzz, and enhance the Strip's legendary reputation as a "hot" destination where the "cool" people came to play. During the course of this process, the Strip only grew—and with it the surrounding "city" it powered. But the roots of this process went back to the postwar years. As early as the 1950s, Las Vegas and the Strip possessed more nationally known resorts than Reno (although Harold's Club and maybe Harrah's were well known). Tourists were far more aware of the Flamingo, Frontier, Sahara, Sands, and Desert Inn than they were of the Mapes and El Cortez. Even before the advent of Caesars Palace, Las Vegas was considered a "hot" place to visit—a place where the stars hung out—a haven for the "in crowd." And Las Vegas has retained that reputation for the last half century. It was the place to see the Rat Pack (or the Clan, as they called themselves), Elvis, the Beatles, and the Rolling Stones as well as the Grateful Dead. It was the place that all the major acts in show business wanted to play, from Eddie Cantor, Nat King Cole, and Sophie Tucker to Siegfried and Roy, Celine Dion, and Lady Gaga. Reno may have been a happening place in the early decades of the twentieth century, but in later years it never recaptured that magic and made little effort to do so.

The Strip increasingly offered visitors a vacation playland. It was a place where tourists could experience a faux but sumptuous version of Italy, Paris, ancient Egypt, and imperial Rome. By 2000, if not earlier, the Strip was, in the words of Steve Wynn, "the highest-energy midway in the world," with its pyramids, medieval castles, Eiffel towers, and dazzling spectacle architecture.[6] In contrast, Reno lacked the WOW factor. For the most part, the city never really offered visitors sights they could not see at home. Like the city of Las Vegas, gambling was Reno's major draw. True, the city's western mountains were majestic and its river was bucolic, but Lake Tahoe—one of America's greatest natural wonders—was more than fifty miles away from Reno and nestled in a high mountain range.

Reno gaming executives also struggled with the residents' preference for lower taxes and managed growth. The seeds of the community's interests in keeping Reno a small city lay in the subregion's conservatism and thrift. The appeal of HUD's 1972 conference on managed growth in Portland, and of Portland itself as a model of urban development in a bucolic setting, lay in Reno's historic identity as a transfer point for people and goods headed elsewhere. After 1868 Reno became more than a river crossing for wagons headed south to the Comstock; the city functioned as a vibrant railroad center. Commercial Row, fronting today's train tunnel, bustled with businesses that relied on train and wagon traffic. Even in the 1930s when Nevada's liberal divorce law drew hundreds of western, eastern, and midwestern socialites to the city's party-time atmosphere, gambling remained a secondary industry—housed in the saloons, gambling halls, and clubs that entertained thousands, but not millions, of visitors who came to and through Reno on business or on vacation. By the 1960s gambling had replaced divorce as the city's best-known industry. Gambling expanded slowly in the postwar decades, as more affluent and mobile Americans toured the scenic West and escaped the confines of postwar mainstream culture.

But despite its notorious reputation as a maverick city that catered to vice, Reno had never truly been a *resort* city with tourism as its main industry. Reno's identity lay elsewhere. Reno was a university town, but, even more important, it was a railroad town—a transportation and transshipment center with numerous businesses, including bottling plants, wood-working mills, and meatpacking factories, as well as surrounding farms and ranches that fed off railroad commerce. It was a town that embraced Progressive reform in the early 1900s—a place where many residents looked askance at the growing number of clubs dealing cards and selling booze. Many Renoites lived in small homes on tree-shaded streets that resembled the neighborhoods in so many other American small towns. These residents often did not work in the gaming district and relied on mainstream industries for their livelihood. This type of person, in later years, constituted a substantial part of the community that questioned the need for large casino resorts. Locals also worried about the effects of transforming their beloved city into a honky-tonk and eventually a full-fledged metropolitan area like Las Vegas. They looked not so much eastward to the endless desert that seemed like such an opportunity to Las Vegas investors, but westward toward the fir-lined, snow-capped Sierra and thought of Portland, Seattle, and other green places whose residents were determined to restrain development, slow growth, and preserve the natural beauty of their surrounding environment.

Both Reno and Las Vegas began as railroad towns, but in 1903 Reno got the profitable repair shops in the form of neighboring Sparks, which was close enough to function as a multiplier for the bigger city's economy. On the other hand, Las Vegas lost its shops to Caliente in 1922 after the national railroad strike ended. So Las Vegas had to look for another industry to ensure its future, and in 1931 Hoover Dam tourism and the legalization of wide-open gambling rescued the city from oblivion. As a result, Las Vegans were not as divided over casinos and tourism as Renoites were in later years. Still, in the 1960s—even in Las Vegas residents and politicians such as Mayor Oran Gragson sought to restrict the growth of gaming by preserving the city's red-line ordinance that confined unrestricted gaming licenses to a narrow zone downtown near the railroad station. Much like the small business owners in downtown Reno, the shop owners around Fremont Street also sought to maintain Las Vegas's small-town identity by not allowing slot joints and bars to proliferate. But unlike Reno residents, Las Vegans had to contend with, and at times cooperate with, the Strip city to their south.

In his 1999 study of Las Vegas, sociologist Mark Gottdiener applied normalization theory to Las Vegas's metropolitan area to explain its development. He defined normalization as the process by which "a new residential area develops the practices and institutions of civic life that are essential characteristics of communities in more developed parts of the country and which contribute to the social stability of the region." He concluded that in the 1980s and '90s, there was a growing convergence between Las Vegas and mainstream urban development in the United States.[7] It took the form of master-planned communities; stepped-up resident resistance to developers attempting to rezone neighborhoods for major commercial developments; growing pressure to fund schools, colleges, and universities; and increased civic activity in general. Historian Hal Rothman noted in a 2001 review that as the twenty-first century began and America "moved toward Las Vegas, the desert city responded by moving toward the nation."[8] But in Reno the normalization process went a bit further, as many residents openly questioned the commitment of their business and political leaders to a future based heavily on rapid growth driven by casino gambling.

At the same time, taxes played a major role in the process to control growth. Unlike the Strip city in southern Nevada, Reno-area residents did not want to build a new high school every two years or spend millions to extend infrastructural systems and street networks miles outward to accommodate the vast population needed to serve millions of tourists. Residents in the city of Las Vegas were never far from this position themselves. Support to maintain the town's red-line ordinance was strong. Las Vegans did not want casino resorts taking over the CBD and invading their neighborhoods. Into the twenty-first century the city government granted unlimited gaming licenses to only a select few resorts, usually on the edge of town, and only after much consideration. On the other hand, Clark County commissioners were more liberal with their zoning policies for many decades and more welcoming of a resort that was likely to draw tens of thousands of tourists and reinforce the Strip city's continued growth and hegemony. It was this process in the Strip city, even more than events transpiring in the central city of Las Vegas, that helped create a true metropolitan area by 1960 and a metropolis of two million by 2007.

Unlike Roy Bankofier, Jud Allen, and other Reno growth advocates, Oran Gragson and his predecessors firmly believed in the red line and sought to preserve it. Just as Reno's retail businesses and professional people did not want casinos and slot arcades spreading down to and beyond the Truckee River, so too Mayors Gragson, Briare, Lurie, Jones, and the media, as well as downtown businesses and residents, did not want slot arcades lining the roads around Fremont Street or *unrestricted* gaming venues, with all kinds of games, popping up all over town. Cities, and especially downtown CBDs, were not the most conducive environments for modern gaming-tourism to prosper. From the nineteenth century into the twentieth, the stage station–railroad station vicinity of any town presented an ideal venue for the small-time clubs of that period. But in more modern times the crowded CBD was not the preferred setting for casinos. Mainstream downtown businesses did not want to coexist with the party-time, all-night atmosphere created by blocks of casinos.

For Las Vegas and Reno, two cities desperately trying to revitalize their downtown areas, casinos were not conducive to the process. A 2012 article in the *New York Times* reported that Reno's casino operators had done little to promote that city's downtown revitalization efforts. As historians David Schwartz, Bryant Simon, and others have noted, casino resorts historically tried to contain their gamblers and guests.[9] They did not (and still do not) want them parading up and down the streets for hours, chatting in coffee shops, patronizing sidewalk cafés, and browsing through dozens of stores. Although Las Vegas's downtown gaming establishments nightly concede lost business for ten minutes each hour to the Fremont Street Experience, it is only for the lucrative purpose of attracting more visitors from the Strip. Casino managers really do not want their guests strolling down to Fremont Street East for a few hours. Although they have never said it publicly, it does not bother them that the Neonopolis Mall remained a commercial black hole for years, separating the big casinos to its west from Fremont East. They were surely delighted that the Tamares Group renovated and reopened the aging Plaza Hotel at the head of Fremont Street. The last thing downtown gamers wanted was for that hotel to close and have the city or some friend of the city buy it and then implode it to provide an Appian Way from the Fremont Street Experience to the Smith Center, Symphony Park's trendy restaurants, the Las Vegas Premium Outlets retail mall, and other developments that would someday appear. In short, an outlying district such as the Strip or the Atlantic City Boardwalk—not a CBD—is really the most conducive environment today for large casinos to prosper in a metropolitan area.

Multiple factors were responsible for limiting the expansion of Reno's tourist-gaming industry. It was not just the people of Reno who moved their city away from its 1970s growth agenda. Despite the hopes of local boosters and gaming executives, external factors also played a major role in killing their dream. Late-century tourists did not flock to Reno as they did to Las Vegas, Orlando, Honolulu, and other vacation destinations. Reno was not just cold in the winter; it was also a stark place with a lot of old buildings and signs of blight—even before the hotels began to close their doors in the 1990s. In the eyes of many tourists who came to Reno on vacation to gamble and relax, the 1970s downtown streetscape in and around the river was full of derelicts, panhandlers, and a lot of older buildings. Although many of these structures certainly interested historic preservationists, they were a different group of visitors from the ones who came to gamble and relax in the modern, vacation-promoting environment that most resorts tried to present. The El Cortez, J. C. Penney's, and F. W. Woolworth—even the old apartment houses of midcentury—were remnants of a bygone era compared to the gleaming glass towers of Harrah's, the Flamingo, and other places downtown. The stores and streetscape that greeted visitors to Reno in the 1970s and '80s could have been in downtown Tacoma, Cheyenne, or Saginaw.

The same was true of downtown Las Vegas, although it lacked some of the seediness that continues to plague sections in and around downtown Reno. Once visitors stepped away from the casino core on Fremont Street, the old Cornet Store, J. C. Penney's, Sears, and Woolworths were just as dated as anything in Reno. Even more depressing were the dingy-looking hardware, linoleum, drapery, and furniture stores that filled Main and Commerce Streets, along with the backdrop of ancient railroad structures just to the west. Along with the pawn shops, jewelry stores, and liquor outlets that lined the streets of both Reno and Las Vegas, the downtown cityscape lying beyond the neon world of clubs and casinos was not a beckoning one when compared to the festival spirit thriving in Manhattan, San Francisco, Chicago, Atlanta, and other American downtowns undergoing an urban renaissance, much less the carnival atmosphere of the Strip.

Late-twentieth-century conventioneers and vacationers preferred a modern-looking streetscape, which was what the Strip presented, albeit in an extreme form. Every resort was not just a casino resort with a pool, but, increasingly, each comprised multiple restaurants and attractions, which made it, in the words of Steve Wynn, a "theme park." The city of Las Vegas, like the city of Reno, did not have nearly enough attractions to lure the tens of millions of tourists needed to become a "hot" destination, much less an exploding metropolis. But Las Vegas did have one thing Reno lacked: a dynamic Strip city south of town with iconic resorts that increasingly took the Las Vegas brand to new heights nationally and globally.

The presence of transcontinental railroad lines was another factor that affected the development of both Reno and Las Vegas. In Las Vegas, as in Reno, railroad trains traveled constantly through the center of town. But unlike Las Vegas, whose tracks lay west of the Strip and Fremont Street, Reno's tracks were a major impediment, crossing the CBD at grade in the middle of the casino core between the Eldorado Hotel and Harolds Club. Las Vegas and the Strip city were relatively quick to route east-west auto traffic over or under the tracks. The City of Las Vegas and the Union Pacific constructed the Bonanza Underpass for cars in 1935 and the Charleston Underpass in 1949.[10] Though paralleling the Strip, the railroad was always on the margins of the gaming district and not in the center, as it was in Reno. Into the twenty-first century the railroad cars halted normal street traffic in Reno, while train horns roused tourists from their sleep in hotels just a few feet away. It cost Reno millions of dollars to fund the ReTRAC project. Las Vegas, on the other hand, was spared this expense. Although trains still run outside through mostly open terrain, the city's ability to convince the Union Pacific to move its yard operations out of town and its success in purchasing those yard lands gave Las Vegas the space and opportunity to revitalize a large portion of downtown without having to engage in costly litigation and the demolition of large buildings. In the Strip city, the county commissioners also eliminated virtually all of the grade crossings on major arteries west of the big resorts and farther out in the southern suburbs.

Annexation also affected the development of Reno and Las Vegas. In the case of Reno, the steady outward expansion of the municipal limits allowed the city to control the lucrative tax base generated from most of the major resorts that appeared in the Truckee Meadows. This separated Reno from Las Vegas, which failed to capture the valuable lands on its southern periphery. Reno never had to annex a large tract of county land hosting a Strip of valuable resorts. Over the years Reno undertook multiple annexations, acquiring new subdivisions sprouting near its edges that lacked schools, sewers, and other urban services.[11] Unlike Las Vegas, water was not something Reno's suburbs needed. Even though Reno had the Truckee, which provided a convenient supply, wells were not scarce in the Truckee Meadows, given the huge Sierra snowpack just west of town. Even with the formation of a special service district, the Truckee Meadows Water Authority did not materially affect Reno's ability to annex outlying lands.

But, unlike Reno, Las Vegas had little to offer the Strip and the small archipelago of unincorporated towns surrounding it. The emerging Strip and its suburbs fought off determined annexation efforts by Las Vegas in 1946, 1951, and 1978.[12] The early Strip did not need that much water. There was no city water company anyway, just the railroad. Thanks to 11,900-foot Mount Charleston west of town, there was plenty of well water for the early hotels, outlying ranches, and the relatively small amount of homes and apartment complexes sitting on county land. The creation of the Las Vegas Valley Water District and its initiation of service in 1954 eliminated another reason for the emerging Strip area to join the central city.

The creation of the Clark County School District in 1955 eliminated yet another reason. County residents could now send their kids to good schools without having to become part of Las Vegas. Joining the big city's school system and plugging into its water supply are what usually forced suburban towns to join Boston, New York, Chicago, and other big cities in the years before 1900. But Las Vegas is the only major US metropolitan area that began in the twentieth century when many factors started making it easier for suburbs to remain independent. The emergence of special service districts was one such factor. Special service districts saved the Strip suburbs from having to build their own schools, libraries, and waterworks. Las Vegas had a police department, but its reputation for corruption tarnished its image enough that county residents stayed with the Sheriff's Office—until 1973, when Las Vegas and Clark County officials decided to merge their respective forces and create the Metropolitan Police Department.[13] In 1953 Clark County started its own fire department to serve the Strip city and created sanitary districts to lay sewer lines in a determined effort to relieve residents from their unwanted dependence upon cesspools. Similarly, the county built its own wastewater treatment plant and road networks, using its expanding tax base to finance the urban services that residents wanted.[14] As a result, the county commissioners eliminated the conditions that in other metro areas would have promoted the central city's annexation efforts. In the process, county leaders kept the emerging Strip city intact. They also kept property taxes lower than those in Las Vegas, because Strip resort property taxes funneled so much more money into county coffers that taxes were less for houses in the county than for homes of comparable size in the city. This differential only helped draw more residents and builders to the Strip city, where people could live east, west, or south of the growing job zone on Las Vegas Boulevard South, which soon became the valley's real nucleus.

Aside from annexation efforts, railroad issues, managed-growth concerns, and the suitability of downtown for casino gambling, Reno also suffered from divisions within its gaming community. Take, for instance, the question of where to locate the city's new convention center in the 1960s. Business and political elites split, with those favoring the urban periphery triumphing over Bill Harrah, Charlie Mapes, and other gamers operating major establishments downtown. There was also disunity within the town's gaming community. Even in the 1950s and '60s when Reno's gaming industry was growing downtown, the seeds of future trouble were already evident. The hotel owners themselves were atomized, too often pursuing their own interests. As Jud Allen observed, men like Charles Mapes and William Harrah rarely talked to each another. They were also stingy in supporting the chamber of commerce's marketing efforts. By contrast, in Las Vegas the hotels in the city and the resorts on the Strip worked together in the 1940s within the city's chamber of commerce, using its various advertising firms to generate reams of valuable publicity about the place. In the mid- to late 1940s these firms created the very successful Live Wire Fund and the Desert Sea News Bureau, which helped publicize the Las Vegas area for many years.

But, as in Reno, divisions eventually arose, although for different reasons. In the southern metropolis, as the line of resorts on the Strip grew larger and became more numerous and more well known, their interests began to diverge from the gaming emporiums and smaller hotels downtown. By the 1950s management at the Flamingo, Desert Inn, Tropicana, and other resorts no longer fully cooperated with their Fremont Street counterparts in supporting Las Vegas's marketing efforts. Gradually, the big resorts established their own marketing departments and, by 1955, began working more closely with the newly created Fair and Recreation Board. But gaming operators within the city did cooperate and work harmoniously with the chamber. So, the situation in southern Nevada was different from that in the North, because the Strip resort owners began to see themselves as a separate entity from Fremont Street gaming, with different interests and clientele. Strip executives also began to realize they were competing directly with Fremont Street and therefore could best market the special resort amenities they offered with their own promotional campaign. However, by the 1970s and '80s, while each resort and downtown hotel still generated its own promotional material, they increasingly worked together through the Las Vegas Convention and Visitors Authority to promote Las Vegas as a national and even an international market.

The missed opportunities are probably what upset Reno-area boosters such as Jud Allen the most. Whereas Las Vegas gamers exploited every chance that came along, much like a wily card player in a game of gin rummy, Reno's leaders missed their share of opportunities. For example, in the late 1970s the Walt Disney Company spent several million dollars on plans for a wilderness theme park near Independence Lake in the Sierra. Such an attraction would have brought thousands of people and families to a safe wilderness area, preserved in its natural state, where tourists could enjoy outdoor activities during the day. Being the nearest city and jetport to the facility, Reno would have become the park's major gateway.

In the end, Allen recalled, "government bureaucrats and environmentalists" blocked Disney's project.[15] But, as he noted in exasperation, state and Reno-area officials did virtually nothing to stop them.

In Reno even the university exerted a drag on the gaming industry. City and gown played different roles in Reno and Las Vegas. Arriving in 1885, twelve years before Reno was incorporated as a formal city, the young college exerted a noticeable influence upon the community it overlooked from its hillside vantage point north of downtown. In the years after 1900 its president allied with progressive reformers in town to try to ban gambling, dispossess brothels, and enforce Prohibition. They had some initial success. Later, in the 1970s and '80s, professors such as the late and highly respected William Eadington, director of the Institute for the Study of Gaming and Commercial Gambling and chair of the 1974 blue-ribbon panel on economic growth, were outspoken in urging the various panels and reformers to support managed growth and economic diversification in a concerted effort to reduce the town's reliance on gambling. Growth advocates in the local business and gaming communities resented this activist stance. In fact, as Mayor Bennett recalled in her 1989 reminiscence, university faculty "always had to be careful about what [they] said on the growth issue and probably still [do].... There was a lot of pressure and heat put on a number of professors at the university about this growth situation." Members of the business community mentioned, even occasionally in the newspapers, that "they didn't like contributing to the university when some professors were speaking against what they thought were their growth interests."[16]

In contrast, UNLV's college predecessor, Nevada Southern, did not even get a campus until 1957, nearly a half century after Las Vegas became an incorporated city and almost twenty years after the Strip was born. The campus was not even in Las Vegas but instead grew up several miles south in the Strip city. Over the years, UNLV presidents and faculty supported the Strip's growth, knowing that any substantial increase in gaming revenues would mean more buildings and staff for the school. The Hotel College, created in 1969, enjoyed an especially close relationship with the Strip resorts, training their future employees at all management levels. In short, whereas UNR sometimes challenged its city's various vice economies, the Strip city in southern Nevada faced no such threat from UNLV.

Despite all of their differences, the city of Las Vegas and the city of Reno possessed many similarities. Although Las Vegas had a larger valley, was farther south, and enjoyed milder winters and easier geographic access from California, both cities began with railroad economies and both grappled with the spread of gaming in their downtown central business districts. In both cities midcentury residents did not want gambling to spread and thought gamers had too much control of city hall. Over time, both cities became overly reliant on gaming and suffered from declining gaming revenues in the 1990s. But Las Vegas had the Strip on its southern border, and despite its conflicts with the county over annexation and other issues, the Strip city invigorated the entire metropolitan area. It awarded the city of Las Vegas and the surrounding valley a prosperity that Reno never experienced and many rounds of growth that most Renoites did not want.

The key was that the Las Vegas area remained a hot spot, attracting generation after generation of visitors from the 1940s into the twenty-first century. After 1960 it was not so much the city, but the Strip that did it. Although they certainly improved their appearance and appeal in later years, 1950s Virginia Street and Fremont Street were then little more than glorified replicas of the honky-tonk midway of clubs in Frank Capra's "Pottersville," depicted in his 1946 film *It's a Wonderful Life*. But the Strip was always a different place. The key was the Strip's clustering effect, not of small clubs as on Fremont and Virginia Streets, but of sprawling hotel properties, in a steadily expanding, though often discontinuous, line down US 91. As early as the 1950s the Strip's low-slung, modern-looking resorts, separated only by small patches of western desert, gas stations, and other small businesses—featuring television and Hollywood stars performing live onstage, risqué lounge acts, palatial gardens, and showgirls cavorting in sun-drenched pools, all staged in a casino-charged atmosphere—captured the imagination of American tourists. After dark these places lit up in a blaze of signage, enhanced by glamorous neon, to celebrate the night.

There were actually two Strips: the early one, more suburban and low-rise, and the later one, more urban and high-rise, with major resorts, packed closer together than ever before—virtually one after another. The first Strip lasted until century's end and still lingers in a few spots today; the new Strip debuted with the Mirage in 1989 and continued to upstage its storied predecessor with iconic megaresorts, fronted now by densely populated sidewalks and buildings, into the twenty-first century. One could argue too that Caesars Palace, Kirk Kerkorian's MGM Grand, and perhaps also his International were precursors of the second Strip. To be sure, this

"New Las Vegas" of the 1990s and 2000s owed much of its life to the advent of corporate gaming, which awarded Strip executives access to the billions in capital they needed to replace aging hotels with dazzling successors. Gone were the Thomas Hulls, the Wilbur Clarks, and the Jay Sarnos, replaced by the Steve Wynns, the Sheldon Adelsons, and the Jim Murrens, along with a small army of architects, designers, and other visionaries who embraced the future. Together, they helped transform the Strip from a popular American destination into a permanent World's Fair, boasting resort pavilions dedicated to leisure, gambling, and self-indulgence.

Cities such as Reno and Las Vegas, with their grid of blocks and lots downtown, were not structured spatially to compete with this evolving spectacle, nor could they. Over time Reno was especially vulnerable, given its cold winters and the later diffusion of Native American gaming across California and the Northwest. Reno will always be Reno; thanks to its historic gaming legacy, it will always draw more than its share of tourists and convention delegates. But the area's gaming industry began to constrict in the late twentieth century, and the city will have to develop new industries if it is to grow and prosper in the twenty-first century.

The Great Recession catalyzed the process. The decline of Reno's gaming sector antedated the recession, but this economic downturn was a shock to both metropolitan areas and to the state, triggering an overdue dialogue regarding the value of diversification. There was more of a sense of urgency in Reno, which did not have a world-famous Strip of resorts to help cushion the recession's shock. Indeed, the Reno-Sparks metropolitan area needed a rapid infusion of new industry to offset the losses in gaming and tourism. But in the South, too, UNLV and other community voices forced a dialogue on the subject. The Las Vegas area will probably climb out of the recession in the next few years and continue to grow, as the demand for its leisure services picks up. But even Las Vegas will not maintain the rate of growth it has long enjoyed forever. Nevada can no longer rely as much on the Strip for its revenues as it did in earlier decades. As one UNR study pointed out, the Strip successfully diversified its dining, retail, gaming, and other products after 1990 and thus attracted more visitors and locals. The Great Recession hit the Strip resorts hard. The consolidation of resort ownership into a few large gaming companies certainly strengthened many Strip resorts. But as UNR gaming analyst William Eadington later noted, the latter displayed an "irrational exuberance" between 2004 and 2007, investing almost thirty billion dollars in new hotels and large expansions, some of which was lost to the recession. As he explained, commitments to building new resorts or to leveraged buyouts dangerously increased debt loads, which, during the economic downturn, nearly bankrupted Caesars Entertainment, MGM Mirage, Station Casinos, and other gaming companies.[17] The four Strip megaresorts that did open between 2004 and 2007—Wynn, Encore, Palazzo, and City Center—while popular, did not substantially increase demand in the Las Vegas market. Nevertheless, the annual number of visitors to Las Vegas has increased since 2010.

Obviously, the ability of Steve Wynn, Sheldon Adelson, and MGM Mirage to penetrate the Asian markets in Macau and Singapore has allowed them to offset losses they suffered during the recession in America. Indeed, by 2006 Macau passed Las Vegas in gross gaming revenues and by 2012 had pulled far ahead, with Singapore coming up fast on the Strip, too. This has been good for the stockholders of American companies, but as Eadington correctly observed, building more Venetians, MGM Grands, and other Las Vegas–style resorts in Asia will not substantially help Las Vegas. Why? Because baccarat has contributed heavily in recent decades to Strip profits, and if Asian high rollers, who prefer this game, play in Asia, it could mean a significant drop in gross gaming revenues for the state's biggest metropolitan area. For Eadington, who forty years ago chaired Reno's blue-ribbon panel on growth and advised that city, almost prophetically, to rely less in the future on its gaming industry, the advice is now for Las Vegas and the state to do the same and begin placing more emphasis on diversification and education. Historically, the ruling elites and residents of Nevada's two metropolitan areas have been exceptionally flexible, embracing vice industries in the 1930s to survive and prosper even as other American cities rejected them, and now embracing any traditional or cutting-edge industry promising to diversify their economies and promote growth.

Today, these leaders and residents have little choice. Though still a vital component of Las Vegas's economy and the state's, casino tourism will not be the panacea it was in the past. It is becoming increasingly clear that as more American cities and nations legalize gaming and as more Las Vegas–type megaresorts are inevitably built, no longer just in China and the Caribbean, but in Europe, Florida, New York, Chicago, New Orleans, and elsewhere, Las Vegas tourism—even in the Strip city—will eventually flatten out for the long term. Of course, the Genting Group's new Strip resort—just like Caesars Palace in the 1960s, MGM Grand in the 1970s, the new south Strip resorts of the 1990s, and the new center Strip resorts of the 2000s—will draw more tourists to Las Vegas for the foreseeable future. The opening of large and exciting new resorts has always helped Las Vegas remain fresh and at the cutting edge, which invariably attracts more tourists. But that formula will not work forever in an increasingly saturated market. Both the Reno and the Las Vegas areas learned a valuable lesson in recent years: they, like Nevada, can no longer rely solely on the easy money that flowed into the state's casinos during past decades. Increasingly, these metropolises will need to attract new industries. Gaming scholar Bo Bernhard recently noted that Macau has not deprived Las Vegas of jobs but actually contributed some. Indeed, he argued, "Most of the major gaming corporations [now] have Asian analysis departments," and he suggested that Macau's spectacular growth has "made Las Vegas the corporate headquarters for the gaming industry."[18] This may well be true, but the brightness of Las Vegas's future will hinge more on economic diversification than on gaming alone.

A combination of such new industries as oil production, solar power and renewable energy, data storage, drone development and testing, medical schools at both UNR and UNLV that not only expand local medical services but also support a vibrant biomedical research sector, along with federal research grants and private-public partnerships involving UNR and UNLV, as well as the construction of Interstate 11, linking Canadian and Mexican markets (via Tucson, Phoenix, Las Vegas, Reno, and perhaps Boise), will all have to be part of the Silver State's new equation for growth and prosperity in the twenty-first century. Some of this will require the state to spend more money than ever before to boost its economy and generate more revenue, but conservative constituencies and their political representatives will just have to bend on that to safeguard Nevada's future. Diversification can only invigorate Las Vegas, Reno, and the rest of the state. Of course, the two universities will play a key role in this effort. They will make excellent partners for big research grants, but it should be noted that Boise did not need a Carnegie top-tier research university to power the growth of computer-related companies in its metropolitan area. As Steven Hill, director of Nevada's economic development office, has pointed out, information technology companies do not necessarily need a Stanford or a Berkeley nearby to conduct their innovative research. They need an educated workforce, and in many cases private or public colleges can provide the computer-industry certification programs that most company employees will need. But a strong metropolitan university or two with advanced research infrastructures and faculty are key to attracting *major* federal grants and forming the public-private partnerships necessary to, as President Smatresk put it, "access cutting-edge science facilities."[19]

Over the next few decades Nevada will have to undertake a more determined effort to create a better-educated workforce than its casinos, mines, and ranches ever needed. Its success in doing this and in meeting the other challenges posed by America's knowledge-based economy will be crucial to the state's development and that of its two metropolitan areas. Like Texas, Arizona, Utah, and other states, Nevada must be innovative and use its metropolitan areas to attract new industries. Reno and Las Vegas can easily serve this purpose, because, at different moments in the past, both cities have embraced the future with their maverick leisure economies. As Kristi Overgaard, the executive who is leading brand development efforts for Switch, recently noted, "We need to emphasize that Las Vegas has the undercurrent of 'anything is possible.' Here we are in the middle of the desert yet we have New York City on one corner and Paris on another. There's energy night and day. And for the most part our leaders say, 'You want to do that? Okay.'"[20]

Along with maintaining a business-friendly climate, leaders in Reno, Las Vegas, and the state will need to think as imaginatively in the future as they have in the past. They need to do this if they hope to attract the right combination of industries that will trigger a renaissance of growth and prosperity reminiscent of the last century, when the two little cities used gaming and tourism in a magical way to vault their state and themselves from obscurity to stardom.

NOTES

ABBREVIATIONS

LVRJ	Las Vegas Review-Journal
LVS	Las Vegas Sun
NSJ	Nevada State Journal
REG	Reno Evening Gazette
RGJ	Reno Gazette-Journal

INTRODUCTION: Reno, Las Vegas, and the "Strip City"

1. Alicia Barber, *Reno's Big Gamble: Images and Reputation in the Biggest Little City*, 66–71, 128–36, 141–46. See also appropriate sections of William Rowley, *Reno: Hub of the Washoe Country, an Illustrated History*.

2. Although there are many works relating to the Las Vegas Strip or downtown gaming history, there are few scholarly histories of the metropolitan area. See Eugene P. Moehring, *Resort City in the Sunbelt: Las Vegas, 1930–2000*. A more recent survey, written more for the reading public, is Eugene P. Moehring and Michael S. Green, *Las Vegas: A Centennial History*. Another insightful work is John M. Findlay, *People of Chance: Gambling in American Society from Jamestown to Las Vegas*.

3. Moehring and Green, *Las Vegas*, 60–61.

4. City of Henderson, *50 Years: An American Journey*, 3–14. The actual author is Matthew Lay.

5. In his first book gaming historian David Schwartz made a convincing argument for referring to substantial hotel-casinos in Reno, Las Vegas, and elsewhere as "casino resorts." I will also use this term throughout this book. Smaller places, often lacking a hotel, will be referred to as gambling clubs and halls. See David G. Schwartz, *Suburban Xanadu: The Casino Resort on the Las Vegas Strip and Beyond*, 3.

6. Moehring, *Resort City in the Sunbelt*, 43–50.

7. For more on the Sunset Strip and its clubs in this period, see *Sunset Strip: A Film by Hans Fjellestad* (2013). See also http://www.examiner.com/article/sunset-strip-a-doc-film-about-famed-hollywood-street-on-showtime.

8. Paul J. Vanderwood, *Satan's Playground: Mobsters and Movie Stars at America's Greatest Gaming Resort*.

9. Even into the 1970s the city of Las Vegas continued to control the vast majority of administrative agencies as well as lawyer's offices. See Betty Yantis, *Fact Book for Las Vegas and Clark County*, 8-1, 8–10.

10. Übergeographer Joel Kotkin popularized the idea of edge cities in an American *and* global context in the 1980s. However, Joel Garreau formally coined the term *edge city*. See Garreau, *Edge City: Life on the New Frontier*.

11. http://www.atributosurbanos.es/en/terms/edge-city/.

12. This is not Alan Hess's "strip city," which would encompass the Strip "city district" and the Las Vegas metropolitan area it encouraged. Instead, the Strip city in this book refers to those county lands lying within the Las Vegas valley that are bounded by Las Vegas–North Las Vegas on the north, Henderson–Boulder City on the south and southeast, the Lake Mead Recreational Area on the east, and the Spring Mountains National Recreation Area and Red Rock Canyon National Conservation Area on the west. In short, my Strip city comprises a significant part of the metropolitan area but not all of it. Certainly, Strip-city economic activity has encouraged a "bedroom suburb" population multiplier in the four surrounding cities, but they also have casinos, military bases, factories, and other small industries of their own that have contributed, quite apart from the Strip resorts, to the development and overall population of the Las Vegas metropolitan area. See Alan Hess, *Viva Las Vegas: After Hours Architecture*, 112, 114, 117.

1 | RENO AREA: Gambling Gains Ascendancy, 1945–1970

1. See relevant sections of Barber, *Reno's Big Gamble*, and appropriate websites for each casino mentioned in "Nevada Club Reno: All About Historical Downtown Reno Casinos," http://www.oldreno.net/.

2. Ibid. See also relevant sections of Dwayne Kling, *The Rise of the Biggest Little City: An Encyclopedic History of Reno Gaming, 1931–1981;* and the "Old Reno" website, http://www.oldreno.net/.

3. Barber, *Reno's Big Gamble*, 147–48, 180; Moehring, *Resort City in the Sunbelt*, 29–82.

4. Barber, *Reno's Big Gamble*, 149–50, 190. Residents and the Chamber of Commerce spoke frequently of the "Real Reno" where people lived as opposed to where tourists gambled (92, 190), and even prominent travel reporters such as Phyllis Zauner willingly humored city promoters by publicizing this idea ("Finding the Real Reno"). See also City of Reno, *City Services: Trends and Issues*.

5. *NSJ*, June 26, 1946, 4.

6. See *Statutes of the State of Nevada at the Forty-Seventh Session of the Legislature* (Carson City: State Printing Office, 1955), chap. 383, 719–27, for the law enabling certain large counties to create fair and recreation boards. It was later amended to allow a name change to "convention authority." See also Carol Infranca, *Reno-Sparks Convention and Visitors Authority: A Brief History*, booklet (Reno-Sparks Convention and Visitors Authority, 1996).

7. Jud Allen, *Life Without a Safety Net: An Insider's View of War, Hollywood, and Reno*, 150.

8. *REG*, February 13, 1960, 3.

9. Sparks Centennial Book Committee, comp., *History of Sparks*.

10. Ibid.; http://en.wikipedia.org/wiki/John_Ascuaga%27s_Nugget_Casino_Resort.

11. W. Rowley, *Reno*, 70. For the situation in Phoenix, see Philip VanderMeer, *Desert Visions and the Making of Phoenix, 1860–2009*, 72–74, 129–33. For Dallas, see Robert B. Fairbanks, "The Good Government Machine: The Citizen's Charter Association and Dallas Politics, 1930–1960."

12. *REG*, October 1, 1969, 4.

13. W. Rowley, *Reno*, 70; Barbara Bennett, *Mayor of Reno and Community Activist*, 26.

14. Moehring, *Resort City in the Sunbelt*, 123.

15. *REG*, January 27, 1960, 1.

16. *REG*, January 28, 1960, 4.

17. Paul A. Leonard, *Tales of Northern Nevada—and Other Lies Recalled by a Native Son, Journalist, and Civic Leader*, 147–50; Regional Planning Commission for Reno, Sparks, and Washoe County, *Regional Planning Report, 1974*, 1.

18. Pete Cladianos, *My Father's Son: A Gaming Memoir*, 275.

19. Allen, *Life Without a Safety Net*, 165–66.

20. Ibid., 202–3.

21. Ibid., 155, 165–66.

22. *REG*, 20 May 1970, 1.

23. For a brief history of Reno-Tahoe International Airport, see http://www.rgj.com/article/20070109/NEWS10/701090336/The-history-Reno-Stead-airport. The histories provided in airport authority annual reports and other sources are too brief.

24. *REG*, February 15, 1960. See the special color issue, which showcased Reno for visitors to the Squaw Valley Winter Olympics (11).

25. *REG*, March 9, 1968, 1.

26. W. Rowley, *Reno*, 75.

27. Allen, *Life Without a Safety Net*, 146–47.

28. Ibid., 152.

29. http://dailysparkstribune.com/view/full_story/3190699/article-The-man-who-brought-us-the-Fun-Train-giant-slot-?instance=news_your_sparks_page.

30. Leonard, *Tales of Northern Nevada*, 132–33.

31. W. Rowley, *Reno*, 66.

32. *REG*, May 8, 1970, 1. Plans to improve downtown Reno date from the early 1930s. See Downtown Renovation Association, "A New Voice for Downtown Reno," File 91-49/4/30, Drackert Collection, Mathewson-IGT Knowledge Center, University of Nevada, Reno. See also Regional Planning Commission for Reno, Sparks, and Washoe County, *Two Cities on a River: A Citizen's Guide to Planning for Reno-Sparks*, 14.

33. *REG*, May 8, 1970, 1.

34. Ibid.

35. *REG*, May 7, 1970, 4. The city funded a downtown redevelopment plan to broaden support for its initiative. See Livingston and Balayney, City and Regional Planners, San Francisco, *Reno Downtown Redevelopment Plan, Urban Renewal Feasibility Survey*.

36. *REG*, September 2, 1970, 4; Allen, *Life Without a Safety Net*, 222.

37. *REG*, September 2, 1970, 2.

38. *NSJ*, June 7, 1946, 4.

39. *NSJ*, September 13, 1951, 2.

40. *NSJ*, April 9, 1978, 5.

41. Ibid.

42. *NSJ*, September 13, 1951, 12. See the "For Lease" advertisement in *REG*, September 13, 1950, 19.

43. *NSJ*, June 7, 1946, 4.

44. *REG*, May 11, 1970, 1.

45. Ibid., 1–2.

46. Ibid., 2.

47. *REG*, May 20, 1970, 1. See the population for each decade in http://en.wikipedia.org/wiki/Reno,_Nevada.

48. *REG*, October 1, 1969, 19.

49. *REG*, September 9, 1969, 1.

50. Ibid.

51. Even before the wave of hotel construction of the 1970s began in earnest, the number of building permits issued in the Reno-Sparks metropolitan area was impressive. See Regional Planning Commission for Reno, Sparks, and Washoe County, *Regional Planning Report, 1974*, 35.

52. *REG*, May 19, 1970, 7; May 20, 1970, 1.

53. *NSJ*, June 7, 1946, 4; Moehring, *Resort City in the Sunbelt*, 294.

54. *REG*, May 23, 1977, 4; Eugene P. Moehring, "Tumult in Playland: The Annexation-Consolidation Controversy in the Las Vegas Metropolitan Area" 5, 3, 14; *LVRJ*, January 20, 1979, 7.

55. Washoe Council of Governments, *Areawide Water Quality Management Plan Phase 1*, 1.

56. *LVRJ*, January 20, 1979, 7.

57. *Reno News & Review*, June 28, 2012, 6–7.

58. Allen, *Life Without a Safety Net*, 202; *NSJ*, June 13, 1960, 1.

59. *NSJ*, September 21, 1975, 4. For an insightful account of the minority casino business in Reno during the 1950s and '60s, see Lai King Chew, *The Cosmo Club and Reno's Chinese Community*, 27–64, 65–74.

60. Moehring, *Resort City in the Sunbelt*, 195–202. For the Great Society's programs in Reno, see, for example, Economic Opportunity Board of Washoe County, Annual Report, September 1971–September 1972. The first five leaves of the report summarize the programs before major budget cuts hit.

61. For minority census data in the Reno area, see Campbell Gibson and Kay Jung, *Historical Census on Population Totals by Race, 1790–1990, and by Hispanic Origin, 1790–1990, for Large Cities and Other Urban Places in the United States*, US Census Bureau, Working Paper no. 76 (February 2005), table 29, "Nevada." See also http://diversitydata.sph.harvard.edu/Data/Profiles/Show.aspx?loc=1144.

2 | LAS VEGAS AREA: Laying the Foundation, 1945–1975

1. For good coverage of the early enthusiasm about the postwar Strip and city as a new travel destination, see Lucius Beebe, "Las Vegas"; and Gladwin Hill, "Atomic Boomtown in the Desert" and "Klondike in the Desert."

2. Moehring, *Resort City in the Sunbelt*, 41–72. See also Hal Rothman, review of *Las Vegas: The Social Production of an All-American City*, by M. Gottdiener, Claudia C. Collins, and David R. Dickens, *H-Urban*, February 2001.

3. Moehring, *Resort City in the Sunbelt*, 62.

4. Ibid., 216. In 1955 the city of Las Vegas resolved to push hard at the state legislative session for legislation permitting the creation of a convention authority. See Las Vegas City Commission, *Minutes*, March 2, 1955, 437. For the bonding authorization to build the convention center, see Clark County Commission, *Minutes*, February 2, 1956, Ordinance 67.

5. *LVS*, February 17, 1970, 3. For the Nashville controversy, see Raymond A. Mohl, "The Interstates and the Cities: Highways, Housing, and the Freeway Revolt," http://www.prrac.org/pdf/mohl.pdf, 31. See also Raymond A. Mohl, "Planned Destruction: The Interstates and Central City Housing," 226–45. For the situation in Nashville and Chicago, see ibid., 235, 237. For more on the Dan Ryan Expressway plowing its way through the south side, see Harold B. Mayer and Richard C. Wade, *Chicago: Growth of a Metropolis*, 445.

6. Eugene P. Moehring, *UNLV: A History of the University of Nevada, Las Vegas*, 11.

7. *LVRJ*, May 19, 1961, 18.

8. *LVRJ*, January 1, 1968, 3.

9. Ibid.; Moehring, *Resort City in the Sunbelt*, 118, 120–22.

10. LVRJ, January 1, 1968, 3.

11. Ibid.

12. *LVRJ*, January 1, 1963, 14. For the best discussion of the metropolitan area's water needs and the plans to meet them, see Las Vegas Valley Water District, *Master Water Plan, Las Vegas Valley*.

13. Florence Lee Jones and John Cahlan, *Water: A History of Las Vegas and the Las Vegas Land and Water Company*, 2:44.

14. Ibid., 74; *LVRJ*, January 3, 1962, 28.

15. A. D. Hopkins and K. J. Evans, *The First 100: Portraits of the Men and Women Who Shaped Las Vegas*, 202.

16. *LVRJ*, January 2, 1966, 38.

17. *LVRJ*, November 2, 1962, 3. In the 1950s Mayor C. D. Baker and city commissioners installed parking meters all through downtown and at a rapid rate. See, for example, Las Vegas City Commission, *Minutes*, May 18, 1955, 516; June 6, 1956, 276.

18. Hopkins and Evans, *The First 100*, 146–47; Amy Bridges, "Politics and Growth in Sunbelt Cities," 88–89. The events in Reno mirrored those in other western cities such as Albuquerque and to some extent in Las Vegas. See Carl Abbott, *How Cities Won the West: Four Centuries of Urban Change in Western North America*, 189–90. There was a similar process in some of Texas's cities as well as elsewhere in the urban Sunbelt. See, for instance, Thomas A. Baylis, "Leadership Change in Contemporary San Antonio," 99–100.

19. Scrapbook, 1974, Series 5, Box 25, Folder 1, Oran Gragson Collection, Special Collections, Lied Library, UNLV; *LVRJ*, March 1, 1974, n.p.

20. Moehring, *Resort City in the Sunbelt*, 294; *LVRJ*, March 3, 1960, 1–2.

21. *LVRJ*, May 15, 1960, 1. For the history of Clark County's wastewater filtration efforts, see http://www.clarkcountynv.gov/Depts/parks/Documents/centennial/history/history-waterreclamationdistrict.pdf.

22. The best source for flood control in Las Vegas is Jarvis Marlow, "'Taming the Waters That Taketh from the Devil's Playground': A History of Flood Control in Las Vegas, Nevada, 1955–2010."

23. *LVRJ*, January 1, 1963, 1.

24. *LVRJ*, January 1, 1965, 1–2.

25. *LVRJ*, January 3, 1965, 18.

26. Ibid.

27. *LVRJ*, June 1, 1969, 25.

28. *LVRJ*, November 11, 1960, 4.

29. *LVRJ*, November 4, 1968, 38.

30. *LVRJ*, August 25, 1960, 30; September 5, 1960, 16.

31. *LVRJ*, February 25, 1960, 5; March 3, 1960, 3.

32. *LVRJ*, June 12, 1963, 1. For a key meeting with architects to examine plans for the new airport, see Clark County Commission, *Minutes*, March 6, 1959.

33. *LVRJ*, June 12, 1963, 1.

34. *LVRJ*, January 10, 1963, 24; November 11, 1963, 1–2; January 6, 1964, 1.

35. *LVRJ*, January 9, 1964, 1, 32.

36. Oran Gragson to James D. Richardson, HUD regional administrator, August 24, 1970, Series 3, Box 6, Folder 3, Gragson Collection, Special Collections, Lied Library, UNLV; *LVS*, December 31, 1974, 11.

37. *LVRJ*, July 19, 1964, 4.

38. See also Moehring, "Tumult in Playland." A good overview of early Boulder City is Dennis McBride, *In the Beginning: A History of Boulder City, Nevada;* and relevant sections of Joseph Stevens, *Hoover Dam: An American Adventure*.

39. UNLV Center for Gaming Research, *Las Vegas Strip Casino Employment: Productivity, Revenues, and Payroll, a Statistical Study, 1990–2011*, 1–9; *LVRJ*, July 21, 1964, 3.

40. *LVRJ*, January 3, 1965, 13.

41. *LVRJ*, January 2, 1966, 10.

42. City of Henderson, *50 Years: Henderson, an American Journey*, 48–55. Jones and Cahlan, *Water*, 2:21, 22, 23, and esp. 47. Greenspun exerted a major influence over the development of Henderson as well as the Las Vegas area. For a brief but informative view of Greenspun's influence, see Michael S. Green, "Hank Greenspun: Where He Stood."

43. *LVRJ*, May 23, 1961, 1–2. See also Eugene P. Moehring, "Laying the Foundation for the Future: Las Vegas Mayor Oran Gragson, 1959–1975" (unpublished manuscript, 2012), 9–13.

44. Ibid.

45. Ibid., 19–20.

46. *LVRJ*, June 2, 1965, 38.

47. Excellent early coverage of the race problem and civil rights effort in Las Vegas can be found in Perry B. Kaufman, "'The Best City of Them All': A History of Las Vegas, 1930–1960," 326–94. See also Moehring, *Resort City in the Sunbelt*, 184–89. Several contemporaries helped put these issues in perspective. See relevant sections of James McMillan, *Fighting Back: A Life in the Struggle for Civil Rights from Oral Histories with James B. McMillan;* Jamie Coughtry, ed., *Lubertha Johnson: Civil Rights Efforts in Las Vegas, 1940s–1960s;* and Elizabeth Nelson Patrick, ed., *Oral Interview of Reverend Prentiss Walker*.

48. Kaufman, "'Best City of Them All,'" 195–98. For the consent decree, see James P. Kraft, *Vegas at Odds: Labor Conflict in a Leisure Economy, 1960–1985,* 136–37. See also an excellent oral history study that highlights the importance of unions in a casino workplace: Susan Chandler and Jill B. Jones, *Casino Women: Courage in Unexpected Places.*

3 | RENO AREA: The Growth Wave Rises and Recedes, 1970–1990

1. *NSJ,* April 2, 1978, 5.

2. Ibid. The initiative involving the blue-ribbon panels is referred to as the Washoe County Blue Ribbon Task Force on Growth. See the task force's *Blue Ribbon Task Force Program: Growth and Development, Reno, Sparks, and Washoe County, Nevada; Committee on Water, Report I,* C2–C3, C19, C21–C22. The panel also recommended metering water use and establishing a water authority for the area. AP-C6–AP-C7, C33; Washoe County Blue Ribbon Task Force on Growth, *Summary of Findings and Recommendations,* 7–11; *NSJ,* April 2, 1978, 5.

3. *NSJ,* April 2, 1978, 5.

4. Ibid. Washoe County Blue Ribbon Task Force on Growth, *Committee on Air Pollution, Report II,* 7–12, 14–26; Washoe County Blue Ribbon Task Force on Growth, *Summary of Findings and Recommendations,* 13–15. See also *NSJ,* April 2, 1978, 5. For more on Portland's efforts in the 1970s to reduce sprawl, see Carl Abbott, *Portland: Planning, Politics, and Growth in a Twentieth-Century City,* 250–58.

5. For a good description of the Virginia Street Mall project, see Downtown Foundation, Reno Downtown Redevelopment folder, "Virginia Street Mall," File 91-49/4/30, Drackert Collection, Mathewson-IGT Knowledge Center, University of Nevada, Reno.

6. *REG,* June 8, 1938, 1; Washoe County Blue Ribbon Task Force on Growth, *Blue Ribbon Task Force Program,* 29–35.

7. *REG,* January 27, 1979, 4.

8. Ibid.

9. Washoe County Blue Ribbon Task Force on Growth, *Committee on Housing, Report III,* 23, 47; *NSJ,* April 3, 1978, 5.

10. Washoe County Blue Ribbon Task Force on Growth, *Committee on Housing,* 28–33. The panel also urged the cities to change their zoning laws to allow more high-density dwellings. Ibid., 41; *NSJ,* April 3, 1978, 5.

11. *NSJ,* June 29, 1978, 4.

12. Washoe County Blue Ribbon Task Force on Growth, *Committee on Design, Report No. 5,* 2–4; Barber, *Reno's Big Gamble,* 197. Barber's views are reinforced by two other distinguished Nevada historians. See Eric Moody and Guy Rocha, "The Rise and Fall of the Reno Stockade."

13. Bryant Simon, *Boardwalk of Dreams: Atlantic City and the Fate of Urban America*, 195, 197, 199; Barber, *Reno's Big Gamble*, 215.

14. *NSJ*, April 5, 1978, 4.

15. Ibid. See also US Department of Transportation, Federal Aviation Administration, *Environmental Impact Assessment Report, Land Acquisition Program, Reno International Airport, Reno, Nevada*.

16. *NSJ*, April 6, 1978, 4. There are two reports: the majority report by William Eadington and growth-control supporters is Washoe County Blue Ribbon Task Force on Growth, *Economics of Growth Committee, Report VII*, see 1–6, 23–26, and the minority report of businessman Wayne Dennis and his supporters, appended to it as pages 42–79 and with a separate publication date (January 30, 1974).

17. Washoe County Blue Ribbon Task Force on Growth, *Economics of Growth Committee, Report VII*, 27–30; Carl Abbott, *The Metropolitan Frontier: Cities in the Modern American West*, 102–3; Abbott, *How Cities Won the West*, 205; Carl Abbott, *The New Urban America: Growth and Politics in Sunbelt Cities*, 215–17.

18. Washoe County Blue Ribbon Task Force on Growth, *Economics of Growth Committee*, 1–6, 23–26; Bennett, *Mayor of Reno*, 25.

19. Ibid., 26.

20. *NSJ*, April 8, 1978, 4.

21. Ibid.

22. See Deirdre Coakley, Hank Greenspun, and Harry C. Gerard, *The Day the MGM Grand Hotel Burned*, 165–68, for the numerous code violations that led to the disastrous conflagration, the lessons from which eventually upgraded hotel fire-safety standards worldwide.

23. *NSJ*, April 13, 1978, 8.

24. Ibid.

25. Ibid. For downtown revitalization, see Greater Reno-Sparks Chamber of Commerce, *Operation Pride: Downtown Revitalization Plan*, brochure (Greater Reno-Sparks Chamber of Commerce, 1983). See also the positive message sent by the chamber of commerce to downtown businesspeople. Tom Fiannaca, president, Greater Reno-Sparks Chamber of Commerce, "Chamber of Commerce to Downtown Business Leaders," August 19, 1983, File 91-49/4/30, Drackert Collection, Mathewson-IGT Knowledge Center, University of Nevada, Reno.

26. *NSJ*, April 1, 1978, 4.

27. *NSJ*, May 2, 1975, 7.

28. *NSJ*, May 2, 1978, 8.

29. Barber, *Reno's Big Gamble*, 196; *Wall Street Journal*, May 7, 1978, 2; *NSJ*, May 2, 1978, 8.

30. *NSJ*, May 2, 1978, 8.

31. Ibid.

32. *NSJ*, April 12, 1978, 8.

33. Ibid.

34. *NSJ*, April 9, 1978, 9.

35. Ibid.

36. Ibid.; Paul Starrs, Heather Van Wormer, and Jean Harrah, *Downtown Reno and the Railroad: A Report of the Project on Historical Growth and Development of Downtown Reno.*

37. *NSJ*, April 9, 1978, 12.

38. Bennett, *Mayor of Reno*, 50.

39. *NSJ*, April 12, 1978, 9.

40. Ibid.

41. See the population table in City of Reno, *Reno City Profile* (Reno, 1982); and *NSJ*, September 22, 1976, 2.

42. Bennett, *Mayor of Reno*, 47.

43. Ibid.; W. Rowley, *Reno*, 79.

44. Bennett, *Mayor of Reno*, 44.

45. *NSJ*, September 18, 1976, 1–2.

46. *NSJ*, May 5, 1978, 2.

47. *NSJ*, May 7, 1978, 4.

48. Bennett, *Mayor of Reno*, 63.

49. *NSJ*, May 2, 1975, 7; Allen, *Life Without a Safety Net*, 158.

50. *NSJ*, July 13, 1979, 24. US Environmental Protection Agency and City of Reno, *Environmental Impact Statement Reno-Sparks Joint Water Pollution Control Plant Cross-Town Sewer and Lawton-Verdi Interceptor Extension*, 1–3, 1–10, 1–14.

51. http://en.wikipedia.org/wiki/Eldorado_Hotel_Casino; *NSJ*, June 29, 1978, 8–9.

52. See relevant sections of Kling, *Rise of the Biggest Little City*.

53. *NSJ*, April 9, 1978, 5.

54. For more on efforts to improve water quality, see Washoe Council of Governments, *Areawide Water Quality Management Plan Phase 1*. See also *NSJ*, April 9, 1978, 5.

55. *LVRJ*, September 22, 1976, 8.

56. The airport authority was approved on May 12, 1977. *Statutes of Nevada*, 1977, vol. 2, chap. 474, 968–77. As the 1980s progressed, the cost of running even a smaller international airport became substantial. See, for instance, Reno-Tahoe International Airport, *Comprehensive Annual Financial Report for July 1, 2006–June 30, 2007* (Reno and Sparks: Airport Authority of Washoe County, Nevada, 2007), 1; and Airport Authority of Washoe County, Nevada, *Comprehensive Annual Financial Report for the Fiscal Year Ended June 30, 1987* (Reno and Sparks: Airport Authority of Washoe County, Nevada, 1987), 1–2.

57. Moehring, *Resort City in the Sunbelt*, 62–63.

58. Barber, *Reno's Big Gamble*, 191; W. Rowley, *Reno*, 67–68, 79; US Department of Commerce, Bureau of the Census, *1980 Census of Population and Housing*, 1, 10–12.

59. Bennett, *Mayor of Reno*, 58.

60. Ibid., 49.

61. Ibid., 35.

62. Barbara N. Land and Myrick Land, *A Short History of Reno*, 120–21.

4 | LAS VEGAS AREA: Recession Turns to Boom, 1975–2007

1. For an informative account of how promoters viewed Las Vegas's future during the mid-1970s, see Las Vegas Chamber of Commerce, *Where Is Las Vegas Going? Get the Full Facts of the Present and Future Economy of Las Vegas*.

2. Moehring, *Resort City in the Sunbelt*, 115–22, 263–76. See also Schwartz, *Suburban Xanadu*. For Las Vegas's promotional efforts to draw more tourists and businesses to the area, see, for instance, Las Vegas Chamber of Commerce, *Where Is Las Vegas Going?*

3. Gottdiener, Collins, and Dickens, *Las Vegas*, 107.

4. The best coverage of Las Vegas's real estate development from the 1970s to 2000 can be found in Geoff Schumacher, *Sun, Sin, and Suburbia: An Essential History of Modern Las Vegas*, 137–47.

5. Ibid., 144–49, 228–31.

6. For more on the transition from Las Vegas Transit to the CAT bus system, see http://en.wikipedia.org/wiki/Las_Vegas_Transit.

7. For Broadbent's public life, see http://www.lasvegassun.com/news/2003/aug/11/longtime-public-servant-broadbent-dies/#axzz2VOrMr82p. A good source for the airport's construction and various expansion projects is Daniel Bubb, *Landing in Las Vegas: Commercial Aviation and the Making of a Tourist City*.

8. Las Vegas Convention and Visitors Authority, "Executive Summary," in *Las Vegas Visitor Profile, Calendar Year 2012*, 24. The percentage of visitors arriving by air has held at roughly this percentage for the past decade.

9. For the city of Las Vegas's population, see the demographics chart in http://en.wikipedia.org/wiki/Las_Vegas#Demographics.

10. Schumacher, *Sun, Sin, and Suburbia*, 117–32. See also Phil Hagen, *The Meadows School: Celebrating 25 Years*.

11. Schumacher, *Sun, Sin, and Suburbia*, 174, 190.

12. For a brief overview of early plans for Lake Las Vegas, see Eugene P. Moehring, "Growth, Services, and the Political Economy of Gambling in Las Vegas, 1970–2000," 78; and Pat Mulroy to Eugene Moehring, September 24, 2013.

13. For the best coverage of the CCFCD's efforts to control flooding, see Marlow, "Taming the Waters."

14. Steve Sloan, "Wynn Plunks Down $2.7 Billion on Las Vegas Strip," *USA Today*, April 22, 2005, D1; *LVRJ*, December 26, 1993, 15D–16D; February 15, 1998, 5E; October 15, 1998, 1A; Hess, *Viva Las Vegas*, 114. For an overview of this resort's significance at the time, see Joel Stein, "The Strip Is Back."

15. *LVRJ*, December 14, 1995, 1C; May 16, 1995, 7C. The concept of the Mirage Revolution was first developed in Eugene P. Moehring, "Las Vegas," 161–62. In earlier decades a few hotels opened gourmet rooms run by chefs who were more locally than nationally famous. In 1957, for instance, Perino's in the Tropicana was run by prominent Los Angeles restaurateur Tony Perino.

16. *LVRJ*, October 10, 1993, 1A. For New York–New York, see January 3, 1997, 1A. For the $6.7 billion offer and the later sale as well as other key transactions and deals for Wynn, see http://www.onlinenevada.org/steve_wynn.

17. *LVRJ*, June 20, 2004, 3E.

18. See George Stamos's articles in *LVRJ*, November 27, 1989, 1B, 4B–5B. See also *LVRJ*, August 24, 1993, 1A–2A.

19. *LVRJ*, June 20, 1990, 1A; October 10, 1993, 1A.

20. *LVRJ*, June 8, 1996, 7E; February 28, 1999, 1A, 22A–23A; February 2, 1999, 1A, 1D–2D; March 3, 1996, 7E.

21. *LVRJ*, August 29, 1999, 1A; July 21, 1999, 1D, 2D.

22. *LVS*, February 4, 2002, 1E, 4E; October 31, 1996, 1E. Andres Martinez, *24/7: Living It Up and Doubling Down in the New Las Vegas*, offers a lively account of the 1990s "New Las Vegas."

23. http://en.wikipedia.org/wiki/Las_Vegas_Monorail. For illustrations of the 1960s and early '70s plans for a Las Vegas monorail, see letter from Aerial Transit Systems of Nevada, February 21, 1971, Series 3, Box 12, Folder 10, Gragson Collection, Special Collections, Lied Library, UNLV, as well as other pictures and documents referring to the "Harrod Super Train," March 1967; and *LVRJ*, March 1, 1974, n.p. For Reno's reaction, see *REG*, January 11, 1999, 4A.

24. *LVRJ*, August 31, 1991, 1A. Of course, there had been plans, as early as the 1970s, to revitalize downtown. See Burrell Cohen, development consultant, and James McDaniel, architects, "An Action Plan for Downtown," prepared for the Downtown Hotel Association (unpublished, Las Vegas, 1975).

25. *LVRJ*, June 16, 2007, 3D. Goodman had many significant accomplishments as mayor. See appropriate sections of Oscar Goodman with George Anastasia, *Being Oscar: From Mob Lawyer to Mayor of Las Vegas, Only in America*.

26. http://www.apnewsarchive.com/1996/Vegas-Dome-Planned-To-Seat-110-000/id-a2cb2b48472427af9dfd67e1b34d30d4.

27. *LVRJ*, December 14, 1995, 1B, 7B.

28. *LVRJ*, April 30, 1996, 1A; May 1, 1996, 1A; September 2, 1999, 1D, 2D.

29. For a sampling of Las Vegas red-line and gaming-license policies, see Las Vegas City Commission, *Minutes*, 9:36, 38–41, 55. For coverage of the abolition of Las Vegas's red-line policy, see *LVRJ*, February 2, 1989, D7; and February 9, 1989, B1, B8.

30. *LVRJ*, February 2, 1989, D7; February 9, 1989, B1, B8; Ron Lurie, personal communication with Eugene Moehring, June 12, 2012.

31. *LVRJ*, February 9, 1989, B8.

32. See *NRS* 463.3084, 463.308, and 463.3086.

33. Clark County was also engaged in a substantial planning and updating process to guide the location of resorts as well as future commercial and residential developments. See, for instance, Clark County Planning Commission, *Comprehensive Plan, Clark County, Nevada*. For the J. W. Marriott, see http://en.wikipedia.org/wiki/JW_Marriott_Las_Vegas. For the Santa Fe Station, see http://en.wikipedia.org/wiki/Santa_Fe-Station.

34. For minority census data in the Las Vegas area, see Gibson and Jung, *Historical Census*, table 29, "Nevada" (see chap. 1, note 61).

35. *LVRJ*, September 9, 2012, 6B.

36. Gibson and Jung, *Historical Census*, table 29, "Nevada."

37. Ibid. For more on the minority population in the Las Vegas area, see US Department of Commerce, Bureau of the Census, *County and City Data Book, 1962*, 596; US Department of Commerce, Bureau of the Census, *County and City Data Book, 1977*, 696; and US Department of Commerce, Bureau of the Census. *County and City Data Book, 1983*, 740.

38. *LVRJ*, February 9, 2005, 1D, 4D; February 14, 2007, 10.

39. *LVRJ*, September 15, 2005, 1D, 3D; October 28, 2003, 1D, 3D.

40. *LVRJ*, July 30, 2004, 1A, 4A.

41. *LVS*, June 15, 2006, 1, 3; *LVRJ*, February 26, 2004, 1D, 3D; March 13, 2007, 1D, 4D; June 20, 2007, 1D, 3D; August 2, 2008, 4A.

42. *LVRJ*, July 7, 2004, 1D, 3D.

43. For the Palazzo, see *LVRJ*, January 13, 2008, 1E, 5E. For Steve Wynn's actions, see *LVRJ*, December 16, 2007, 1E, 4E.

44. *LVRJ*, April 25, 2005, 35A. An informative account of the key figures, such as Steve Wynn, who built some of Las Vegas's most important hotels at different times in its history can be found in Jack E. Sheehan, ed., *The Players: The Men Who Made Las Vegas*.

45. *LVRJ*, May 1, 2005, 1E, 4E.

46. *LVRJ*, December 21, 2008, 1E, 5E.

47. *LVS*, December 23, 2008, 3; *LVRJ*, December 21, 2008, 1A, 2A.

48. *LVRJ*, December 16, 2007, 1E, 4E.

49. *LVRJ*, March 13, 2007, 1D, 3D.

50. Ibid. For good coverage of the locals' gambling scene at these suburban resorts, see appropriate sections of Rex J. Rowley, *Everyday Las Vegas: Local Life in a Tourist Town*.

51. *LVRJ*, August 1, 2011, 1A, 4A.

52. *LVRJ*, April 27, 2008, 1E, 5E.

53. *LVS*, June 15, 2006, 1, 3; *LVRJ*, May 17, 2007, 1D, 4D; September 24, 2011, 1.

54. *LVRJ*, December 14, 2010, 1, 3; September 24, 2011, 1.

55. *LVS*, April 8, 2006, 1–2.

56. *LVRJ*, May 8, 2004, 1E.

57. *LVRJ*, December 25, 2005, 1D, 2D, 3D.

58. *LVRJ*, March 27, 2005, 30A–31A.

59. *LVS*, September 1, 2006, 1–2.

60. *LVRJ*, December 21, 2003, 1B, 10B.

61. *LVS*, September 17, 2006, 9.

62. For the Blue Diamond Road improvement project, see http://www.r2h.com/t-blue.html.

5 | RENO AREA: Transition and Depression, 1990–2014

1. http://en.wikipedia.org/wiki/Reno_Air; Reno-Sparks Convention and Visitors Authority, *Visitor Profile Study, 1985 Summary Report*, n.p. See "Summary of Findings" near the front.

2. Reno-Sparks Convention and Visitors Authority, *Marketing Report, 1987*, 15. For an evaluation of the decline in convention delegates during the 1980s, see Reno-Sparks Convention and Visitors Authority, *Decade of the 1980s*, 76–81, 96, 99, 101.

3. *LVS*, August 15, 1997, 1; W. Rowley, *Reno*, 76; LVRJ, July 9, 1997, 10B; April 17, 1998, 1A, 5A; *LVS*, January 12, 1997, 5D. The inspiration for Senator Titus's plan was Portland. See Abbott, *Portland*, 257–58, for the "Urban Growth Boundary."

4. http://en.wikipedia.org/wiki/Silver_Legacy_Resort_Casino.

5. http://en.wikipedia.org/wiki/Atlantis_Casino_Resort.

6. Barber, *Reno's Big Gamble*, 223.

7. The *Reno Evening Gazette* and *Nevada State Journal* merged in print on October 1, 1983, becoming the *Reno Gazette-Journal*. *RGJ*, February 21, 2003, 1A, 6A.

8. For more on tribal casinos in the Northwest states, see http://www.indiancasinos.com/oregon,shtml, http://www.indiancasinos.com/washington/shtml, and http://www.indiancasinos.com/idaho.shtml.

9. http://en.wikipedia.org/wiki/Grand_Sierra_Resort.

10. http://en.wikipedia.org/wiki/The_Montage_Reno.

11. For the 1998 visitor profile, see *RGJ*, July 4, 1999, 1E, 5E–6E; and William Eadington, *Gaming and Nevada's Economic Future: The Challenges Ahead, Directions, 2011*.

12. Ibid.

13. Ibid.

14. Ibid.

15. http://www.vegastripping.com/news/blog/1673/murky-future-for-reno-casinos-/. For Mandelstam's comments, see *NSJ*, April 24, 1983, 1F, 2F, File 91-49/4/30, Drackert Collection, Mathewson-IGT Knowledge Center, University of Nevada, Reno. Of course, Reno also had its supporters. See Tom Chiarella, "The Dirtiest Secret in Nevada."

16. Cladianos, *My Father's Son*, 266.

17. http://www.vegastripping.com/news/blog/1673/murky-future-for-reno-casinos-/.

18. *RGJ*, February 21, 2003, 1A, 6A.

19. *RGJ*, October 28, 2001, 5E.

20. *RGJ*, January 11, 1999, 4A. See also Reno-Sparks Convention and Visitors Authority, *Marketing Report for 1990*.

21. *RGJ*, January 11, 1999, 4A.

22. Ibid.

23. *RGJ*, January 11, 1999, 5A.

24. http://www.rtcwashoe.com/public-transportation-5. For a critical view of Keene, see Cladianos, *My Father's Son*, 278.

25. For Eadington's comments regarding Reno and Lake Tahoe gambling as a declining tourist draw, see http://www.lasvegassun.com/news/2010/jul/23/q-william-eadington/#axzz2Y2COO2w7.

26. *RGJ*, January 11, 1999, 4A.

27. *RGJ*, July 28, 1990, 3. See also special section (18).

28. *RGJ*, July 23, 1990, 3. See also Sierra Pacific Resources, *Business Portrait of Reno-Sparks*, 5th ed. (1993), 11, 15; and Sierra Pacific Resources, Economic Development Department, *Discover It: Downtown Reno, Live, Work, Play* (ca. 2007), 10.

29. The bowling stadium was one of the more controversial projects, because it was a relatively expensive project not built for residents but more for special tournaments designed to attract tourists. See Bill Barol, "Lanes Paved with Gold."

30. Mary Ringhoff and Edward Stoner, *The River and the Railroad: An Archaeological History of Reno*, 57–58.

31. http://www.downtownmakeover.com/1-15-11-ReTrac-Retrospect.asp; Steve Varela, City of Reno, Director of Public Works, *Final Proposed ReTRAC Project Plan, Prepared for US Department of Transportation, Federal Highway Administration and State of Nevada, Department of Transportation, Prepared by Steve Varela, Director of Public Works, City of Reno*. See also Air Sciences, Inc., Prepared for Nevadans for Fast and Responsible Action, *Analysis of Air Emission Increases Resulting from the Union Pacific and Southern Pacific Railroad Merger and Effects on the Management of the Air Resource of the Truckee Meadows Nonattainment Area*, 1.

32. Barber, *Reno's Big Gamble*, 193.
33. Ibid.; *NSJ*, September 18, 1975, 4.
34. *NSJ*, September 18, 1975, 12.
35. http://www.newsreview.com/reno/reno-scape/content.question?old-19196.
36. Ibid.
37. http://articles,latimes.com/1997-01-04/news/mn-15395_1_flood-water.
38. For median incomes in Reno neighborhoods, see http://www.areavibes.com/reno-nv/neighborhoods/east+reno/areavibe/.
39. http://doublediamondranch.org/.
40. http://Renotahoe.about.com/od/neighborhoodprofiles/a/damonteranch.htm.
41. For Kiley Ranch, see http://www.nevadabusinessreport.com/stories/html/2006/10/02/162.php. See also http://www.thebizscoop.com/2011/11/kiley-ranch-sale-is-the-largest-3rd-party-trustee-sale-in-therenosparksareas-history1.
42. Ibid.
43. http://www.rgj.com/article/20090827/BIZ908270342. For the Silver Legacy's bankruptcy filing, see http://www.bloomberg.com/news/2012-05-18/circus-eldorado-joint-venture-seeks-bankruptcy-in-nevada-1-.html.
44. For the Atlantis Sky Bridge, see http://www.visitrenotahoe.com/media/news-releases/?564%5Bcommands%5D=view&64%5Bid%5D=225.
45. One can determine the square footage available for meetings by consulting the websites of each facility mentioned.
46. http://edawn.otoip.net/news/publications/columns/03-08-2009/edawn-column-for-the-reno-gazette-journal-for-sunday,-march-8,-2009.
47. For C. A. Howlett's comments, see http://nj.npri.org/nj98/09/cover_story.htm.
48. *Boise Weekly*, September 2–8, 2009, 11–14.
49. Ibid.
50. Ibid. For the reference to Boise State, see http://bsgift.org/boise_state_university. See also Heike Meyer, "Boise Idaho: An Overview of the High Technology Economy in the Treasure Valley," http://www.idahotechconnect.com/Documents%20and%20Settings/7/Site%20Documents/Boise_Issue%20Paper_Feb%202008_Final.pdf.
51. Bennett, *Mayor of Reno*, 60. Sparks also funded a vigorous redevelopment effort of its own in the early twenty-first century. See, for example, City of Sparks Redevelopment Agency, *Redevelopment Agency of the City of Sparks, Final Budget*.
52. http://www.csmonitor.com/2001/0313/p12s1.html.
53. *LVRJ*, June 27, 2012, 1D.

6 | LAS VEGAS: Depression and Some Recovery, 2007–2014

1. *LVRJ*, December 11, 2008, 1D.
2. *LVRJ*, February 28, 2009, 1D, 2D; February 7, 2007, 3D.

3. *LVRJ,* February 23, 2008, 3D. For more on the Sahara's history before its demise, see Eugene P. Moehring, "The Sahara Hotel: Las Vegas' 'Jewel in the Desert,'" in *Stripping Las Vegas: A Contextual Review of Las Vegas Casino Resort Architecture,* edited by Karin Jaschke and Silke Otsch, 13–40. The Sahara was also part of the unique architectural style first chronicled in the classic book by Robert Venturi, Denise Scott Brown, and Steven Izenour, *Learning from Las Vegas: The Forgotten Symbolism of Architectural Form.*

4. *LVS,* August 9, 2009, 1, 8, 9.

5. *LVS,* November 29, 2009, 1, 9, 10.

6. *LVS,* March 28, 2009, 1, 3; March 3, 2009, 1, 2.

7. http://www.marketwatch.com/story/terry-lanni-once-ceo-of-mgm-dies-at-68-2011-07-15.

8. *LVRJ,* May 20, 2013, 1, 4.

9. *LVS,* May 20, 2013, 1, 4; *LVRJ,* June 4, 2013, 5E; September 23, 2013, 3B. Pat Mulroy to Eugene Moehring, September 24, 2013.

10. *LVRJ,* March 1, 2009, 1A, 26A; June 2, 2011, D2.

11. *LVS,* January 3, 2006, 7.

12. *LVS,* February 23, 2006, 3.

13. *LVS,* May 11, 2009, 8.

14. *LVS,* July 20, 2008, 1, 8.

15. It was not until 2013 that home prices began to rebound and plans were announced to resume building at Inspirada and other projects. See LVRJ, January 11, 2014, 1D, 3D; and January 14, 2014, 1E, 2E.

16. *LVRJ,* July 20, 2008, 1E, 4E.

17. *Las Vegas Business Press,* March 2–8, 2009, 10; *LVRJ,* December 30, 2012, 3E.

18. *LVRJ,* July 1, 2009, 7A.

19. *LVRJ,* September 28, 2011, 1B, 5B. As late as 2007 enrollment was still increasing in the metropolitan area. See Clark County School District, *Comprehensive Annual Financial Report... Finance and Operations Division, Fiscal Year Ended June 30, 2007,* iv, v.

20. *Time,* August 24, 2009, 22.

21. *LVRJ,* December 12, 2010, 20A–21A; *LVS,* February 12, 2010, 1–22.

22. *LVRJ,* December 14, 2010, 1A, 8A.

23. *LVS,* July 23, 2011, 4; *LVRJ,* July 12, 2013, 3D.

24. *LVRJ,* April 16, 2005, 1D, 3D.

25. *LVS,* August 10, 2010, 5.

26. *LVS,* July 25, 2004, 1J; June 27, 2004, 1D, 4D. In the late 1980s and early 1990s officials began stressing the need for water conservation and devising ambitious construction projects to provide more water for the metro area's future population.

See the population projections and other relevant graphs in Las Vegas Valley Water District, *General Information*, n.p. A voter-approved sales tax increase of .25 percent in 1998 helped fund the SNWA's construction projects. An excellent source for the development of the SNWA is Christian S. Harrison, "Desert Paradigm: Las Vegas, the Southern Nevada Water Authority, and Water Politics in the Colorado River Basin."

27. *LVS*, July 25, 2004, 1J; June 27, 2004, 1D, 4D.

28. *LVRJ*, July 28, 2004, 1B, 3B.

29. *LVRJ*, April 22, 2007, 1D.

30. *LVRJ*, January 21, 2011, 1A, 2A; March 3, 2011, B1.

31. *LVS*, December 14, 2010, 1, 3.

32. For more on mixed-use developments in Las Vegas, see http://www.lasvegastodayandtomorrow.com/page9mixed.htm.

33. http://www.reviewjournal.com/real-estate/firm-certifies-mountains-edge-providence-ranks-top-5-national-sales.

34. *LVS*, March 28, 2004, 1F, 3F.

35. http://www.lasvegassun.com/news/2006/jun/25/smith-center-wont-be-cheap/#axzz2XTnSJSaL.

36. *LVRJ*, May 15, 2005, 33A, 34A.

37. *LVRJ*, September 23, 2003, 1D, 4D. For more on downtown revitalization, see *LVS*, January 7, 2014, 1, 5. See also Christopher Hall, "Vegas on Fire."

38. *LVRJ*, December 19, 2004, 40A–41A.

39. *LVRJ*, May 10, 2006, 1A–3A.

40. *LVRJ*, September 2, 2012, 3. For a good description of the museum, see http://en.wikipedia.org/wiki/Neon_Museum.

41. http://en.wikipedia.org/wiki/Las_Vegas_Springs_Preserve; http://www.nevadaculture.org/.

42. *LVS*, January 18, 2007, 2. For a glimpse of Hsieh's philosophy, see appropriate sections of Tony Hsieh, *Delivering Happiness: A Path to Profits, Passion, and Purpose*.

43. http://en.wikipedia.org/Mob_Museum.

44. *LVRJ*, February 2, 2011, 1A, 4A; September 26, 2011, 1B, 3B.

45. *LVS*, March 28, 2012, 1, 4; 20; *LVRJ*, April 20, 2012, 1D, 3D; http://www.inc.com/issie-lapowsky/tony-hsieh-vegas-downtown-project-strides.html. For the Container Park, see *LVS*, December 1, 2013, 10.

46. http://www.8newsnow.com/story/22553506/report-nevada-ranks-near-bottom-for-science-and-tech-jobs.

47. *LVS*, May 14, 2013, 5. For the MGM Resorts International arena behind New York–New York, see *LVRJ*, November 5, 2013, 1A, 4A. See also Hall, "Vegas on Fire."

48. *LVS*, June 11, 2008, 1, 2.

49. *LVRJ*, December 24, 2006, 1E, 3E.
50. *LVRJ*, April 4, 2010, 1E, 4E.
51. *LVRJ*, March 4, 2004, 1D, 7D; June 28, 2005, 1D. A good overview of downtown's revitalization as of mid-2013 can be found in *LVRJ*, June 30, 2013. See the special section entitled "Delivering a New Downtown."
52. *LVRJ*, January 1, 2006, 1E, 4E.
53. *LVRJ*, September 30, 2011, 1D, 3D; March 13, 2012, 1D, 4D. For the Downtown Grand, see *LVRJ*, October 28, 2013, 1A, 8A.
54. *LVRJ*, March 3, 2012, 3B. For a more critical view of Goodman, see *Review-Journal* columnist John L. Smith's book *Of Rats and Men: Oscar Goodman's Life from Mob Mouthpiece to Mayor of Las Vegas*.
55. *LVRJ*, June 14, 2011, 1D, 2D.
56. http://www.lasvegassun.com/news/2011/jul/01/another-low-ranking/#axzz2XTnSJSaL.
57. For more on Switch, see http://en.wikipedia.org/wiki/Switch_Communications.
58. *LVRJ*, March 12, 2007, 1D, 4D.
59. Ibid.
60. *LVS*, January 25, 2010, 1, 3; January 18, 2012, 1, 2.
61. *LVRJ*, April 19, 2012, B2; *LVS*, July 5, 2011, 1, 5.
62. Ibid.
63. Neal Smatresk and William Boldt, e-mails to Eugene Moehring, January 25 and February 2, 2013. See also Brian Greenspun's columns on Brookings coming to UNLV in *LVS*, September 8, 2009, 1; September 13, 2009, 1.
64. *LVS*, September 8, 2009, 1; August 26, 2009, 1.
65. For the Lincy Institute proposal, see the ten-page "Organizational Unit Proposal, Lincy Foundation," prepared by Neal Smatresk and William Boldt based on input from Lindy Schumacher, Nevada's representative for the Lincy Foundation (UNLV, July 31, 2009).
66. *LVRJ*, January 6, 2011, 7B.
67. Las Vegas Chamber of Commerce, "Dr. Neal Smatresk Talks Economic Diversification and Education." See also http://www.lasvegassun.com/news/2011/apr/21/unlvs-overture-business-execs-includes-tour/.
68. *LVRJ*, January 6, 2011, 7B.
69. *LVS*, September 9, 2009, 1, 3. For Smatresk's announcement, see http://news.unlv.edu/article/state-university-address-now-available-online. For more on the Carnegie Foundation for the Advancement of Teaching's classifications, see http://classifications.carnegiefoundation.org/ and http://www.unlv.edu/president/tier1/faq.
70. Neal Smatresk, "A Message for the UNLV Community from President Neal Smatresk," e-mail, September 7, 2010.

71. *LVS,* June 15, 2011, 1, 3, 9. For more on the earlier phase of downtown Phoenix's transformation, see VanderMeer, *Desert Visions,* 324–36.

72. Ibid.

73. *LVRJ,* March 5, 2013, 1A, 4A. See also the editorial on 8B.

74. See the KLAS-TV report on rising North Strip land values after the Genting Group's announcement at http://www.8newsnow.com/story/21815993/new-projects-could-spark-north-strip-redevelopment. *LVS,* August 1, 2013, 8.

75. *LVS,* April 20, 2013, 6.

76. *LVRJ,* January 27, 2013, 1E, 2E.

77. http://www.vegasinc.com/news/2013/feb/26/nevada-development-authority-gets-new-name-new-hom/.

7 | RENO AND LAS VEGAS AREAS: A Comparative View

1. Bennett, *Mayor of Reno,* 48.

2. Early maps of the town clearly show the relative lack of space on the outskirts of Las Vegas (but within the city line) for resort hotels, while the lots along Fremont Street are larger and clearly the best place for commercial establishments such as casinos. See Sanborn Map Company, "Insurance Maps of Las Vegas, Nevada."

3. Barber, *Reno's Big Gamble,* 85.

4. John F. Cahlan, personal communication to Eugene Moehring, June 14, 1986.

5. Elaine Wynn, personal communication to Eugene Moehring, April 21, 2005.

6. Eugene P. Moehring, "City and Spectacle: How Steve Wynn Changed the Las Vegas Landscape," 202.

7. Gottdiener, Collins, and Dickens, *Las Vegas,* 127.

8. Rothman, review of *Las Vegas,* by Gottdiener, Collins, and Dickens, *H-Urban,* February 2001.

9. Schwartz, *Suburban Xanadu,* 7; Simon, *Boardwalk of Dreams,* 199.

10. Charles Hall Paige and Associates, *Historic Preservation Inventory and Guidelines: City of Las Vegas,* 101, 84.

11. For a list of Reno and Sparks annexations from 1868 just to 1974, see Regional Planning Commission, *Regional Planning Report, 1974,* 29.

12. For Las Vegas's various attempts to annex the Strip, see Moehring, "Tumult in Playland."

13. Moehring, *Resort City in the Sunbelt,* 145.

14. Ibid., 145–46.

15. Allen, *Life Without a Safety Net,* 215–16.

16. Bennett, *Mayor of Reno,* 28.

17. *LVRJ,* October 21, 2007, 2J–3J.

18. *LVRJ,* April 22, 2012, 1E.

19. *LVS*, September 1, 2013, 5. See also Robert Lang's article in *LVS*, September 8, 2013, 5. For drone development, see *LVRJ*, December 31, 2013, 1A, 8A; for more on Interstate 11's potential impact on Las Vegas's economy, see 1A, 17A–20A. For more on UNLV's proposed medical school, see the consultant's report: Tripp-Umbach, "Economic Impact of Medical Education Expansion in Nevada: Economic Impact Assessment and Recommended Approach," October 24, 2013. The Nevada Board of Regents actively recruited a development dean in the spring of 2014 and pushed for a fall 2016 inaugural class for the new UNLV medical school while also seeking public and private funding to expand the UNR medical school to full scale. The ultimate goal was to position the two schools in the near future to pursue biomedical research grants that would help diversify the economies of both metropolitan areas.

20. http://www.vegasinc.com/news/2012/nov/05/how-nevada-trying-grow-its-tech-sector-and-succeed/.

BIBLIOGRAPHY

NEWSPAPERS

Boise Weekly
Las Vegas Business Press
Las Vegas Review-Journal
Las Vegas Sun
Nevada State Journal
New York Times
Reno Evening Gazette
Reno Gazette-Journal
Reno News & Review
USA Today
Wall Street Journal

GOVERNMENT PUBLICATIONS

Air Sciences, Inc., Prepared for Nevadans for Fast and Responsible Action. *Analysis of Air Emission Increases Resulting from the Union Pacific and Southern Pacific Railroad Merger and Effects on the Management of the Air Resource of the Truckee Meadows Nonattainment Area.* October 1997.

City of Henderson. *50 Years: Henderson, an American Journey.* Henderson, 2004.

City of Reno. *City Services: Trends and Issues.* August 1944.

City of Sparks. *City of Sparks Redevelopment Agency, Final Budget.* May 24, 2004.

Clark County, Board of Commissioners, *Minutes, 1909–1960.* Clark County Government Center.

Clark County Planning Commission. *Comprehensive Plan, Clark County, Nevada.* 6 vols. Las Vegas, 1981.

Clark County School District. *Comprehensive Annual Financial Report... Finance and Operations Division for Fiscal Year Ended June 30, 2007.* Las Vegas: Clark County School District, 2007.

Economic Opportunity Board of Washoe County. *Annual Report, September 1971–September 1972.* Reno: Economic Opportunity Board of Washoe County, October 1972.

Las Vegas, Board of City Commissioners. *Minutes, 1911–1959.* Printed edition at Special Collections, Lied Library, University of Nevada, Las Vegas.

Las Vegas Convention and Visitors Authority. *Las Vegas Visitor Profile, Calendar Year, 2012.* San Francisco: GLS Research, 2012.

Las Vegas Valley Water District. *General Information.* Las Vegas, 1991.

———. *Master Water Plan, Las Vegas Valley.* Las Vegas: Boyle Engineering, 1970.

Livingston and Balayney, City and Regional Planners, San Francisco. *Reno Downtown Development Plan, Urban Renewal Feasibility Study.* May 1970.

Regional Planning Commission for Reno, Sparks, and Washoe County. *Regional Planning Report, 1974.* Reno: February 1975.

———. *Two Cities on a River: A Citizen's Guide to Planning for Reno-Sparks.* February 1, 1966.

Reno-Sparks Convention and Visitors Authority. *Decade of the 1980s.* Reno, 1991.

———. *Marketing Report, 1987.* Reno: Reno-Sparks Convention and Visitors Authority, 1988.

———. *Marketing Report for 1990.* Reno: Reno-Sparks Convention and Visitors Authority, 1991.

———. *Visitor Profile Study, 1985 Summary Report.* Los Angeles: Western International Research, 1986.

Reno-Tahoe Airport Authority. *Comprehensive Annual Financial Report for the Year Ended June 30, 2007.* Reno: Reno-Tahoe Airport Authority, 2007.

Ringhoff, Mary, and Edward Stoner. *The River and the Railroad: An Archaeological History of Reno.* Reno: University of Nevada Press, 2011.

Sanborn Map Company. "Insurance Maps of Las Vegas, Nevada." Rev. ed. 1928. Reprint, New York: Sanborn Map Company, 1961. In *Fire Insurance Maps of Nevada Communities, 1877–1972.* Reno: Nevada Historical Society, 1995.

UNLV Center for Gaming Research. *Las Vegas Strip Casino Employment: Productivity, Revenues, and Payroll, a Statistical Study, 1990–2011.* Las Vegas: UNLV Center for Gaming Research, March 2012.

US Department of Commerce, Bureau of the Census. *1980 Census of Population and Housing.* Washington, DC: US Government Printing Office, 1983.

———. *County and City Data Book, 1962.* Washington, DC: US Government Printing Office, 1962.

———. *County and City Data Book, 1977.* Washington, DC: US Government Printing Office, 1978.

———. *County and City Data Book, 1983.* Washington, DC: US Government Printing Office, 1983.

US Department of Transportation, Federal Aviation Administration. *Environmental Impact Assessment Report, Land Acquisition Program, Reno International Airport, Reno, Nevada.* July 1976.

US Environmental Protection Agency and City of Reno. *Environmental Impact Statement Reno-Sparks Joint Water Pollution Control Plant Cross-Town Sewer and Lawton-Verdi Interceptor Extension.* US Environmental Protection Agency and City of Reno, 1975.

Varela, Steve, City of Reno, Director of Public Works. *Final Proposed ReTRAC Project Plan, Prepared for U.S. Department of Transportation, Federal Highway Administration and State of Nevada, Department of Transportation, Prepared by Steve Varela, Director of Public Works, City of Reno.* Reno: Public Works Department, May 7, 1999.

Washoe Council of Governments. *Areawide Water Quality Management Plan, Phase I.* Washoe County, NV: November 1975.

Washoe County Blue Ribbon Task Force on Growth. *Blue Ribbon Task Force Program: Growth and Development, Reno, Sparks, and Washoe County, Nevada.* Reno: Regional Planning Commission of Reno, Sparks, and Washoe County, 1973–74.

———. *Committee on Air Pollution, Report II.* February 1974.

———. *Economics of Growth Committee, Report VII.* December 30, 1973.

———. *Summary of Findings and Recommendations.* October 1973.

OTHER SOURCES

Abbott, Carl. *How Cities Won the West: Four Centuries of Urban Change in Western North America.* Albuquerque: University of New Mexico Press, 2008.

———. *The Metropolitan Frontier: Cities in the Modern American West.* Tucson: University of Arizona Press, 1993.

———. *The New Urban America: Growth and Politics in Sunbelt Cities.* Chapel Hill: University of North Carolina Press, 1987.

———. *Portland: Planning, Politics, and Growth in a Twentieth-Century City.* Lincoln: University of Nebraska Press, 1983.

Allen, Jud. *Life Without a Safety Net: An Insider's View of War, Hollywood, and Reno.* Marcelline, MO: Wadsworth, 1997.

Barber, Alicia. *Reno's Big Gamble: Images and Reputation in the Biggest Little City.* Lawrence: University Press of Kansas, 2008.

Barol, Bill. "Lanes Paved with Gold." *Time,* September 18, 1995, 94.

Baylis, Thomas. "Leadership Change in Contemporary San Antonio." In *The Politics of San Antonio: Community, Progress, and Power*, edited by David R. Johnson, John A. Booth, and Richard Harris, 95–113. Lincoln: University of Nebraska Press, 1983.

Beebe, Lucius. "Las Vegas." *Holiday*, December 12, 1952, 106–8, 132–37.

Bennett, Barbara. *Mayor of Reno and Community Activist.* Interviewed by Helen W. Blue and R. T. King. Reno: University of Nevada Oral History Program, 1989.

Binion, Lester Ben. *Some Recollections of a Texas and Las Vegas Gaming Operator.* Reno: University of Nevada Oral History Program, 1973.

Bridges, Amy. "Politics and Growth in Sunbelt Cities." In *Searching for the Sunbelt: Historical Perspectives on a Region*, edited by Raymond Mohl, 85–104. Knoxville: University of Tennessee Press, 1990.

Bubb, Daniel. *Landing in Las Vegas: Commercial Aviation and the Making of a Tourist City.* Reno: University of Nevada Press, 2012.

Cahlan, John. *Reminiscences of a Reno and Las Vegas, Nevada, Newspaperman, University Regent, and Public-Spirited Citizen.* Reno: University of Nevada Oral History Program, 1970.

Chandler, Susan, and Jill B. Jones. *Casino Women: Courage in Unexpected Places.* Ithaca, NY: ILR Press, 2011.

Charles Hall Paige and Associates. *Historic Preservation Inventory and Guidelines: City of Las Vegas.* San Francisco: Charles Hall Paige and Associates, May 31, 1978.

Chew, Lai King. *The Cosmo Club and Reno's Chinese Community.* Interviewed by Hwa-di Broadhead and Michael Broadhead. Reno: University of Nevada Oral History Program, 2000.

Chiarella, Tom. "The Dirtiest Secret in Nevada." *Esquire*, October 2007, 153–56.

Cladianos, Pete. *My Father's Son: A Gaming Memoir.* Interviewed by R. T. King. Reno: University of Nevada Reno Oral History Program, 2002.

Coakley, Deirdre, Hank Greenspun, and Harry C. Gerard. *The Day the MGM Grand Hotel Burned.* Secaucus, NJ: Lyle Stuart, 1982.

Coughtry, Jamie, ed. *Lubertha Johnson: Civil Rights Efforts in Las Vegas, 1940s–1960s.* Reno: University of Nevada Oral History Program, 1988.

Eadington, William. *Gaming and Nevada's Economic Future: The Challenges Ahead, Directions, 2011.* Reno: Institute for the Study of Gambling and Commercial Gaming, February 3, 2011.

Fairbanks, Robert B. "The Good Government Machine: The Citizen's Charter Association and Dallas Politics, 1930–1960." In *Essays on Sunbelt Cities and Recent Urban America*, edited by Robert B. Fairbanks and Kathleen Underwood, 125–50. Austin: University of Texas Press, 1990.

Findlay, John M. *People of Chance: Gambling in American Society from Jamestown to Las Vegas.* New York: Oxford University Press, 1986.

Garreau, Joel. *Edge City: Life on the New Frontier.* New York: Anchor Books, Doubleday, 1991.

Goodman, Oscar B., with George Anastasia. *Being Oscar: From Mob Lawyer to Mayor of Las Vegas, Only in America.* New York: Weinstein Books, 2013.

Gottdiener, M., Claudia C. Collins, and David R. Dickens. *Las Vegas: The Social Production of an All-American City.* Malden, MA: Blackwell, 1999.

Green, Michael S. "Hank Greenspun: Where He Stood." In *The Maverick Spirit: Building the New Nevada,* edited by Richard O. Davies, 74–95. Reno: University of Nevada Press, 1998.

Hagen, Phil. *The Meadows School: Celebrating 25 Years.* Las Vegas: Creel, 2009.

Hall, Christopher. "Vegas on Fire." *Via: Your AAA Magazine* (Nevada ed.), November–December 2013, 20–22.

Harrison, Christian S. "Desert Paradigm: Las Vegas, the Southern Nevada Water Authority, and Water Politics in the Colorado River Basin." PhD diss., University of Nevada, Las Vegas, 2014.

Hess, Alan. *Viva Las Vegas: After Hours Architecture.* San Francisco: Chronicle Books, 1993.

Hill, Gladwin. "Atomic Boomtown in the Desert." *New York Times Magazine,* February 11, 1951, 14.

———. "Klondike in the Desert." *New York Times Magazine,* June 7, 1953, 14, 65, 67.

Hopkins, A. D., and K. J. Evans, eds. *The First 100: Portraits of the Men and Women Who Shaped Las Vegas.* Las Vegas: Huntington Press, 1999.

Hsieh, Tony. *Delivering Happiness: A Path to Profits, Passion, and Purpose.* New York and Boston: Business Plus, 2010.

Jaschke, Karin, and Silke Otsch, eds. *Stripping Las Vegas: A Contextual Review of Las Vegas Casino Resort Architecture.* London: Verso, 2003.

Jones, Florence Lee, and John C. Cahlan. *Water: A History of Las Vegas and the Las Vegas Land and Water Company.* 2 vols. Las Vegas: Las Vegas Land and Water Company, 1975.

Kaufman, Perry B. "The Best City of Them All: A History of Las Vegas, 1930–1960." PhD diss., University of California, Santa Barbara, 1974.

Kling, Dwayne. *The Rise of the Biggest Little City: An Encyclopedic History of Reno Gaming, 1931–1981.* Reno: University of Nevada Press, 2000.

Kraft, James P. *Vegas at Odds: Labor Conflict in a Leisure Economy, 1960–1985.* Baltimore: Johns Hopkins University Press, 2010.

Land, Barbara N., and Myrick Land. *A Short History of Las Vegas.* Reno: University of Nevada Press, 1999.

———. *A Short History of Reno.* Reno: University of Nevada Press, 1995.
Las Vegas Chamber of Commerce. "Dr. Neal Smatresk Talks Economic Diversification and Education." *Business Voice,* November 2010, 6, 26, 28.
———. *Where Is Las Vegas Going? Get the Full Facts of the Present and Future Economy of Las Vegas.* Las Vegas: Las Vegas Chamber of Commerce, 1974.
Leonard, Paul A. *Tales of Northern Nevada—and Other Lies Recalled by a Native Son, Journalist, and Civic Leader.* Interviewed by Mary Ellen Glass. Reno: University of Nevada Oral History Program, 1980.
Marlow, Jarvis. "'Taming the Waters That Taketh from the Devil's Playground': A History of Flood Control in Las Vegas, 1955–2010." Master's thesis, University of Nevada, Las Vegas, 2011.
Martinez, Andres. *24/7: Living It Up and Doubling Down in the New Las Vegas.* New York: Dell, 2000.
Mayer, Harold B., and Richard C. Wade. *Chicago: Growth of a Metropolis.* Chicago: University of Chicago Press, 1969.
McBride, Dennis. *In the Beginning: A History of Boulder City, Nevada.* Boulder City, NV: Chamber of Commerce, 1981.
McMillan, James. *Fighting Back: A Life in the Struggle for Civil Rights from Oral Histories with James B. McMillan.* Interviewed by Gary E. Elliott and narrative interpretation by R. T. King. Reno: University of Nevada Oral History Program, 1997.
Moehring, Eugene P. "City and Spectacle: How Steve Wynn Changed the Las Vegas Landscape." *Wynn Magazine,* premiere issue, 2005, 200–202.
———. "Growth, Services, and the Political Economy of Gambling in Las Vegas, 1970–2000." In *The Grit Beneath the Glitter: Tales of the Real Las Vegas,* edited by Hal K. Rothman and Mike Davis, 73–98. Berkeley: University of California Press, 2002..
———. "Las Vegas." In *American Tourism: Constructing a National Tradition,* edited by Mark J. Souther and Nicholas Dagen Bloom, 157–66. Chicago: Center for American Places at Columbia College Chicago, 2012.
———. *Resort City in the Sunbelt: Las Vegas, 1930–2000.* 2nd ed. Reno: University of Nevada Press, 2000.
———. "Tumult in Playland: The Annexation-Consolidation Controversy in the Las Vegas Metropolitan Area." *Nevada Historical Society Quarterly* 53, no. 2 (2010): 80–107.
———. *UNLV: A History of the University of Nevada, Las Vegas.* Reno: University of Nevada Press, 2007.
Moehring, Eugene P., and Michael S. Green. *Las Vegas: A Centennial History.* Reno: University of Nevada Press, 2005.
Mohl, Raymond A. "Planned Destruction: The Interstates and Central Housing." In *From Tenements to the Taylor Homes: In Search of an Urban Policy in Twentieth-*

Century America, edited by John F. Bauman, Roger Biles, and Kristin Szylvian, 231–45. University Park: Pennsylvania State University Press, 2000.

Moody, Eric, and Guy Rocha. "The Rise and Fall of the Reno Stockade." *Nevada* (April–June 1978): 28–30.

Patrick, Elizabeth Nelson, ed. *Oral Interview of Reverend Prentiss Walker*. Las Vegas, 1978.

Rothman, Hal K. *Neon Metropolis: How Las Vegas Started the Twenty-First Century*. London: Routledge, 2002.

Rowley, Rex J. *Everyday Las Vegas: Local Life in a Tourist Town*. Reno: University of Nevada Press, 2013.

Rowley, William D. *Reno, Hub of the Washoe Country: An Illustrated History*. Woodland Hills, CA: Windsor, 1984.

Schumacher, Geoff. *Sun, Sin, and Suburbia: An Essential History of Modern Las Vegas*. Rev. ed. Las Vegas: Stephens Press, 2012.

Schwartz, David G. *Suburban Xanadu: The Casino Resort on the Las Vegas Strip and Beyond*. New York: Routledge, 2003.

Sheehan, Jack E., ed. *The Players: The Men Who Made Las Vegas*. Reno: University of Nevada Press, 1997.

Simon, Bryant. *Boardwalk of Dreams: Atlantic City and the Fate of Urban America*. New York: Oxford University Press, 2004.

Smith, John L. *Of Rats and Men: Oscar Goodman's Life from Mob Mouthpiece to Mayor of Las Vegas*. Las Vegas: Huntington Press, 2003.

Sparks Centennial Book Committee, comp. *History of Sparks*. Reno: Dynagraphic Printing, 2004.

Starrs, Paul C., Heather Van Wormer, and Jean Harrah. *Downtown Reno and the Railroad: A Report of the Project on Historical Growth and Development of Downtown Reno, Nevada*. Reno: University of Nevada Sponsored Projects Office, 1997.

Stein, Joel. "The Strip Is Back." *Time*, July 26, 2004, 22–34.

Stevens, Joseph. *Hoover Dam: An American Adventure*. Norman: University of Oklahoma Press, 1988.

VanderMeer, Philip. *Desert Visions and the Making of Phoenix, 1860–2009*. Albuquerque: University of New Mexico Press, 2010.

Vanderwood, Paul J. *Satan's Playground: Mobsters and Movie Stars at America's Greatest Gaming Resort*. Durham, NC: Duke University Press, 2010.

Venturi, Robert, Denise Scott Brown, and Steven Izenour. *Learning from Las Vegas: The Forgotten Symbolism of Architectural Form*. Cambridge, MA: Harvard University Press, 1977.

Yantis, Betty. *Fact Book for Las Vegas and Clark County*. Las Vegas: UNLV Center for Business and Economic Research, 1977.

Zauner, Phyllis. "Finding the Real Reno." *Travel*, December 1971, 56.

INDEX

Abajian, Tori, 192
Abbott, Carl, 52, 79, 99
Aces Ballpark, 154
Adelson, Sheldon, 116, 117, 128, 130–31, 178
Agua Caliente (Tijuana), 4
air pollution, 71–72
Airport Authority of Washoe County, 97–98
airport construction: Las Vegas area, 6, 42–43, 57–59, 98, 109, 179–80; Reno area, 21–23, 87, 97–99
Aladdin, 117, 131
Algiers Hotel, 128
Aliante, 134
Aliante Station, 132, 134
Allen, Dick, 81
Allen, Jud: on building of Reno's convention center, 17, 19–20; involvement in and views on Reno's promotional efforts, 12–13, 23, 24, 25, 30, 38, 96, 151, 152, 153, 221–22; on Reno's economic growth and development, 28, 82, 96–97, 102, 140
American Institute of Architects, 156
American Nevada Corporation, 64, 106
America West Airlines, 109
annexation efforts, 61, 219–20
Anthem community, 111
Antholis, William, 200
"antigrowth activists," 79. *See also* managed-growth debates
Aoyama, Fred, 33
Apple, Inc., 167
Aqua Blue, 176

Arch Drug, 38
arena projects, 121, 192–93
Aria, 172, 178
Arizona Charlie's, 104
Arizona State University (ASU), 203–4
Artown Festival, 154
Ascuaga, John, 14
Atlantic City (NJ), 30, 76, 94, 103, 162
Atlantis, 19, 132, 141, 152, 162
Atlantis Sky Bridge, 161

baccarat, 225
Baker, Bud, 15, 30, 52
Baker, C. D., 15, 52
Bally's, 114, 117, 142, 162
Bankofier, Roy, 15, 27–28, 31–32, 33
Barber, Alicia, 11, 75, 156, 210
Barden, Don, 195
Baring, Walter, 24, 25, 73
Barrick Gaming Group, 194
Basic Magnesium, 2, 42, 63, 64
Battenburg, John, 102
Bayley, Warren and Judy, 116, 212
Baylis, Thomas, 52
Bechtel Corporation, 179
Beers, Bob, 135
Bellagio, 113, 212
Benedict, Alvin, 81
Bennett, Barbara: on county planning, 93; on economic growth and development, 16, 79, 80, 89, 91, 92, 100–101, 153, 166; on Reno's lack of a strip, 208–9

259

Bennett, Tony, 3
Bennett, William, 115–16
Benninger, Fred, 83–84, 86
Benston, Liz, 130
Bergman, Wall, and Associates, 170
Bernhard, Bo, 206, 226
Berns, Dave, 199, 203
Bible, Alan, 47, 48, 49
Biggest Little City Committee, 101–2
Biglieri, Clyde, 82, 89
Bilbray, James Sr., 59–60
Bill's Gamblin' Hall, 205
Bingo Palace, 104, 131
Binion, Benny, 41
Binion's Horseshoe Casino, 41
"Black Springs," 39
Blasco, Joe, 106
Blue Diamond Road, 137
blue-ribbon task force: on aesthetic design and streetscape issues, 75–77; on air pollution and related railroad problems, 71–74; formation of, 69–70; on housing issues, 74–75; later redevelopment efforts rooted in, 156; on physical growth and managed growth, 77–80; on water-related issues, 70–71
Boca Park shopping center, 184
Boeing Air Transport Company, 21
Bogart, Carl, 73, 157
Boise (ID), 79, 164–66
Boise State University, 165–66
Boldt, William, 200
Boulder City, 5, 36, 135, 137
Boulder Club, 41
Boulder Dam project, 2
Boulder Station, 131
Boulevard Mall, 50
Boyd, Sam, 68
Boyd Group, 120, 127–28
Briare, William, 37, 60, 61, 101, 119
Bridges, Amy, 51
Broadbent, Robert, 109, 118
Brookings Institute, 200
Brookings Mountain West, 200–201, 203
Brown, Jerry, 93
Bruce Woodbury Beltway, 107–8

Bryan, Richard, 200
Buckley, Barbara, 137
Burke, Don, 23–24
bus systems, 34, 108, 150–51

Caesars Entertainment, 131, 132, 142, 205
Caesars Palace, 45, 104, 114, 117, 132
Caesars Palace flood, 112
Caesars World, 143
Cahlan, John, 211
California Hotel, 104, 120
Callister, Matt, 107
Cannery, 132
Cannon, Howard, 48, 49, 54, 58
Canyons community, 110
Carano, Don, 95, 140
Carson City, 33
Cartier Avenue Urban Renewal Project, 62, 63
Casazza, Ralph, 21
Cashell, Bob, 155, 163
Cashman Center, 131
casino industry. *See* gaming-tourist industry
Castaways, 45, 132
Centennial Coliseum, 16–21, 87. *See also* Reno-Sparks Convention Center
Centennial Plaza Transit Center, 150–51
Centennial Springs, 133
Century Riverside Theatre, 153
Cherches, Charles, 101
Cherry, Sam, 187
Chiarella, Tom, 146
Chih-Cheng, James, 125
Chinatown Plaza, 125
"Chinatown" (Strip city), 125
Chism, John, 27
Christian Science Monitor, 166
CIM Group, 194
Circus Circus, 115–16, 142, 212
Cisco Systems, 166
Citifare bus system, 108
Citizens Area Transit, 108
City Center (Project City Center), 126, 171–72, 178–79
Civic Center Drive, 62
Civic Center (North Las Vegas), 62

Index

Civil Aeronautics Board, 58
civil rights issues, 37–40, 67–68
Cladianos, Pete, 18, 33, 146, 147
Clark, William, 2, 72
Clark County commissioners, 6–7
Clark County Courthouse, 56
Clark County Fair and Recreation Board, 44, 57. *See also* Las Vegas Convention and Visitors Authority
Clark County Regional Flood Control District, 112
Clark County Regional Planning Council, 60
Clark County School District, 54, 90, 177
Clark County Water Reclamation District, 53
Club Cal Neva, 10, 12, 141, 148
CNBC poll, 196–97
Collins Brothers Corporation, 106
Colonial Inn, 141
Colony, 9, 96
Colony Resorts, 170
Colorado River Compact of 1922, 48
combined-use projects. *See* mixed-use projects
Comdex, 117
Commercial Center, 50
Commercial Row, 8
commission government, 51
computer industry, 164–67, 190–92, 197, 226–27
Comstock, 95, 141
consent decrees, 68
Container Park, 191
convention facilities and industry: Las Vegas area, 6, 44, 57, 131, 180–81; Reno area, 16–21, 84–85, 139–40, 150, 161–62
Corey, Jim, 50
corporate gaming, 224
Cosmopolitan, 178
cost of living, 135, 176
Cragin, Ernie, 52
Crandall, Michael, 195
Cromwell hotel, 205
Crouch, Jordan, 21
Crow, Michael, 203–4
Curtis, Mark, 101
Curve condominiums, 133

Cyan community, 160
Cyphers, Amanda, 136

Dalitz, Moe, 42
"Dancing Waters" show, 113
Davis, Sammy, Jr., 3, 9
defense spending, 47
Del Webb, 105, 110, 111, 134, 143
Dennis, Wayne, 78
Desert Inn, 3, 12, 45, 115, 128
Desert Inn Super Arterial, 6, 107
Desert Sea News Bureau, 221
Desert Shores, 106
Deutsche Bank, 178
Diamonte Ranch, 161
Digital Royalty, 191
Dion, Celine, 173
discrimination. *See* civil rights issues
District community, 108, 133
divorce industry, 1–2, 8, 10–11
D Las Vegas, 195
DLJ Merchant bank, 132
Donner, Andrew, 190–91
Double Diamond Ranch, 159, 160
Douglas Alley, 8
Downtown Grand, 195
downtown redevelopment (Las Vegas): efforts in 1990s, 119–22; efforts in 2000s and impact of Great Recession, 184–96; limiting factors, 216–18; red-line reform, 29, 64–65, 122–24, 216
downtown redevelopment (Reno): efforts in 1980s, 101–2; efforts in 1990s and 2000s, 153–58; limiting factors, 216–18; Project RENOvation in 1960s, 26–28, 101; red-line reform, 15, 26, 28–33, 216
Drai, Victor, 130, 205
Dream Fund, 201
Dubai World, 172
Dunes, 3, 12
Dunn, Allen, 26–27
Durant, Marcel, 89

Eadington, William, 78, 151, 224–25
Echelon Place, 127–28, 133
Eckert, Robert, 80

Economic Development Authority of Western Nevada, 163
economic diversification efforts, 162–68, 196–204, 225–27
Economic Opportunity Board of Washoe County, 39
"edge cities," 5–6
education issues (Las Vegas area): public school expansion and enrollment, 54–55, 177; rise and growth of NSU, 44, 47, 55–56; state budget cuts and underinvestment, 163–64, 197, 198, 200, 201; UNLV relationship to gaming community, 222; UNLV role in economic diversification, 200–204, 226–27; UNLV stadium project, 192–93
education issues (Reno area): public school expansion, 34–35, 89–90; state budget cuts and underinvestment, 163–64, 197, 198, 200, 201; UNR role in economic diversification, 202, 226–27
Elad Group, 133
El Cortez, 9, 41
Eldorado, 41, 95, 142
El Rancho Vegas, 3
Encore, 130, 177, 212
Enron, 197
"enterprise zones," 123
"epitome districts," 157
Esposito, Joseph, 84, 85–86
Ethel M (Mars) Chocolates, 162
Evans, Ken, 147
Excalibur, 116

Fabulous Flamingo, 3
fair employment practices bill, 67
fair housing bill, 39
Fashion Show Mall, 126
Fazio, Tom, 128
federal consent decrees, 68
Feldman, Alan, 129
Ferraro, Bob, 137
Fertitta, Frank, Jr., 131
Fifth Street School, 188
Fine, Mark, 106, 186
Fitzgerald, Lincoln, 95

Fitzgeralds, 75, 195
Flamingo, 45, 117, 143
Flexible Gunnery School, 3
floods and flood control, 54, 111–13, 158–59
Foley Federal Building, 47
Foliot Furniture, 196
Fontainebleau, 128, 133, 171
foreclosure crisis, 175–76
Forum Shops, 114
Four Queens, 45
Fourth Street Station, 150
Franklin, George, 64, 65
Frazier, Maude, 34
Freeport Law, 79
freeways. *See* roads and road construction
Fremont East, 189
Fremont East Entertainment District, 121
Fremont Hotel, 41, 45
Fremont Street, 2–3
Fremont Street Experience, 121, 193
Frontier Hotel, 45
Fun Flights, 24, 38
"Fun Train," 23–24, 144
furniture expos, 185–86

Gabrielli, John, 92
Galleria Mall, 108
gambling industry. *See* gaming-tourist industry
gaming licenses, 26, 28
gaming-tourist industry (Las Vegas area): challenges of mid- to late 1970s, 103–4; creativity, reputation, and visual appeal of the Strip, 211–13, 223–24; divisions between downtown and the Strip, 221; downtown redevelopment and, 216–17; impact of Great Recession on, 169–79, 193–95, 224–25; Mob presence and, 42; need to diversify beyond, 225–27; "New Las Vegas" era, 113–18; postwar growth of, 41–42, 45; prerecession boom, 126–34; recent signs of the Strip's economic recovery, 205–6; red-line reform, 29, 64–65, 122–24, 216; ties to city hall, 51–52; UNLV's relationship to, 222. *See also* Strip city and the Strip

gaming-tourist industry (Reno area): boom in 1970s and '80s, 94–97; decline during 1990s and 2000s, 139–48; divisions and missed opportunities, 220–22; downtown redevelopment and, 216–17; economic diversification beyond, 162–68, 225–27; factors limiting expansion of, 217–18; housing issues and, 74–75; impact on cityscape, 75–77; local ambivalence and opposition toward, 11, 29–31, 35–36; MGM Grand construction and related growth debates, 80–89; postwar boom in, 8–12; promotional efforts, 11–13, 23–24; red-line reform, 15, 26, 28–33, 216; ties to city hall, 87; UNR's relationship to, 222
Garreau, Joel, 5–6
Gaughan, Jackie, 194
Gehry, Frank, 185
gender discrimination, 68
Genting Group, 205
Gibbons, James, 200
Glick, Milton, 201, 202
Goett, Gary, 175
Gold Coast, 104
Golden Bank Club, 8
Golden hotel, 9
Golden Nugget, 41, 193, 194, 195
Golden Phoenix, 143
Goldman Sachs, 156, 170
Gold Spike, 194
Goodman, Carolyn, 51, 110, 121, 196
Goodman, Oscar, 121, 184, 186–87, 190, 192, 195
Goolsby, John, 123
Gottdiener, Mark, 215
government reform: Las Vegas area, 15, 51–52, 60–61; Reno area, 15–16, 36–37, 93–94
Gragson, Oran, 15, 29, 50, 52, 64–66
Gramercy Capital, 170
Grand Canal Shoppes, 117
Grand Central Hotel project, 193
Grand Sierra Resort, 143, 162
Grand Vacations Club, 127
Graves, Dick, 14

Great Recession: impact on Las Vegas area, 169–84, 193–95, 224–25; impact on Reno area, 160–61
Greenbaum, Gus, 42
Greenspun, Brian, 200
Greenspun, Hank, 67, 106
Green Valley, 106–7, 108
Greg Street controversy, 83
Griffin, Jeff, 155, 166
Griffin, Merv, 103
Griffith, R. E., 3, 65
Guinn, Kenny, 68, 125, 200

Hacienda, 3, 212
Hall, Jerry, 86–87
Hampton Inn, 159
Hard Rock Hotel, 132
Harmon Hotel, 172
Harolds Club, 2, 8, 12, 13, 141, 148
Harrah, William, 9, 12, 13, 30, 74, 85
Harrah's, 8, 9, 12, 148, 159, 192
Harrah's Entertainment, 175
Harrah's Marina, 76
"Harrah's World" project, 85
Harris, Len, 9
Harveys Inn, 93
Heidrich, Delbert, 35
Helldorado Rodeo, 11
Henderson: growth and development of, 3, 5, 42, 63–64, 110, 111, 135–36; impact of Great Recession on, 174–75, 177
Hess, Alan, 113
Hewlett-Packard, 164
Hicks, Marion, 3
Hidden Valley, 159
Hill, Steven, 226
Hills community, 110
Hilton, 116–17, 127, 142, 143
Hilton Lake Las Vegas & Spa, 173
historic preservation, 188–90
Historic Reno Preservation Society, 150
Hlusak, Bob, 117
Holiday, 9, 30, 85, 96, 141
Hollingsworth, Somer, 196, 197–98
Holsum Lofts, 187
homeless problems, 146–47

Horseshoe, 9, 96, 141
hospital projects, 56–57
Hot August Nights, 145
Hotel Apache, 41
Hotel Last Frontier, 3
hotel/motel room tax, 16, 20
House of Blues, 118
housing issues (Las Vegas area): cost of living increases, 135; impact of Great Recession on housing market, 175–76, 184, 193; residential segregation, 39, 68; rise of master-planned communities, 105–7, 110–11
housing issues (Reno area): affordable housing concerns, 87; blue-ribbon panel on, 74–75; residential segregation, 39; suburban development and national housing crisis, 159–61
Houston (TX), 76
Howard Hughes Corporation, 110, 123
Howlett, C. A., 164
Hsieh, Tony, 189, 190–91, 195
Hubbard, Eddie, 21
Hubbard Field, 21–22
Hughes, Howard, 45, 110
Hughes Corporation. *See* Howard Hughes Corporation
Hull, Thomas, 3, 65
Hyatt Regency Lake Las Vegas, 173
Hydro-o-Dynamic Corporation, 196

iGO, 166
Imperial Palace, 104
Inspirada project, 174–75
International/Las Vegas Hilton, 45, 104, 117
Interstate 15, 25, 44, 51, 54, 107
Interstate 80, 14, 24–25, 71
Intuit, 166
It's a Wonderful Life (film), 223
Ivana Las Vegas, 176

J. C. Penney's, 79
Jerde, Jon, 121
Jet, 118
John Ascuaga's Nugget, 9, 14, 148, 162
Jones, Cliff, 3

Jones, Jan, 119, 120, 121, 186, 192
Joseph Magnin (store), 29
Juhl, 193
Julian, Joe, 57–58

Kam Sang, 173
Kashani, Jack, 185
Keene, Phil, 149–51
Kellar, Charles, 38, 68
Kennedy, A. H., 52
Kerkorian, Kirk, 45, 114–15, 200
Kiley Ranch, 160, 161
Kirman, Richard, 163
Kiwi Program, 47
KLAS-TV, 45
Koll Real Estate Group, 120
Koolhaas, Rem, 117
Krystal Sands, 176

La Concha Motel Office, 188
Lady Luck, 194, 195
Lake-Evans blocks, 38
Lake Las Vegas, 111, 173–74
Lakes community, 106
Lake Tahoe, 12, 93, 144–45
Landmark Hotel, 45
Landry's Restaurant, 194
land values, 176, 197–98
Lang, Robert, 202, 204
Lanni, Terence, 172
Las Vegas & Tonopah Railroad, 2
Las Vegas area: compared to Reno area (*see* Reno–Las Vegas comparisons); early history of, 2–3; normalization process, 215; Reno as trailblazer for, 7; rise and growth of Strip city and the Strip, 3–7. *See also* Strip city and the Strip
Las Vegas area (1945–75): civil rights issues and gender discrimination, 38–39, 67–68; expansion of other public facilities, 56–59; government reform and attempted service consolidation, 15, 51–52, 60–61; growth in North Las Vegas and Henderson, 61–64; growth in resort and defense sectors during 1960s, 44–45, 47–48; postwar boom, 41–44; red-line

reform and managed-growth debates, 64–67; rise and growth of NSU, 44, 47, 54–56; tax issues, 59–60; traffic issues, 50–51; water-related issues, 43–44, 48–50, 53–54

Las Vegas area (1975–2007): challenges of mid- to late 1970s, 103–4; downtown re-development, 119–22; flood-control efforts, 111–13; growth of suburbs and exurbs during 2000s, 134–38; migration and suburban development, 104–11; monorail system construction, 118–19; "New Las Vegas" era, 113–18; population growth and diversity, 124–26; prerecession boom, 126–34; red-line reform, 122–24

Las Vegas area (2007–14): building projects pursued despite recession, 179–84; downtown redevelopment and historic preservation, 184–96; economic diversification efforts, 196–200; impact of Great Recession, 169–79; role of UNLV in economic diversification, 200–204

Las Vegas Arts District, 187
Las Vegas Beltway, 6
Las Vegas Chamber of Commerce, 58
Las Vegas city hall, 56
Las Vegas Club, 41, 194
Las Vegas Convention and Visitors Authority (LVCVA), 57, 133–34, 180–81, 198. *See also* Clark County Fair and Recreation Board
Las Vegas Convention Center, 180–81. *See also* convention facilities and industry
Las Vegas Downtown Project, 191
Las Vegas Hilton, 45, 104, 170
Las Vegas Library, 188
Las Vegas Metro Chamber of Commerce, 201
Las Vegas Monorail Company, 118
Las Vegas Premium Outlets, 186
Las Vegas Redevelopment Agency, 119
Las Vegas Review-Journal, 47, 56, 57, 58, 59, 66, 183, 201
Las Vegas Sands, 170
Las Vegas Sands Convention Center, 131
Las Vegas Springs Preserve, 189
Las Vegas Strip, 46. *See also* Strip city and the Strip

Las Vegas Sun, 203
Las Vegas Taxpayers' Association, 52
Las Vegas Townsite, 72
Las Vegas Transit, 34
Las Vegas Valley Water District, 43–44, 48, 50, 63, 70
Latimore, Joseph, 27, 81–82
Laub, William, 196
Lawrence, Cliff, 90
Laxalt, Paul, 32, 59, 93
Lear Industries, 23
Leasure, Larry, 148
Leonard, Paul, 24
Lewis, Pat, 81
Lewis Homes, 110
Liberace, 8
Lied Discovery Children's Museum, 188
Lincy Foundation, 200
Lincy Institute, 200, 201, 203
Linq, 132
Livestock Events Center, 20
Live Wire Fund, 221
Lloyd George Federal Courthouse, 120
L'Octaine Apartments, 187
Longoria, Eva, 178
Los Angeles (CA), 66
Los Angeles Highway, 2
Losee Industrial District, 62
Lou Ruvo Center for Brain Health (Alzheimer's Center), 185, 195
Lucent, 166
Lurie, Ron, 119
Luxor, 116
LVCVA. *See* Las Vegas Convention and Visitors Authority
Lynch, Clay, 60, 62

Macau, 225, 226
Mack, Jerome, 55
Mack, Michael, 182
Main Street Station project, 120
Majestic Realty, 192
managed-growth debates: Las Vegas area, 64, 66–67; Reno area, 16, 79, 88, 99–101, 102, 140, 214, 222
Mandalay Bay, 115, 116

Index

Mandarin Oriental, 172
Mandelstam, Julian, 146
Mapes, Charlie, 13, 30
Mapes Hotel, 9, 12, 96, 102
Mapes Money Tree, 75, 96, 102
Marina, 104, 115
Marnell, Anthony, 174
Marnell-Corrao (builders), 170
Maryland Parkway, 50
master-planned communities, 105–7, 110–11, 160, 184
Mathia, Doyle, 95
Maxim resort, 104
McAfee, Guy, 3
McCarran, Pat, 42
McCarran Airport, 6, 57–59, 109, 179–80. *See also* airport construction
McCarran Boulevard, 108
"McCarran 2000," 109, 179
"McCarran Village," 184
McGaughey, James, 112
McGoldrick, Edward, 17
McGowan, Robert, 148
McMillan, James, 67
Meacham, Warren, 90
Meadowood Mall, 21, 81
Meadows Mall, 52, 64
Meadows School, 110
Medico-Dental Building, 31
meeting industry. *See* convention facilities and industry
Menicucci, Bruno, 16, 36–37, 87, 88–89, 91, 97
Meredith, Byron, 32–33
Meruelo Group, 143
Mesquite, 135
Metropolis condominiums, 176
Metropolitan Police Department (Las Vegas), 61
MGM Grand (Las Vegas), 45, 104, 114–15
MGM Grand (Reno), 80–89, 91, 94, 95, 96–97
MGM Mirage, 115, 126, 170, 171–72, 175
MGM Resorts International, 131, 192, 205–6
Micron, 164
Microsoft, 166
Mike O'Callaghan–Pat Tillman Memorial Bridge, 135

Miller, Bob, 200
Minami Tower project, 120
minority rights. *See* civil rights issues
Mint Hotel and Casino, 41
Mirage, 105, 113, 118, 129, 212
Mirage Revolution, 114. *See also* "New Las Vegas" era
mixed-use projects, 133, 172, 183–84, 186. *See also* City Center
Mob, the, 42
Mob Museum, 190
Molasky, Irwin, 186
Molasky Corporate Center, 187
monorail system, 118–19
Montage condominiums, 143
MonteLago Village, 111
Montreux, 127
Moore, William J., 3, 65, 212
Morgans Hotel Group, 132
Mormon Fort, 188
Moulin Rouge Agreement, 67
Mountain's Edge, 137, 184
Moyer, Donald, 56
M Resort, 132, 174
Mulroy, Pat, 181–82, 189
Munro, Mark, 202
Murren, Jim, 171–72, 178
Museum of Natural History, 188
Muth, Ed, 48

Nangaku, Masao, 120
National Association for the Advancement of Colored People (NAACP), 38, 67
National Bowling Stadium, 145, 153, 162
"National Clean Energy Conference 3.0," 203
Native American casinos, 142, 144, 145
Navegante Group, 194
Nellis Air Force Base, 22, 42, 47
Nellis Industrial Park, 63
Neon Museum (Boneyard), 188
Neonopolis Mall, 120–21
Nevada business environment, 196–97
Nevada Club, 9, 141
Nevada Commission on Economic Development, 163
Nevada Department of Highways, 51

Nevada Development Authority, 196, 198–99
Nevada Discovery Museum, 154
Nevadan/Onslow, 141
Nevada Proving Grounds, 42
Nevada Southern University (NSU), 44, 47, 55–56. *See also* University of Nevada, Las Vegas
Nevada State Journal, 24, 31, 36, 75, 83, 86, 87, 93
Nevada State Museum and Historical Society, 189
Nevada State Office Building, 20
Nevada Tax Commission, 59
Newcomer, Leland, 54–55
New Frontier, 127, 133
Newlands Communities, 187
"New Las Vegas" era, 113–18
Newport Lofts, 178, 187
Newsweek, 94
New York–New York, 115
New York Times, 216
normalization, 215
Northern Nevada Development Authority, 163
North Las Vegas: growth and development of, 3, 5, 42, 61–63, 110, 111, 134, 135; impact of Great Recession on, 177
North Las Vegas Air Terminal, 45
North Las Vegas library, 63
NSU. *See* Nevada Southern University
Nugget (Sparks), 9, 14, 148, 162

O'Callaghan, Mike, 39, 68
Ocean Spray Cranberries, 162
"One Sound State" approach, 163
Onslow, 76, 95, 96
open accommodations, 38, 67
open-housing bill, 68
"orderly growth," 66. *See also* managed-growth debates
organized crime, 42, 190
O'Sheas Casino, 132
Overgaard, Kristi, 227

Palace Club, 9
Palace Station, 131
Palazzo, 128, 130
Palo Alto (CA), 75
Panorama Towers, 176
Paradise township, 61, 125
Pardee Construction Company, 105, 111
Paris–Las Vegas, 116, 117
parking meters, 51
Park Lane Mall, 21
Park Place Entertainment, 117, 142
Parsons, Ed, 89
Paulson, John, 173
Peccole, William, 110
Peccole Ranch, 106
"pedestrianscapes," 113
Penn Gaming, 174
Pennington, William, 115–16
Peppermill, 19, 96, 132, 141, 162
Perini Construction, 172
Perry, Rick, 199–200
Phoenix (AZ), 164, 203–4
Pickford, Mary, 1
Picollo, Marvin, 34, 90
Pioneer Bus Lines, 34
Pioneer Center for the Performing Arts, 20
Pioneer Club, 41
Pioneer (Reno), 141
Pipkin, Charles, 52
planned growth. *See* managed-growth debates
Plaza Hotel, 133, 194
Polyphase Sports and Entertainment, 121
population growth: Las Vegas area, 47, 52, 104–5, 109–10, 124–26, 135, 177; Reno area, 33, 39–40, 90, 100
Portland (OR), 69, 71
Powning Park, 20
Primadonna, 9
Primm, Ernest, 9, 30
Procter Hug High School, 35
Project City Center. *See* City Center
Project RENOvation, 26–28, 101
property taxes, 35, 59
Providence community, 184
public hospital facilities, 56–57
public schools. *See* education issues
Puck, Wolfgang, 114

Pueblo community, 110
Pulte, 161
Pure nightclub, 118

"quality-of-life liberals," 79
Question 10, 107

race books, 65
racial minorities: Las Vegas area, 67–68, 124–26; Reno area, 37–40
Raggio, Bill, 163
railroad issues (Las Vegas area): history and impact of lines, 2, 72, 218; redevelopment of downtown rail yards, 185–86, 187–88
railroad issues (Reno area): creation of ReTRAC, 155–56; "Fun Train" tourist promotion, 23–24, 144; history and impact of lines, 72–74, 218–19
Ramada Reno Hotel Casino, 140
Ravella, 173
Raymond I. Smith Riverwalk, 102, 153, 157
recession. *See* Great Recession
Red Hawk Native American casino, 145
red-line reform: Las Vegas area, 29, 64–65, 122–24, 216; Reno area, 15, 26, 28–33, 216
Red Rock Resort, 131
Red Rock Station, 132
Reed Whipple Center, 188
Regency, 148
regional commissions, 60
Regional Transportation Commission of Washoe County, 94
Regional Urban Design Assistance Team, 156
Reid, Harry, 200
Renaissance Venice, 117
Reno, Major General Jesse Lee, 150
Reno Air, 139
Reno Air Races, 23, 145
Reno area: compared to Las Vegas area (*see* Reno–Las Vegas comparisons); early history of, 1–2; identity issues, 11, 157–58; as trailblazer for Las Vegas, 7
Reno area (1945–70): building of convention center, 16–21; civil rights issues, 37–40; construction of modern jetport, 21–23; as divorce mecca, 8, 10–11; government reform and attempted service consolidation, 15–16, 36–37; growth-related problems, 33–36; improvement of car, bus, and train access, 23–25; postwar gambling boom, 8–12; Project RENOvation, 26–28, 101; red-line reform, 15, 26, 28–33; Reno-Sparks growth capacity and conurbation, 13–14; tourism challenges and promotional efforts, 11–13, 23–24
Reno area (1970–90): airport expansion and modernization, 97–99; blue-ribbon task force on growth and development, 69–80; casino boom in 1970s and '80s, 94–97; downtown redevelopment, 101–2; managed-growth debates, 99–101; MGM Grand construction and related growth debates, 80–89; need for regional government/cooperation, 93–94; public school expansion debates, 89–90; water-related issues, 70–71, 90–92, 94–95
Reno area (1990–2014): decline of gaming-tourist industry, 139–48; downtown redevelopment, 153–58; economic diversification efforts, 162–68; efforts to attract larger conventions, 161–62; floods and flood control, 158–59; suburban expansion and national housing crisis, 159–61; suggestions for tourist industry revival, 148–52
Reno Ballroom, 162
Reno chamber of commerce, 12–13, 23–24
Reno Drive-up Package, 24
Reno Evening Gazette, 17, 24, 27, 28, 32, 35, 73–74
Reno Events Center, 20, 153, 162
Reno Hilton, 142, 143, 148
Reno International Airport, 22. *See also* airport construction
Reno–Las Vegas comparisons: annexation efforts, 219–20; creativity, reputation, and visual appeal, 96, 211–13, 223–24; development of the Strip, 207–9; factors limiting downtown redevelopment, 216–18; gaming community divisions and missed opportunities,

220–22; geographic location, 209–10; growth-related concerns, 210–11, 214–16; impact of Great Recession, 224–25; need for economic diversification, 225–27; railroad issues, 218–19; similarities, 222–23
Reno Livestock Center, 162
Reno Ramada, 95
Reno Redevelopment Agency, 101, 102
Reno Rodeo, 11, 145
Reno Rodeo and Livestock Association, 11
Reno-Sparks Convention and Visitors Authority, 150. *See also* Washoe County Fair and Recreation Board
Reno-Sparks Convention Center, 161. *See also* Centennial Coliseum
Reno-Sparks Sewage Treatment Plant, 70, 71, 86, 95
Reno-Stead airport, 22–23, 98
Reno-Tahoe Airport Authority, 99
Reno-Tahoe International Airport, 21. *See also* airport construction
Reno Transportation Rail Access Corridor (ReTRAC), 155–56
"Reno Unlimited," 26, 82
Reserve resort, 132
residential segregation, 39, 68
Resort at Summerlin, 124
resort industry. *See* gaming-tourist industry
Resorts International, 103
Resorts World Las Vegas project, 205
restricted gaming licenses, 26
Rhodes Ranch, 107
Riddle, Major, 42
Ritz Carlton, 173
Riverboat, 95, 141
Riverside Artist Lofts, 154
Riverside hotel, 9, 12, 85, 96
Riviera, 3
roads and road construction: Bruce Woodbury Beltway, 107–8; in expanding Las Vegas suburbs and exurbs, 63–64, 137–38; Interstate 15, 25, 44, 51, 54; Interstate 80, 14, 24–25, 71; traffic issues, 50–51
room tax, 16, 20
Rose Garden Urban Renewal Project, 63

Rothman, Hal, 215
Rowley, William, 25, 48, 140
RTC Centennial Plaza Transit Center, 150–51
Ruckdeschel, John, 198
Ruffin, Phil, 127
Rush, Bob, 87
Russell, Charles, 34

Sahara (Las Vegas), 3, 12, 45, 116, 170–71
Sahara (Reno), 75, 76, 95
sales tax, 59
Sal Sagev Hotel, 41
Samson, Shawn, 185
Sam's Town, 104
Sandoval, Brian, 163, 199, 200
Sands, 3, 12, 45, 95, 117, 148
Sands Expo Center, 131
San Francisco (CA), 86
Santa Fe Station, 124, 132
Sarno, Jay, 45, 115, 212
Satre, Phil, 171
Sawyer, Grant, 18, 59, 67
Saylor, Don, 60
SBE Entertainment, 170–71
Schaeffer, Glenn, 128–29
schools. *See* education issues
school segregation, 39, 68
Schumacher, Geoff, 106
Schumacher, Lindy, 200
Schwartz, David (historian), 216
Schwarz, David (architect), 185
Scott, Eddie, 38
Scott, Frank, 196
segregation. *See* civil rights issues
senior citizens, 105
septic tanks, 70
sewage treatment issues, 53–54, 90–91, 94–95, 136
Sferrazza, Pete, 102, 140, 153, 155
Shah, Faisal, 165
Shopper's Square, 21
Siegel, Bugsy, 3
Siegel Group, 194
Siena, 140
Sierra Pacific utility company, 92, 100
Silver Dollar, 9

Silver Legacy, 140–41, 161
Silver Spur, 9, 96
Simon, Bryant, 76, 216
Sinatra, Frank, 9
sit-ins, 38
Sixth Grade Busing Plan, 68
skiing, 12
Slattery, James, 67
slow-growth movement, 16. *See also* managed-growth debates
SLS Las Vegas, 171
Smatresk, Neal, 198, 200–203, 227
Smith, Harold, 12, 30
Smith, Raymond I. "Pappy," 12, 23, 30
Smith Center for the Performing Arts, 185, 195
Snow, Bob, 120
Snyder, Donald, 171, 185, 203
Soho Lofts, 187, 193
Sorb-Tech, 166
Southern Highlands, 107, 175
Southern Nevada Industrial Foundation, 196
Southern Nevada Memorial Hospital, 57
Southern Nevada Public Lands Management Act, 111, 134
Southern Nevada Water Authority (SNWA), 181–83, 189
Southern Nevada Water Project, 47, 68
Southern Pacific Railroad, 155
South Meadows development, 159
Southwest Airlines, 109
Southwest Sports, 185
Spago, 114
Spanish Trail, 106
Sparks: conflicts and cooperation with Reno, 83, 92, 93–94; growth and development of, 14, 33, 72, 160
Speakeasy, 141
special service districts, 220
Spectacle architecture, 116, 117
Spring Valley, 105–6
stadium projects, 121, 192–93
Stardust, 3, 12, 127, 212
Starrs, Paul, 88, 157, 158
Starwood Hotels International, 131
"State of the City" address, 202

Station Casinos, 131, 132–33
Stead Air Force Base, 34
Stearns, John, 148–49, 151–52
Stern, Martin, Jr., 45, 104
Sternauer, Bill, 87
Stevens, Derek, 195
Stratosphere Hotel-Casino, 104, 121–22
Streamline condominium tower, 187, 193
Strip city and the Strip: airport construction and expansion, 6, 42–43, 57–59, 98, 109, 179–80; building projects pursued despite Great Recession, 179–84; challenges of mid- to late 1970s, 103–4; Clark County commissioners' role in growth of, 6–7; convention facilities and industry, 6, 44, 57, 131, 180–81; creativity, reputation, and visual appeal of, 211–13, 223–24; divisions between downtown gaming industry and, 221; growth issues and, 66, 79–80, 210–11; Howard Hughes's vital role in, 45; impact of Great Recession on, 169–79, 224–25; as key difference between Las Vegas and Reno, 207–9; Las Vegas's annexation efforts, 61, 219–20; Mob presence in, 42; monorail system construction, 118–19; "New Las Vegas" era, 113–18; NSU/UNLV and, 44, 47, 55–56, 222; prerecession boom, 126–34; recent signs of economic recovery, 205–6; rise and growth of, 3–7; suburban development of, 105–7; wastewater treatment issues in, 53–54
Stupak, Bob, 65, 104, 121–22
Summerlin, 107, 110–11, 134
Summerlin Centre, 184
Summerlin Parkway, 110
Sun City Aliante, 134
Sun City Anthem, 111
Sun City community, 110
Suncoast, 132
Sundance, 104
Sundowner, 85, 95, 148
Sunset Station, 108, 132
Sunset Strip, 3
Switch (data-storage company), 197
Swope, Burton, 86

Index

Tabu, 118
Tahoe Regional Planning Agency, 93
Tamares Group, 194
Tam O'Shanter, 128
Tango Club, 13
Tao nightclub, 118
tax-increment financing, 154–55
tax issues, 35, 59–60, 147–48, 163–64, 215–16
Taylor, Tracy, 182–83
Taylor, William, 62
Technology Business Alliance of Nevada, 192
technology industry, 164–67, 190–92, 197, 226–27
Texas, economic development efforts, 199–200
Texas Station, 132
Thomas, E. Parry, 55, 196
Thomas, Roger, 130
Thunderbird, 3
Thunder Valley Casino Resort, 142
Time, 178
time-share housing, 127
Titus, Dina, 140
Tivoli Village, 133, 183–84
tourist industry. *See* gaming-tourist industry
traffic issues, 50–51
Transcontinental Highway Exposition, 20
Treasure Island, 113, 127
tribal casinos, 142, 144, 145
"Trop 42," 184
Tropicana, 3, 12
Tropicana and Flamingo Washes Project, 112
Tropicana Hotel, 103
Truckee Meadows Regional Planning Commission, 93
Truckee Meadows Water Authority, 94
Truckee River Whitewater Park, 154
Trump, Donald, 103, 126
Turnberry Tower, 176
Turner, Clyde, 140
"two Renos," 11

Union Pacific Railroad, 2, 43, 51, 185
Union Plaza Hotel, 68
Unique Infrastructure Group, 167
United Airlines, 21
United Freeway Association, 25
University Medical Center, 57
University of Arizona, 204
University of Nevada, Las Vegas (UNLV), 163–64, 192–93, 200–204, 222, 226–27. *See also* Nevada Southern University
University of Nevada, Reno (UNR), 163–64, 200, 202, 222, 226–27
University of Utah, 202
unrestricted gaming licenses, 26, 28
U.S. Micro Corporation, 196
US 40, 14, 23
US 91, 2
US 93, 2
US Army Air Corps' Flexible Gunnery School, 3
US Army Corps of Engineers, 54, 112
Utah Science and Technology Research Initiative, 202

Valley Auto Mall, 108
Valley High School, 55
Van Epp, Dan, 185, 188
Vdara, 172
Vegas Heights, 60
Vegas World, 65, 104
Veloce restaurant, 174
Venetian, 116, 130
Virginian, 95, 141
Virginia Street, 2, 8, 157
Virginia Street Mall, 71
Viva Project, 132
Vo Tech, 55

Wadsworth, 72
Waldorf Club, 9
Walker, Randall, 179–80
Walt Disney Company, 221
warehousing industry, 162
Washoe Council of Governments, 36, 37, 69, 93
Washoe County Courthouse, 36
Washoe County Fair and Recreation Board, 12, 16–17, 18, 20. *See also* Reno-Sparks Convention and Visitors Authority

Washoe County Regional Planning Commission, 17, 36, 69, 93
Washoe County School District, 34–35
Washoe County Teacher's Association, 34
wastewater treatment issues, 53–54, 90–91, 94–95, 136
water meters, 48
water-related issues (Las Vegas area): creation of the Las Vegas Valley Water District, 43–44; floods and flood control, 54, 111–13; Henderson and, 63; sewer infrastructure and wastewater treatment, 53–54, 136; water supply concerns and pipeline project, 48–50, 181–83
water-related issues (Reno area): blue-ribbon panel on, 70–71; floods and flood control, 113, 158–59; wastewater treatment and water supply concerns, 90–92, 94–95
Webb, Del, 41
Western Air Express Airport, 42
Western Airlines, 22
Western High School, 55
Western Hotel, 194
western-themed tourism, 11, 149–50
Westin Hotels, 173
West Street Plaza, 154
Whipple, Reed, 50

Wild Island, 154
Wilkerson, Billy, 3, 65
Williams, Paul, 188
Williams, Thomas, 3
Winchester, 61
Wingfield Park Amphitheater, 153
Wingfield Park area, 154
WinTech, 191
Woodbury, Bruce, 107, 112
wood products industry, 13, 162
Woolf, Larry, 194
Wooster, Earl, 15, 30
World Market Center, 185–86
World Series of Poker, 41
Wright, Jim, 111
Wynn, Steve: iconic building projects of 2000s, 128–29, 130, 131; purchase of Golden Nugget, 41; on Reno tourism, 149; role in building the "New Las Vegas," 113–14, 115, 211–12
Wynn Las Vegas, 113, 126, 128, 177
Wynn Resorts, Ltd., 170

XS nightclub, 118, 130

Yoder, Michael, 191

Zappos.com, 189, 190–91